"Jerry has given us a ⎵⎵⎵⎵⎵⎵⎵⎵⎵⎵⎵
this book. Relevant, tho⎵⎵⎵⎵⎵⎵⎵⎵
each Psalm to everyday ⎵⎵⎵⎵⎵⎵⎵⎵
savor and to share. Dor⎵⎵⎵⎵⎵⎵⎵⎵
inspires us to deeper enga⎵⎵⎵⎵ with the Scriptures as ⎵⎵⎵⎵⎵
his own habits of prayer reflection morning by morning."
—*Mike Treneer, International President*
The Navigators

"It has been said that to read the Psalms is to know the heart of David. I hasten to add that to understand and appreciate the heart of Jerry Rankin, one should read his meditations on these same Psalms. Not only have I come to know him better, but I've grown closer to my heavenly Father through his inspiring devotional thoughts."

—*Ed Cox, Director*
International Prayer Strategy Office, IMB

"As his pastor, I've come to know and love Jerry Rankin's heart for God. Yet reading through *In the Secret Place* allowed me to know and appreciate his heart even more. My wife Loree and I read it at night together for our devotions. This is not a commentary, though he has the mind to produce one. It is an inspiring journal of Jerry's pilgrimage of leaning on God."

—*Mark Becton, Pastor*
Grove Avenue Baptist Church, Richmond, VA

"In Psalms 46:10, God instructs us to be still before Him, that we might align our heart with His and allow Him to guide us onto paths that honor and glorify Him. In his book, *In the Secret Place,* Jerry Rankin carefully and lovingly guides us on an adventure into the heart of God and His Word. Laying out each Psalm in a personal and understandable application, this book is a wonderful tool to help the reader be still and listen, and deepen one's understanding and love for God."

—*Bob Cresson, president*
Wycliffe Bible Translators, USA

"Jerry Rankin has given me a fresh new perspective on the Psalms, my favorite book of the Bible. He has an amazingly powerful and personal way of connecting the psalmist's heart with my own day-to-day world. His reflections are theologically penetrating, powerfully personal, and deeply rooted in years of leadership experience. *In the Secret Place* has helped me fall in love with God all over again. I can't think of a better way to start my day."
—*Arlene Richardson, Pioneers Mission Agency*
and Founder of Heartcraft

"In this engaging and transparent look into the Psalms, Jerry Rankin calls us to confession, holiness, and praise of God. He urges us to practice the presence of Christ, pursuing humility with an absolute trust in God and His sufficiency. This missions leader joins the psalmist in calling us to the nations, telling them of our powerful and loving God. Every leader must read this book, as a prevalent theme is Dr. Rankin's identification with the psalmist as he responds in faith to frequent and undeserved criticism that inevitably comes to a spiritual leader."

—*Clyde Meador, Executive Vice-President*
International Mission Board

"Jerry Rankin's personal devotional reflections on the Psalms came from the heart of a man who loves God supremely. His meditations reveal the depth of His own experience of walking in intimate fellowship with God. *In the Secret Place* will nourish your soul and fuel the fire of your devotion to live for the glory of God among all nations."

—*Al Jackson, Pastor*
Lakeview Baptist Church, Auburn, AL

"If you want to go deeper in Christ and experience a victorious Christian life, you have to dive deeper into the Psalms. Jerry Rankin, who has a heart after God, is well-qualified to guide us in this mining expedition. He knows the Lord and knows the Psalms. Using *In the Secret Place* in one's devotional reading will give a growing knowledge of both."

—*John Marshall, Pastor*
Second Baptist Church, Springfield, MO

"To read the collected Psalms is to walk on holy ground. In many of them, David, as shepherd, soldier, and king, opens wide the pages of his diary and allows us to look into the inner sanctuary of his heart. In a similar fashion, this book by Jerry Rankin invites us into his own heart. Here you will find how the Psalms have brought joy and strength to his life. You will feel the pulsebeat and grasp the burdens of the man who shepherds the largest missionary team in the evangelical world. And you will be challenged and encouraged for your own pilgrimage of faith."

—*Tom Elliff, pastor, writer, teacher, former SBC president,*
and IMB senior vice-president

In the Secret Place

JERRY RANKIN

In the Secret Place

A PILGRIMAGE

THROUGH

THE PSALMS

B&H
PUBLISHING GROUP

NASHVILLE, TENNESSEE

© 2009 by Jerry Rankin
All rights reserved.
Printed in the United States of America

978-0-8054-4881-8

Published by B&H Publishing Group
Nashville, Tennessee

Dewey Decimal Classification: 242.5
Subject Heading: DEVOTIONAL LITERATURE \
BIBLE. O.T. PSALMS—INSPIRATION \ CHRISTIAN LIFE

Unless otherwise noted, Scripture quotations
are from, New American Standard Bible, NASB, © the
Lockman Foundation, 1960, 1962, 1963, 1968,
1971, 1972, 1973, 1975, 1977; used by permission.
Other Scripture versions include NKJV, New King James
Version, copyright © 1979, 1980, 1982, Thomas Nelson,
Inc., Publishers and KJV, the King James Version.

1 2 3 4 5 6 7 8 • 13 12 11 10 09

Dedication

Dedicated to my six grandchildren

Zachary, Joseph, Samuel, Anna Grace, Mia, and Gloria

*With the desire that they have
a heart for God,
a love for His Word,
a commitment to His will,
stand in awe of His sovereignty and grace,
and live for His glory and praise!*

Foreword

I was about five years old when I received from my parents a children's illustrated Bible for Christmas. It was the version many children received at a young age—a thick hardcover with colorful pictures interspersed throughout that illustrated the Bible stories. Noah and the ark, Jonah and the whale, David conquering Goliath, and the pictures of a smiling Jesus surrounded by children.

It was with this Bible that I learned all the books of the Old and New Testaments and began to learn about the stories contained within. I remember the encouragement my parents gave me about the importance of spending time every day in personal Bible reading. I loved that Bible; it sits on a shelf in my home today, marked with awkward scrawling of a child just learning to write. Some additional artwork can be found in the inside covers and throughout the pages as well, most certainly the doodles of a restless child in church.

As a child I was usually one of the first ones up in the mornings. It was during these cool, tropical mornings in Indonesia that I received a visual imprint that taught me more than I ever could have learned from a book or verbal lesson. Tip-toeing quietly out of my room, I would make my way through our house to a back corner where my dad had his office set up. His desk, which still sits in his house today, was a large wooden carved desk with deep drawers and pull-out center console that smelled of ink and paper. It contained all sorts of treasures with which curious little boys love to tinker when their dads aren't around. But in the quiet of the morning, I could be assured that my dad would be sitting at that desk, his Bible open before him and his hands clasped beneath his chin. His expression—to a child—was furrowed and weighty. I knew this was not a time to crawl under the desk and play.

In his responsibilities as a church planter in Indonesia with the (then) Foreign Mission Board, he would travel to villages all over East Java preaching, teaching, and training national leaders. As I grew older, I came to understand what was transpiring during those solemn times in the morning. These were moments that were foundational to my father's life. This was his fuel. He drew his strength and inspiration from the pages of the Scriptures, and his meditations and times of prayer and petition were for people I didn't even know and for burdens I couldn't even begin to grasp at my young age. Many times I would retreat back to my favorite corner in my room with my own Bible. I did this because this is what I saw my father doing.

Two decades later I received another Bible. I was in my midtwenties, married with a newborn son. I found myself in a place of wanting more of God. I was struggling with a desire to live a life of impact and relevance, but more often I felt as if my life was stuck in a cycle of mere religious practice and dutiful, shallow church involvement. My father had recently been elected to lead the International Mission Board, an appointment that brought my parents back to the United States after twenty-three years of overseas service. I was grateful for the fact that having them back in America meant more opportunities for time as a family and the chance for my son to have his grandparents in the same country. This time we were together in Dallas; my parents were in town for a meeting. At a moment when my wife and mother were consumed with the antics of my young son, I found myself pouring out to my father the deep frustrations I was feeling.

His response to me was a simple question; the basic discipleship inquiry: "Are you in the Word?" It wasn't issued as a challenge or delivered with condemnation, but the simplicity of the question pierced me and instantly brought me back to that childhood memory of my father sitting at his desk. I admitted that I felt mired in a spiritual desert, where the Scriptures—which I knew with my mind were alive and active and sharper than any two-edged sword—were thumping hollow in my spirit.

"Here," he said. "I want you to have this." With that he handed me a Bible. I had my own Bible; several, in fact, were on my shelf at home. There was nothing magical about this brown, leather New International Version, but holding this Bible made me feel as if I were a new believer receiving a Bible for the very first time. It was his Bible. He encouraged me to read it daily, and outlined for me the simple pattern of his own morning habit, which always begins with a chapter in Psalms. Meditate on them, he encouraged me. Read them aloud and ask God to speak through the passage. Write down reflections, application, inspiration, personal prayers.

That time of encouragement was monumental to my faith walk. My dad's words and prayers for me were not just a shot in the arm, but it was a time of renewal to the realization of the necessity of being completely reliant on God and His grace and love to make it through the day. That Bible contained not only the inspired words of God given to man, but it contained evidence of my own father's journey—his neatly written notations and underlining of passages that gave me an understanding that I was not alone; that others had walked before me with similar struggles and petitions for greater strength and humility.

I was given a portion of my inheritance two years ago when my father presented me with a spiral-bound manuscript of this book. *In the Secret Place* is a deep, personal compilation of my father's lifelong pilgrimage through the book of Psalms. As I integrated the manuscript with my own personal moments of reading, passages of Scripture came alive to me once again. I saw how the Psalms ministered to him in times of struggle, disappointment, betrayal, and doubt. I came to know passages that had served to inspire my father and passages that helped him lead his family and stay true to his calling of bringing a message of redemption to a lost and dying world. Much like that first children's Bible, his reflections and heartfelt pictures helped illustrate the beautiful truths revealed in the tapestry of a life committed to Jesus Christ.

Sharing this book with you is much like opening the door to our family. But the beauty of it is that, while it is a glimpse into one man's meditations, it reveals the foundational truth found in Psalm 78:4: "We will tell to the generation to come the praises of the LORD, and His strength and His wondrous works that He has done."

—Russell Rankin

Preface

I have a reputation among family and staff of being a well-organized, detailed person. Granted, the neatness of my office and a controlled agenda would substantiate that perception. However, few would be aware of the exasperation I live with in being surrounded by mountains of papers and folders in my attic office at home. It is probably a legacy I unconsciously acquired from my mother of never throwing away an article, note, or scrap of paper that may one day be useful. Never mind that I have never mastered a filing system that would enable instant retrieval. In fact, it would not be a coincidence but a miracle of God if I were able to remember and put my hand on a reference I recalled having read that would be relevant to a current need.

I learned long ago the benefit of journaling, writing insights from Scripture and recording what seemed to be impressions from the Lord in times of meditation. While some of these are filed systematically, or by dates, the notebooks have accumulated over the years. Among all of these, notes made from a repetitive reading of the Psalms over the years were the ones I found myself actually reviewing and using in devotionals and testimonies. During a sabbatical in the summer of 2004, I was working feverishly for long hours on several writing projects that have now been published. It was in the momentum of actually seeing these books materialize that I realized God had given me subject matter that was far more valuable. Inspired by a few attempts to reduce some of my notes on the Psalms to a readable format that might be meaningful to others, I pressed forward with the project, writing one or two each day. The following pages of introduction will explain the background and process more thoroughly, but needless to say, the blessing of reliving and capturing the message of each Psalm became an intimate walk with the Father in which I felt I was entering into that secret place of His presence.

I am grateful for Bobbye, my wife, whose own consistent devotional time each morning has been an encouragement and influence. Her love for God and His Word is evident to all who know her. I have been blessed by the privilege of living with her and witnessing the evidence of her time "in the secret place." Her pattern of memorizing and quoting entire Psalms created an awareness of how powerful these passages of Scripture are. Confident of her faithful intercession and support, I was encouraged to press forward with the project. Her feedback after reading and meditating on my reflections helped to improve the relevancy of the content and style of communication.

I also want to thank staff and colleagues at the International Mission Board who did double duty in covering responsibilities to allow me the needed time of rest and respite during my sabbatical to complete this and other projects. Special thanks are due to Anita Bowden who graciously and constructively edited the material. This volume is offered not as something that would be a credit to the author but as a gift to the Father and those whom He desires to draw into His presence.

Introduction

For many years it has been my practice to begin my morning quiet time with the Lord by reading a Psalm and usually a chapter from the Gospels. This wasn't an intentional formality, and even when I tried to get away from the pattern for the sake of variety and freshness in devotional reading, I would find myself drawn back to the Psalms. It seemed something was missing in proceeding with a study of other portions of the Bible or praying without, first, that focus on the worship passages of Psalms. They seemed to bring to my awareness the majesty and power of God the Father. They reminded me of His sovereignty and loving-kindness. Reading a Psalm first thing in the morning seemed to put me in touch with the Father's heart and give me a sense of His presence as I unloaded my burdens, interceded for others and desperately sought His wisdom and will for the day. Likewise, a chapter from the Gospels simply made Jesus real to me.

I grew up being trained as a child to practice "daily Bible readings." It was something my parents held me accountable for as much as taking out the trash, brushing my teeth, or doing my homework. As I grew in my relationship with the Lord and began to formulate personal values as a teenager, a disciplined "quiet time" of Bible study, reading devotional books and systematic approaches to prayer became a regular practice, though done more often as a habit and formality than from a motivation and desire to know God more intimately.

With each ensuing responsibility of ministry that emerged in adulthood, culminating in missionary appointment, and later, demanding leadership roles, I recognized a greater need for God's power and blessings, and I consciously determined to get more serious about my prayer time. The busyness and demands of juggling a multiplicity of tasks with limited time, demands of travel and irregular schedules always made my resolve short-lived to the point of resorting to grabbing a few brief moments to read a few verses and say a quick prayer before getting on with the more important and pressing agenda of the day.

While leading a church growth strategy study in Japan in 1988, God did something to get my attention. We were finding nothing that would help guide the missionaries to be more effective in their witness and ministry. No one seemed to have found a handle to break through this difficult culture that seemed so resistant to the gospel. Everyone was discouraged. Then in one interview we found an enthusiastic first-term missionary who had planted a relatively large church in his first term that was now starting another mission. He had led to faith and baptized many Japanese men, something others had not been able to do, and he had not used a penny of subsidy. When we asked about his strategy and methodology, his wife interrupted to explain that her husband got up at 5:00 every morning and spent an hour on his knees before beginning his work.

I had read the books on prayer and heard others' testimonies. But for some reason I came to the point of realizing that, if I wanted the assurance of God's hand upon me and my ministry, I had to have a heart for Him that would be reflected in a disciplined time of prayer and fellowship with Him. I needed to spend enough time in the Word to allow God to speak to me. If I were going to preach, inspire, and presume to lead and minister to others, I had to allow Him to speak into my life on His terms. I was shamefully impressed by my own arrogance in expecting Him to guide me, to bless me, to answer my prayers, and to meet my needs when I spent so little time seeking Him. How presumptuous to think I could utter a few stereotyped phrases of prayer to begin the day, and the God of the universe would be obligated to respond to my needs and desires!

At that time I was definitely not a morning person. It wasn't unusual to fellowship with friends well into the night, to watch television and videos late in the evening, or more often, simply to stay up reading and getting work done after the family had gone to bed. But I was impressed that Jesus was a morning person. Even He needed time with the Father and felt the need to arise early, even while it was dark, long before the demanding crowds began to infringe on His time. If Jesus felt it necessary to spend time with the Father and stay in touch with His heart and purpose, how much more important must it be for me. I began to get up at 6:00 to spend a solid half hour in prayer and Bible reading. The time seemed to go by in a flash and was just enough to whet my appetite for more. So I started arising at 5:30 and found the more open-ended time of prayer; pouring out my heart in expressing my feelings, burdens, and concerns; and having time to cover an extensive prayer list, was a blessing I had seldom experienced. Once again the time became inadequate, and I found myself getting up at 5:00, and then at 4:30; and I began to sense the reality of God's presence and assurance of His guidance consistently throughout the day. I discovered personal attacks, conflicts, and criticism did not upset me as before. I became more sensitive to ungodly feelings and attitudes buried deep within my heart that would have given fruition to sinful words or actions had they not been recognized and confessed. But probably most noticeable of all, to myself at least, was an attitude and tendency to be praising the Lord throughout the day as I became constantly aware of His presence.

Before acquiring a coffeepot with an automatic timer, my pattern each morning would be to put on the coffee and, while it was perking, read a Psalm and kneel in just a brief time of worship and focus on the character and nature of the Father that had just been revealed. Not allowing myself to proceed to other needs and petitions, those moments were often a sense of literally placing my head in the Father's lap! With the coffee ready, I would move to the Gospels, read a chapter, and then go back to a more detailed study and reading of my Psalm for the day. Only then would I open my prayer journal and proceed to pray for forty-five minutes or longer. Then the remaining time usually focused on the preparation of messages or devotional studies that became a wealth of resource to draw upon when the need and opportunity arose, often spontaneously.

To maintain a freshness and continued growth in what soon became familiar, I began to make notes on what the

Lord was saying to me in my Psalm for the day. I would read different versions of the Bible and, in subsequent series of going through the Psalms, paraphrase them in my own words, noting applications for contemporary life and writing prayers in an attempt to "pray back" the Word to God. I avoided reading commentaries or other devotional books, though I used them extensively in other studies, not wanting what God was revealing and saying to me to be shaped by others' opinions and insights. Though blessed by unique insights and the wording of various translations, I came to love and rely on the New American Standard Version as my basic and preferred text, which is reflected in these devotionals. Beginning my morning quiet time with reading and meditating on a Psalm has now become such a habitual and meaningful part of my life and pilgrimage, it is something I could not fail to do. In fact, from time to time I have tried to get away from this pattern, but I always find myself drawn back, as something is lacking when I neglect the reading of one or more Psalms in my devotional time each morning.

It would be impossible to capture in a few sentences why this is true, but it has something to do with how the Psalms reveal the nature and character of God. Readers are impressed by His power and authority and majesty as One who is worthy of all worship and honor and praise. The affirmation of His sovereignty and providence helps to put the circumstances and trials that we experience in the context of His purpose. Our fear and reverence for God is enhanced by the descriptions of His wrath and judgment, but His compassion and mercy draw us to Him. He cares for every detail of our lives, and we can be assured that He will guide us according to His will; He will care for us, provide our every need, and vindicate our enemies. The graphic, picturesque language evokes images that stir our emotions and strengthen our confidence. To know that He is our rock, our shield, our fortress, and our strong tower all convey an understanding we need each day as well as the comforting and tender assurances that He is a shepherd enfolding us in His arms. There will be a good bit of repetition in what is shared because the themes and central thoughts are reinforced over and over throughout the Psalms.

I originally wrote these personal thoughts and reflections not to be published and disseminated but that my children and grandchildren might be inspired and encouraged to grow in their intimacy with the Father. They know me in the earthly relationship I have had with them as a father and grandfather. Hopefully they have benefited from my teaching and influence. They are aware of the roles and positions of leadership I have filled. But the lasting legacy I desire to leave is a spiritual one. Through sharing these personal reflections from my own time with the Lord, I pray that they and others might be encouraged to discover that "secret place of the Most High" that they might "abide under the shadow of the Almighty."

My personal habits of a morning devotional time are not necessarily a model for others or pattern that commends itself. It is not the fact of what I have done each morning that is significant, but whether or not it has made a difference in the witness of my life and a Christlike relationship with others. Only family and colleagues can be the judge of that.

These devotionals are not a detailed exegesis or verse-by verse-commentary but simply a compilation of personal thoughts and reflections. They are written from extensive notes made over the years when I paraphrased the passage and noted applications. They are a summary of what I felt God was saying to me personally or wrote out as prayers in an attempt to "pray back" the Word. They reveal what I believe about God and many doctrinal convictions more thoroughly than if I were to attempt to write a textbook on systematic theology. Sometimes they cover the entire Psalm but usually are an expansion of an excerpted theme or primary lesson. It was a challenge to maintain a consistency in limiting each to the same format and length, but I felt being concise would more readily speak the essential truths God would reveal in the passage. Occasionally the length and content of a special Psalm, particularly Psalms 37, 51, and others merited more than one devotional thought. Reviewing Psalm 119 was a mountaintop experience personally as I compiled these notes into eight segments. Perhaps it is the length or the apparent repetition, but we tend to miss the impact of what this reveals regarding the power of the Word of God. The blessing of grasping the depth of God's

Word and finding my own love and devotion to it enhanced was one of the highlights of this literary pilgrimage.

I would readily insist that the entire Psalm be read prayerfully beforehand and these devotionals not be read in isolation of the biblical passage. Readers will probably find them more meaningful by reading one a day, meditating on the Scripture, and allowing the truths and insights to sink in. I do not share this out of a desire to be a model or presume that others would have the same meaningful experience from reading repetitively through the Psalms but that those who are most dear to my heart might be blessed by the legacy of what God has done in my own life and how He has spoken to me.

I could say with John (3 John 4), *"I have no greater joy than this, to hear of my children [and grandchildren] walking in the truth."* It is not my example and influence that will have that result but only their own hunger for God in which pursuing Him becomes the passion of their lives. It is only their desire to know and be obedient to His will and to live their life to the praise of His glory that will keep them in the Word.

My prayer is that these devotional reflections will give each one who reads them a love for the Psalms but, more than that, a love for the God who is revealed in them. I pray that each one will gain insight into practical applications that are personal, unique, and timely for them. And above all it is my desire that I might leave something more valuable than precious memories and joys of relationships and that the legacy I leave with my children and grandchildren would be passed on to their offspring and future generations.

Let the pilgrimage begin . . .

*"He who dwells in the [secret place] of the Most High
shall abide under the shadow of the Almighty."*
(Psalm 91:1 NKJV)

A Fruitful Life

Key Verse: "His delight is in the law of the LORD, and in His law he meditates day and night." (Psalm 1:2)

We are presented with a clear, explicit picture of how to be blessed through a contrasting view of what to do and what not to do. The reference is to a life that fulfills God's purpose, brings glory to Him, and is fruitful in all that God wants us to accomplish. This is all wrapped up in the closing expression of verse 3, *"And in whatever he does, he prospers."* That is certainly the desire of my heart. Why waste time and years in pursuits that do not prosper or that do not result in positive influence in advancing the kingdom of God?

I want to be like that tree planted by streams of water, constantly drawing sustenance, strength, and spiritual nutrients from the Water of Life—one that bears fruit as a natural process of life. A tree does not bear fruit by working or struggling but by simply abiding in the source of life. I want to be "firmly" planted, unwavering in conviction, and not susceptible to temptations. In times of trials, I will not wander from fellowship with the Father because I'm so rooted in Him, the source of strength and blessing.

> **Why waste time and years in pursuits that do not prosper or that do not result in positive influence in advancing the kingdom of God?**

How to receive the blessing and be this kind of person is clearly explained by a graphic contrast. One makes choices not to yield to the influence and counsel of the wicked. One must avoid the activities characterized by worldly values and by walking in places and engaging in things that are self-serving and do not please God. One should never associate with those who make light of spiritual things. We should never get comfortable around those who ridicule a commitment to purity or integrity and disparage the truth of God's Word. These will perish like chaff blown away by the wind when they face the sure judgment of God. There is nothing of eternal, lasting value among the wicked and those characterized by worldly principles and influences.

But the righteous, the one who is blessed and prospers, is the one who remains firmly planted and rooted in God. He focuses on God's truth and meditates on His Word day and night. The key is a consistent discipline and practice of feeding on God's Word—reading it until it becomes a part of one's life—allowing it to shape our worldview, our character, motives, and desires. God's Word and the truth of His promises become not only the source of victory and strength but also the joy and delight of one's life.

PRAYER: *Lord, give me insight and wisdom that I might discern the counsel of the wicked and avoid the subtle influence of those who are cynical and insensitive to Your Spirit; help me avoid situations where I would be influenced by the world and its values. May I find delight in being obedient to Your law and drawing strength from Your Word. Let me be fruitful in season according to Your plan and purpose, never withering in fatigue and discouragement. May I prosper in that which You lead me to do for Your glory.*

God Is Sovereign over the Nations

*Key Verse: Worship the LORD with reverence and rejoice
with trembling. . . . How blessed are all who take refuge in Him!
(Psalm 2:11–12)*

E verything going on around us in the world is a distraction that seems to contradict the sovereignty and purpose of the Father. Global conflicts, oppressive government regimes, massive suffering, and the dominance of evil readily create doubts regarding whether or not God is in control. The absence of any moral conviction in our society and the prominence of materialistic self-serving values make us wonder if the gospel is real. Is it capable of bringing change that affirms the power of God and the redemption assured by Christ's death? Where is the evidence of a living Savior who is Lord of the universe?

When people in the early church in Acts 4 found themselves confronted with persecution, imprisonment, and threats and were soon to experience martyrdom, they prayed this Psalm, asking the question, *"Why do the nations rage? Why do the kings of earth take their stand . . . against the Lord and His anointed?"* We ask ourselves the same question, almost on a daily basis. Why am I confronted with constant conflict, criticism, and stress created by situations and those who seem to have no respect for Christian principles? It is obviously because we live in a rebellious world in which not only individuals but nations and cultures have rejected the lordship of Jesus Christ.

> **God has established His throne in the
> heavens and anointed His Son with all
> power and authority.**

But God, who has established His throne in the heavens and anointed His Son with all power and authority, sees all of this. He laughs at those who in their arrogance and pride will face His judgment and wrath. At a time when I was going through challenges of public criticism and trial, someone wrote a brief note of encouragement that said, "Keep the view from the throne!" What is God's perspective on all that is swirling about us? How does He view the adversity, opposition, and trials we face?

I have often quoted verse 8 as the role of prayer in our task of global evangelization and as a strategy of God being one day exalted among the nations. The nations will become and are His possession. But for the purpose of executing judgment on those who have rejected Him, His wrath will be poured out, and He will *break them with a rod of iron [and] shatter them like earthenware* (v. 9).

This is a reminder of God's sovereignty and power and the certainty of His wrath and justice because of His moral nature. He is a just God who cannot tolerate evil and rebellion in our hearts or among the nations. He has not relinquished His throne regardless of all that is going on in the world. Therefore, we are to worship Him in reverence. Our fear of the Lord should bring us into His presence with trembling but also with rejoicing that the Son has provided us a refuge from His wrath and judgment.

PRAYER: *Lord, You are a holy and righteous God who cannot abide with sin and rebellion that are so characteristic of our world. You have told us to ask You for the nations. They are under Your sovereignty. I plead for them that they might become Your inheritance and might know the Son instead of being subjected to Your wrath and judgment.*

Psalm 3

God Is Our Shield

Key Verse: But Thou, O LORD, art a shield about me, my glory, and the One who lifts my head. (Psalm 3:3)

Few people live such an isolated and benign existence that they don't constantly feel the pressures and demands of life. Responsibilities of family, education, and work force us into relationships with people and subject us to circumstances that create tensions and stress. I often think of the panic attacks we experienced among a massive mob of screaming people in Indonesia or India and the anxiety that comes from feeling out of control. The picture of *"ten thousands of people who have set themselves against me"* (v. 6) is real as I recall congested crowds of people in the marketplaces of Asia. The task of reaching a lost world is overwhelming when we realize that millions of Muslims, Buddhists, and Hindus are set in opposition against our evangelistic witness.

Daily problems that are common to life can be just as formidable as the literal opposition of an adversary. They create self-doubts and a feeling of futility that there is no solution or way of deliverance. Writing assignments, school lessons, or travel schedules may pile up, eliminating balance and margin in life, imposing frustration and robbing us of a sense of peace and well-being. But the psalmist gives assurance that when we cry to the Lord, He hears us and saves us, not just in the sense of redeeming us from sin but from situations and attitudes that would rob Him of His glory.

> *The psalmist gives assurance that when we cry to the Lord He hears us and saves us from situations and attitudes that would rob Him of His glory.*

The Lord is our shield and our glory. I have been through many times of criticism and attacks, but often an impermeable shield seemed to surround me and kept me from being touched or affected by the fiery darts that were intended to hurt. Those who set themselves against me did not diminish, but their attacks did not harm me, my reputation, or my security in the Lord. This came as a result of a commitment to maintain fellowship with the Father. I gloried in Him and His promises in times when it seemed that was all I had. I found that He was the One who did not allow me to become bowed down under the burden and weight of attacks, but He *"lift[ed] my head"* (v. 3) and kept me walking in confidence and faith with my head held high. It is not our performance or what we do but God who gives status and respect.

The beautiful promise of this Psalm is the assurance we can lie down and sleep because God is our shield and glory. There is no cause for restless, sleepless nights with troubling thoughts swirling in our minds. We sleep in peace and awaken refreshed and with assurance, for He is the One who sustains us. We are reminded judgment belongs to the Lord. He will take care of the wicked. The battle is not ours. God's role is salvation and deliverance. His desire is for His people to be blessed.

PRAYER: *Lord, I seem to be surrounded by so many conflicts and controversies. I feel so vulnerable as they attack my mind, creating pressures that overwhelm me. Thank You for being a shield around me today. Surround me with Your presence that I can sleep in peace, and allow me to be touched only by that which will draw me closer to You. Allow me to see Your faithfulness and deliverance that all I do may bring glory to You.*

Assurance of Answered Prayer

Key Verse: But know that the LORD has set apart the godly man for Himself; the LORD hears when I call to Him. (Psalm 4:3)

We can identify with the desperation and plea of the psalmist in the opening verses. Sometimes we feel rejected or maybe are conscious of having made a mistake. Having offended someone, we feel the reproach of a strained relationship. We are out of sorts with God—that sweet fellowship and sense of His presence has vanished—and we plead with Him to answer our prayer, be gracious to us, and relieve our distress.

The contrast is made clear in characterizing one who succumbs to worldly and ungodly attitudes and behavior and what one does who is walking a godly life in the righteousness of the Father. One who is out of fellowship with the Father is attracted to worthless things—values of the world, materialism and entertainment that appeals to baser instincts and passions. Such a person is deceived and misleads others in his example and influence. We recognize our need for God's help. It is not because we are deserving but because of His righteousness that we can expect Him to answer when we call; it is on the basis of His grace that He hears our prayer.

> **It is not because we are deserving but because of His righteousness that we can expect Him to answer when we call.**

Verse 3 is a beautiful reminder that if we live a godly life, it is because God has chosen us and set us apart; it is not for our blessing but for His glory. Why does the godly person have assurance the Lord hears when he calls? It is because we belong to Him and walk in fellowship with Him. Life becomes communion with God in which the Father responds to our pleading and manifests Himself to us in an outpouring of grace.

The person set apart for the Lord is to do four things to maintain that relationship:

- Tremble and do not sin; the fear of the Lord should be a deterrent from sin.
- Meditate and think about the Lord and godly things in times when we are still, while lying in bed or perhaps waiting in a line or stalled in traffic.
- Offer the sacrifices of righteousness; do what is good—"What would Jesus do?"
- Trust in the Lord. Walk in faith, confident that God is leading and enabling us.

The result of being a godly person who walks with God in doing these things is that God is consistently revealing Himself to us and through us. He is *"lift[ing] up the light of [His] countenance upon us"* (v. 6). He puts gladness in our heart, a joy that abounds like the farmer who reaps a prosperous crop beyond all expectations. And we can sleep in peace and dwell in safety. There is no distress, problem, or threat that infringes on our security.

PRAYER: *Lord, there is no goodness at all in me; any element of holiness and godliness comes from You. You have demonstrated grace and mercy in setting me apart from worldly things, but never let me forget it is for Your glory. I encounter so many conflicts and temptations in my mind, but You give a blessed peace and joy in abundance because I rest in You and You alone.*

Our Refuge from Sin

*Key Verse: For it is Thou who dost bless the righteous
man, O Lord, Thou dost surround him with favor
as with a shield. (Psalm 5:12)*

God hears our prayers, answers us, and blesses us. It is not because we are deserving and merit His favor but only because of His moral nature of holiness and righteousness. His attitude toward the unrighteous in verses 4–6 reveals the fact that sin is totally contrary to His nature.

- He does not take pleasure in wickedness.
- Evil shall not dwell with Him.
- He hates workers of iniquity.
- He will destroy those who speak falsehood.
- He abhors the bloodthirsty and deceitful.

This is why Psalm 66:18 tells us, *"If I regard wickedness in my heart, the Lord will not hear."* We cannot be presumptuous, ignore sin in our attitude and heart, and expect God to respond. The psalmist goes on to describe the characteristics of the wicked and those who stand against the righteous man. They are unreliable in what they say; their inward being is destruction; and their own scheming and devices will lead them to judgment. Because of their rebellious nature and the multitude of their transgressions, they will be thrust out of God's presence. There will be no sin in heaven; all who enter God's presence must be cleansed by the blood of Jesus Christ through repentance and faith.

***We cannot be presumptuous, ignore
sin in our attitude and heart, and
expect God to respond.***

But we can come into His presence and take refuge in Him. We can be assured that the Lord will hear our groaning when our burdens are great. He will heed our cry for help, for He is our King and our God. How pleasing it must be to our Lord to hear our voice in the morning as we awaken, revealing our priority to seek His face; we can *"eagerly watch"* (v. 3) for His blessings and how He will answer our prayers through the day.

Therefore we will come into His house, into His presence, because of His *"abundant lovingkindness* (mercy)" (v. 7). In fear and reverence we will worship Him and know that He will lead us in righteousness. He will show us His will and smooth out the problems and conflicting distractions by *"making our way straight"* (v. 8). We will be glad and sing for joy because He is our refuge and shelters us from sin and harm. He blesses us because we love His name and exult in Him. His favor surrounds us and protects us like a shield. The fiery darts and temptations of the evil one and the attacks of unrighteous influences in the world cannot touch us.

PRAYER: *Lord, in the midst of storms and controversies that swirl around me constantly, I'm grateful that You are my refuge. You are sensitive to the groanings of my heart and hear my prayer. In You I find a haven of refuge and respite. In Your presence I find gladness and joy, because I recognize Your favor and praise You as my King and my God. Keep my heart clean from the ways of the wicked and make my way straight as I bow before You.*

Maintaining Faith When
Feeling Forsaken

Key Verse: The LORD has heard my supplication,
the LORD receives my prayer. (Psalm 6:9)

Many think that the life of a Christian should be free from stress and discouragement. We feel guilty when we struggle with times of depression and are unable to claim the promises of abiding joy and peace in the midst of trials. We fail to realize that God allows these experiences in order for us to recognize our own inadequacy, to grow in our faith, and to see Him as our only sufficiency. We must learn that the Father is always teaching us and using circumstances to draw us to Him. The psalmist seems to have learned that when one comes to the end of his rope and is overcome with opposition, the only recourse is to seek the Lord.

Sometimes adversity comes because of who we are in Christ. The opposition and attacks from society and from those who appear to be enemies of the faith are real. Satan is seeking to deprive God of being glorified in our lives by robbing us of the victory that we have been provided. But sometimes these low times come as a result of our own sin and neglecting to nurture our relationship with the Father in consistent prayer and Bible study. They come from yielding to self-serving motives and selfish gain, contrary to the calling and will of the Father, or from seeing things through worldly eyes of carnal values. Whatever the reason, God seems far away, as if He has abandoned us.

> *God allows these experiences for us to recognize our own inadequacy, to grow in our faith, and to see Him as our only sufficiency.*

When there is no sense of God's presence and fellowship with the Father, the emotion and attitude are evident. As the psalmist reflects, *"I am pining away* (v. 2) . . . *my soul is greatly dismayed* (v. 3) . . . *I am weary with my sighing* (v. 6) . . . *I dissolve my couch with my tears"* (v. 6). He pleads, *"do not rebuke . . . nor chasten me* (v. 1) . . . *be gracious to me . . . heal me* (v. 2) . . . *rescue my soul* (v. 4) . . . *save me because of Thy lovingkindness"* (v. 4). We have all been there in feeling there is no relief, no answer, no one cares, the Lord has abandoned us, and plead, *"O Lord—how long?"* (v. 3).

But there is a subtle hint of the answer. We exist to praise the Lord and give thanks to Him. He blesses us because He loves us with an unfailing love, but not for our benefit; it is for His glory. The psalmist reminds the Lord that no one in hell gives thanks to Him. There is no gain in being oppressed unto death. So in confidence he declares that the Lord hears his weeping, heeds his supplication, and receives his prayer. We are able to stand firm against our adversaries, whether people or circumstances, confident that they will be turned back and thwarted. There may be no visible, external evidence, but the reality of the victory comes because of our faith and confidence in the Father and His faithfulness and abundant mercies.

PRAYER: *Lord, I accept the consequences of any unrighteousness I have done. But I am also overcome by being subjected to those who criticize, oppose, and oppress me unjustly. Rather than allowing me to yield to a root of bitterness and bondage to depression, use these experiences to draw me to You. Teach me what I need to learn in order to be restored to an abiding fellowship with You and a sense of Your presence that I might give thanks to You, assured of Your faithfulness and deliverance.*

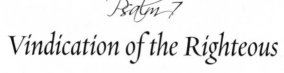

Vindication of the Righteous

Key Verse: Vindicate me, O LORD, according to my righteousness and my integrity that is in me. (Psalm 7:8)

There is a repetitive theme throughout the Psalms and indeed, throughout the Bible, that God is absolutely righteous and worthy of all praise. We are all sinners and deserve the consequences of our wrongdoing. But God is merciful, always ready to forgive, cleanse, and restore when we come to Him in confession and repentance.

The opening verses give us a model of confession—humble recognition that many of our troubles, conflicts in relationships, and turmoil within may be because of our own sin. Have we been guilty of treating others unjustly, condoning evil by simply tolerating worldliness in our indulgence of entertainment and pleasure? Have we taken advantage and *"plundered"* others for our own benefit or gain? If so, we must acknowledge why our soul is torn apart and why we feel that we are being trampled down.

But when we do come under attack and others take advantage of us, we must recognize that it is God's task to deal with it, not ours. Others may malign our reputation and motives, criticize something we have done, or undermine our work. Our security is in the Lord, and we must be confident that He will rise up against the unjust. God reigns on high and will judge the peoples. He is a righteous judge and will in indignation vindicate those who have been wronged and who maintain their integrity. He is our shield. If the wicked adversary does not repent, he brings on himself the deadly judgment prepared by God. The one who conceives mischief and is given to violence is like one who has dug a pit as a trap and then falls into it himself.

> *When we do come under attack and others take advantage of us, we must recognize that it is God's task to deal with it, not ours.*

But the one who can look to God for a refuge and be confident of His intervention and deliverance is the one who is upright in heart. We can expect His help only according to our own righteousness and integrity. Second Chronicles 16:9 says, *"The eyes of the LORD move to and fro throughout the earth that He may strongly support those whose heart is completely His."* A person who is upright in heart is one who is right in his relationship with God and is honest and transparent in all relationships and motives. He is one who reflects holiness, purity, and righteousness in his daily life. God will always vindicate such a person.

So even in the midst of adversity—whether it is people who are creating problems and conflicts or a sense of overwhelming problems and situations that tend to bring us down—we can rejoice and give thanks to God for His righteousness and faithfulness and sing praise to the Lord Most High!

PRAYER: *Lord, I acknowledge and accept the consequences of my sins, whether unrighteous actions, injustice to others or indulging in impure thoughts in my heart. I do not deserve Your mercy. But when temptations or real adversaries come against me, I thank You that You are my refuge, my shield, and my deliverer. You will vindicate me, and I will give thanks and praise Your name.*

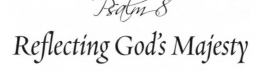

Reflecting God's Majesty

*Key Verse: O LORD, our Lord, how majestic is
Thy name in all the earth! (Psalm 8:1, 9)*

This passage was one that I memorized years ago as a child in Vacation Bible School. It is one that spontaneously flows into my mind and often finds expression on my lips in moments when my personal worship seems to come into touch with the awesome majesty of God. The grandeur and power and glory of God cannot be grasped by the human mind. But this description of meditating upon the things that reflect His majesty represents the extent to which words can attempt to describe it.

Just the name of the Lord is an acknowledgement of His reign and the fact there is nothing that exceeds His power and glory in all the earth. It is reflected in the world He has created from the tiniest atom and molecule to the expanse of the heavens, far beyond what man will ever discover or understand. It is reflected in nature and the creation of life in all its complexities. It is not those who would question or oppose the existence of God, or in worldly wisdom and skepticism presume to try to explain Him, who are able to grasp the reality of His power. It is rather those who claim the innocence and faith of a child.

> *God has displayed His splendor
> and majesty in giving us life.
> Will we display His splendor and
> majesty in the way we live?*

But the awesome, mind-boggling central expression of God's majesty and glory is His creation of us! Our value and self-esteem are affirmed in the fact that we are at the highest level of His plan and purpose in creating the world and all that is in it. We are just a little below the divine nature of God Himself. He chose to create us in His image and has given to us glory and majesty to rule over His creation. He has given us intellect and wisdom and the ability to demonstrate moral values in managing our world and environment for His glory. The birds, the animals, and the fish of the sea, in a beautiful poetic expression, are all under the dominion of man. All the works of God's hands have been put under our feet.

We need to realize that this ordered universe—and the stewardship of managing our environment and the wealth of resources on our planet—is for our blessing and benefit because God cares for us. We are to use them and enjoy them, for the glory of God. Also we should be both humbled and encouraged to realize that each of us is a person of immense value to God. We exist because He loves us and cares for us. He has given us phenomenal potential in a life that is to be lived for Him and for His glory. We are to reflect His majesty and glory daily in our service to others and by living a life of holiness. God has displayed His splendor and majesty in giving us life. Will we display His splendor and majesty in the way we live?

PRAYER: *Lord, Your glory and majesty are beyond comprehension. You have created me for Your glory as the apex of Your handiwork. Help me to be a good steward of the things You have made so that You would be honored and Your majesty reflected in my life. As the crown of Your creation, may those of us who know You be faithful in our witness, that Your lordship and majesty would be known and worshipped in all the earth.*

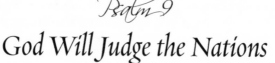

God Will Judge the Nations

Key Verse: I will give thanks to the LORD with all my heart; I will tell of all Thy wonders. I will be glad and exult in Thee; I will sing praise to Thy name, O Most High." (Psalm 9:1–2)

I often quote the passage from Philippians (2:10–11) that says, *"One day every knee will bow and every tongue confess that Jesus is Lord to the glory of God the Father."* The reality is that everyone will acknowledge the lordship of Christ, but for many it will be in judgment, for they never believed on Him as Lord and Savior. This Psalm portrays the judgment of the nations that reject God. It is written as a reflection on the enemies who had already been defeated and peoples who had been subdued in David's reign. But it is also a prophetic passage reflecting the sovereignty of God in judging the nations.

God has not relinquished His throne no matter how strongly world events spin out of control in chaos, and totalitarian authorities subject believers to persecution. Those who reject God and stand in opposition to Him will stumble and perish. They will be turned back. God will rebuke the nations, destroy the wicked, and blot out their name. Their cities will be uprooted, they will come to an end in perpetual ruin, and even the memory of them will perish. This is because God sits on His throne and will judge righteously. He is everlasting, abides forever, and will execute judgment for the peoples with equity. And the standard of equity by which all will be judged will be their relationship to Christ. Romans 2:16 refers to *"the day when, according to my gospel, God will judge the secrets of men through Christ Jesus."*

> **The standard of equity by which all will be judged will be their relationship to Christ.**

So the nations will be snared in their own trap of sin. Rather than yielding in submission to God, they will be caught in the pit they have made to punish and subdue others—that of exalting their own supposed power and authority. They are nothing but men, and the Lord will prevail. But for us who believe and follow God, He is our stronghold. The image of a massive, impenetrable fortress comes to mind. Though we may feel oppressed and go through times of trouble, we know the Lord. We can call upon His name as One we know intimately, and He will not forsake us. We are conditioned in such time of turmoil and confusion to seek the Lord rather than succumb to the pressures and attacks of the enemy. He does not forget us; He is gracious and lifts us up!

Therefore, we will give thanks with all our heart and be glad in Him. We will sing His praises but also tell of His wonders and declare His deeds among the peoples. We should not delight in their judgment and assurance of vindication from the Lord. We should desire that all nations would recognize and fear the Lord.

PRAYER: *Lord, I praise You with my whole heart and thank You that You are my stronghold in times of trouble, pressures, temptations, criticism, and attacks. I will declare Your deeds and tell of Your wonders, for You are sovereign over the nations. You will judge those who do not know You, and I need not fear the affliction of the wicked.*

When the Wicked Seem to Prosper

Key Verse: O LORD, Thou hast heard the desire
of the humble; Thou wilt strengthen their heart,
Thou wilt incline Thine ear. (Psalm 10:17)

The psalmist confronts the ageless rhetorical question, "Why do the wicked prosper?" We want to presume that God judges evil and unrighteousness. We think He should immediately bring down self-serving people with evil motives who take advantage of the afflicted and oppressed. We want to assume they will always suffer the consequences of their evil deeds. The arrogant who thumb their noses at God and His commands will be judged and punished. But our skepticism grows when we do not see it happening. It is natural to begin to doubt the reality of God's concern and His ability to vindicate those who suffer injustices in the world. Worldly values and sinful attitudes are blatant in the sexuality and violence that dominate entertainment on television and that prevail in our postmodern society.

It's reasonable to question, "*Why [does God] stand afar off? Why does He seem to hide Himself in times of trouble?*" (v. 1). However, God does not counter the physical laws of gravity when someone jumps off a building to keep them from being killed. Neither does He intervene to counter the moral laws among those who choose the ways of evil to keep them from impacting others. Those who spurn the Lord and do not acknowledge and respect His lordship and authority act as if He does not exist. In their greediness and pride, they have no inclination to seek the Lord. God's judgments are "*out of . . . sight*" (v. 5) and may not be manifested immediately in a cause-and-effect response, but they are certain.

> *God's judgments may not be manifested immediately in a cause-and-effect response, but they are certain.*

Meanwhile, the wicked are unmoved in their arrogance. They have no reticence in victimizing others, whether through sexual promiscuity, financial fraud, or economic self-gain at the expense of the less fortunate. Their mouths are filled with curses, deceit, and oppression. Their devious and mischievous acts that bring suffering to the unfortunate and innocent are deliberate without conscience or remorse. They are deluded in thinking that God does not see or care and will not require accountability for their evil deeds.

But we should not be disillusioned by appearances and perceived inaction by God. He is king over the nations and sovereign over all in the world whether people acknowledge Him or not. He does hear the desire of the humble and strengthens the hearts of the oppressed when they are mistreated. He will vindicate the victims of evildoers. God's judgment may not be immediately evident, but we must keep the sad realities of the fallen world we see around us in perspective of God's ultimate judgment.

PRAYER: *Lord, let me never lose faith in Your moral nature and the certainty of Your judgment of the unrighteous. Evil and carnality seem so prominent in our world and injustice prevails; those who have no respect for You seem to prosper. Help me not to be deceived by appearances. Strengthen my heart and desire to know You and to remain confident of Your eventual judgment of the wicked. Incline Your ear to hear my prayer that I may walk in faithfulness.*

Making the Right Choice

*Key Verse: For the LORD is righteous; He loves righteousness;
the upright will behold His face. (Psalm 11:7)*

The choice is always whether to trust in the Lord or do it yourself. This decision is being made constantly and not always consciously. Throughout each day we encounter decisions, actions, and recourses to incidents impacting our lives. Even our perceptions determine our attitudes and behavior. To rely upon our own strength and wisdom makes us vulnerable to temptation and susceptible to influences that are contrary to God's will. The "wicked" that lie in wait to attack may not be blatantly evil but simply things that cause us to choose our own will. Self-serving motives and gratification of the flesh may be what robs us of victory. They erode the foundation of trust in God that brings security and confidence.

There are only two choices in every situation—submission to the lordship of Christ or going our own way. Our only refuge and hope is fleeing to God, trusting His power, and resting in Him. He is our protection against temptation and evil influences. These influences are often subtle. We are constantly exposed to worldly and materialistic values that lead to self-serving decisions rather than to that which would glorify God. Such a direction allows our affections to go astray; the enemy is always lurking, seeking to capture our hearts and sabotage the holy and righteous life to which God has called us.

> **To rely upon our own strength makes us
> vulnerable to temptation and to influ-
> ences that are contrary to God's will.**

It is essential to practice a conscious awareness of seeking God constantly. The desires of our heart must be for Him. There is no middle ground. The Lord loves the righteous but hates the wicked. We are constantly being tested to choose that which is contrary to God's will or that which will please and glorify Him. He is sovereign over all whether we acknowledge Him or not, and we will suffer the consequences of His judgment. All power and dominion belong to Him, and we can either choose to serve Him and live for Him or for ourselves.

Paul speaks of our bodies being the temple of the Holy Spirit living within us. We are to glorify God in our bodies by avoiding anything that would defile the temple of God. This has always been a deterrent to me from indulging in sexual impurity, smoking, drinking, and anything that would not glorify God in the temple of my body. We should be reminded that His eyes are always upon us, observing and judging the sons of men.

The reward of choosing righteousness and purity in life is the assurance that the *"upright will behold His face"* (v. 7). The greatest joy is to have a sense of the Lord's presence, for Him to reveal Himself to us and to know that He is, indeed, our refuge from sin.

PRAYER: *Lord, help me resist the inclination to rely upon my own wisdom and strength which makes me vulnerable to temptation. Help me avoid fleeing responsibility and neglecting to run to You for refuge. My natural instincts would lead me to a position in which the enemy would defeat me, but You are my righteousness. I seek You and long to see Your face.*

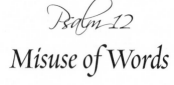

Misuse of Words

Key Verse: The words of the LORD are pure words; as silver tried in a furnace on the earth, refined seven times. (Psalm 12:6)

The Bible reminds us that words are a powerful force for either good or evil. In the third chapter of James, we are told that the tongue can be a source of blessing or cursing, and it reveals what is within one's heart. A person can grow in Christian character and a disciplined life, but the tongue is the most difficult to control. In an instant, without thinking, we can express anger, put down someone with a cutting, sarcastic word, or just verbalize an attitude of complaining and griping—none of which glorifies God. Gossiping and spreading rumors about others stir up contention. Proverbs 26:20 says, *"For lack of wood the fire goes out, and where there is no whisperer, contention quiets down."* In Proverbs 29:20 we are told, *"Do you see a man who is hasty in his words? There is more hope for a fool than for him."* Therefore, *"he who restrains his lips is wise"* (Prov. 10:19).

The psalmist seems to say that this is what brings down many a godly person to defeat. He constantly contrasts the righteous and unrighteous, but the references in Psalm 12 are about the godly person who has ceased to be godly and what has caused the faithful to disappear. It is because they spoke lies and falsehoods to one another and engaged in flattery from a "double heart." Reference to a double heart in the Scripture highlights a devastating characteristic—to have double, conflicting affections or to carry on a pretense of believing and practicing one thing while actually being another. Flattery is a comment which is insincere, saying nice things to or about someone in order to impress or gain favor, when they are not true and not at all what we think in our hearts. It reflects insincerity and a lack of integrity. And we are told the Lord will cut off from fellowship with Him all who speak such things.

> *The words of the Lord are pure. They are for blessing and edification.*

Another example of misusing the tongue is seen in those who are eloquent and persuasive and able to twist and distort issues so that people believe and follow them. They are able to use words to their own advantage and power; it feeds their ego and so exalts their pride that they come to believe they are accountable to no one—no one is Lord over them. While this may sound like a description of some politicians, it is amazing how many preachers seem to fall into this deceptive trap. The result of misusing words to carry on pretense, building up oneself, and putting down others is that someone is always victimized and hurt. The Lord will always side with the afflicted and needy and come to their aid.

In contrast to the pride of the wicked, exalting evil and exerting influence that is worldly and vile, the words of the Lord are pure. They are for blessing and edification. His promises are true and will preserve those who seek refuge in Him and believe.

PRAYER: *Lord, help me not to yield to the subtle temptation of misusing words for self-gain and in ways that would hurt others and dishonor You. Help me to avoid the pretense of flattery that is dishonest and self-serving. Help me always speak with integrity and use my words to edify and bless. Thank You for Your words that are true and dependable.*

Overcoming Depression

Key Verse: How long, O LORD? Wilt Thou forget me forever?
How long wilt Thou hide Thy face from me? (Psalm 13:1)

All of us go through times of discouragement and despair. It may be when plans go awry and we feel out of control. It may be due to a debilitating accident or illness or a financial setback when the bills pile up. It may come due to a conflict with a friend or colleague or maybe strained relationships within the family. We all go through times of self-doubt and cease to find joy and fulfillment in our work or daily tasks. Whatever the reason—and we may not be able to put our finger on it—we feel abandoned by God. The joy of intimacy that comes from a close walk with Him and the sense of His presence are gone. Even our efforts at Bible study and prayer seem empty.

Four times in Psalm 13 the psalmist cries out, *"How long, O LORD?"* (v. 1). How long will you forget me? How long will You hide Your face so that I don't sense the reality of Your presence and blessing? How long must I grovel in the sorrow and agony of soul-searching, feeling sorry for myself and finding no answer? And there always seems to be a cause, someone, something, or some circumstance that is not right, as if an enemy is overpowering us.

> **In times of depression we must be transparent and acknowledge our need and then recognize that God is the answer.**

Our plea to God is appropriate. We must get beyond the personal struggle of trying to work through our problems ourselves. We must avoid those futile efforts to generate feelings of victory through mental attempts of denying reality.

We must be transparent and acknowledge our need and then recognize that God is the answer. Be honest with Him and relinquish the problem to Him, *"casting all your anxiety upon Him, because He cares for you"* (1 Pet. 5:7). Confess Him as your Lord and your God. Believe that He wants to enlighten our eyes to see Him in all His glory. He is not blessed and glorified when we are going through the throes of depression as if we might die. There is no benefit to Him when we are shaken by our adversaries and overcome by our enemies of worry and anxiety.

Victory and release come through trusting in God's mercy and loving-kindness and rejoicing in the salvation God has given us. Victory comes through singing to the Lord, confident that He deals with us in compassion. As Paul expressed it: *"exceedingly abundantly beyond all we could ask or think!"* (Eph. 3:20). Hebrews 11:1 says, *"Faith is the assurance of things hoped for, the conviction of things not seen."* We must believe and trust God in spite of all evidence to the contrary, not because of what we feel and experience but because of His nature and character. Nothing can take our salvation from us. Our security is in Christ. We may go through the valley but must never cease to rejoice in His salvation. And finally, singing to the Lord will bring the ultimate victory because God delights in the praises of His people. He will manifest His presence and restore the joy when we thank Him and praise Him in all things.

PRAYER: *Lord, in times of discouragement and depression when I feel rejected, hear my prayer and reveal Yourself to me. Don't allow me to succumb to doubting Your faithfulness regardless of the circumstances, but guide me always to trust Your loving-kindness. I will rejoice in the salvation You have given me and will sing praise to You, my Lord and my God.*

Psalm 14

Living in a Godless World

Key Verse: There is no one who does good, not even one.
(Psalm 14:3)

When we observe the behavior and attitudes that permeate our society today, there can be little question about the depravity of people who do not know the Lord. In fact, all of us have hearts that are corrupt. Only by God's grace and His redeeming power does anyone have any degree of righteousness. Since Adam, the heart of man is inclined to sin. Corrupt motives are characteristic of our sinful nature; "abominable deeds" are the result. In self-centered pride and arrogance we have convinced ourselves of self-sufficiency and that we are lord of our own lives.

Humanism is the prevailing philosophy in which people exert their own will, feel adequate in their own strength, and have the right to choose their own destiny, no matter who is affected or victimized. People justify doing whatever pleases and gratifies them. There is no absolute truth or moral parameters. This results in a libertarian attitude of "anything goes." It is the natural expression of the flesh, and it characterizes our nature apart from God.

> **There are few true atheists who deny the existence of God but many practical atheists who ignore Him in order to pursue their own desires.**

There are few true atheists who deny the existence of God but many practical atheists who ignore Him and reject Him in order to pursue their own desires and pleasures. For if one denies God, then there is no accountability. While many may take this position due to pseudo-intellectual rationalization, it is foolish to deny the realities that testify to His existence, His sovereignty over the universe, and our need for Him. Nevertheless, this is the human predicament apart from God. We don't understand or seek after God, our hearts are corrupt, our deeds are wicked, and we don't call upon God in times of need.

But we are assured that God is with the righteous generation. He is a refuge for those who are afflicted by having to live in a godless society, ridiculed and shamed for their faith. Just as the *"salvation of Israel [came] out of Zion"* (v. 7) with the coming of Jesus, the Lord will restore His people who are captive to a sinful world. We may bemoan injustices and be subjected to influences and even laws that are contrary to the righteousness of God, such as legalized abortion and denying prayer and religious expression in public places. But we should rejoice and be glad. God is on His throne. He is our refuge, our security, our hope and will reward the righteous whose heart is pure and those who seek to walk in faithfulness in contrast to the ways of the world.

PRAYER: *Lord, it is easy to recognize the godlessness and gross worldliness that characterize our world and society. No one naturally seeks You and does good. It is only by Your grace that our hearts are changed from our corrupt, sinful nature apart from You. Help me not to succumb to the influences and values of the world but look to You for counsel and guidance. You are my refuge; You are my salvation, and I will be glad and rejoice in You.*

Psalm 15

Dwelling in God's Presence

Key Verse: O LORD, who may abide in Thy tent? Who may dwell on Thy holy hill? He who walks with integrity, and works righteousness, and speaks truth in his heart. (Psalm 15:1–2)

Our greatest desire should always be to abide in the presence of the Lord. The greatest joy is to be aware of Him within our lives, throughout the day, and in everything we encounter. God is there. We have access to the Father through Jesus Christ. He will never leave us or forsake us. But how do we experience the abiding? What gives us an awareness of living, dwelling, working, and walking in His holy presence?

Obviously that must be the desire of our heart, the pursuit of our life, the longing within our mind and thoughts. Christ has come to indwell our life; He wants us to enjoy the reality of His presence daily. The psalmist describes five characteristics that must be reflected in our lives and five things we must avoid if we are to be mindful of that reality.

- We must walk with integrity, that is, practice absolute honesty and transparency.
- We must do works of righteousness. This comes not from our ability but because of His righteousness within us, guiding us and empowering us to do what is good.
- We must speak truth in our hearts. It is not just our words; the most devious lies are self-deceit, the pretense of thinking we are something we are not. We will not speak and represent truth if we do not recognize it and acknowledge it within.
- We honor those who fear the Lord. Those are the people who are our models and mentors. We respect them and seek to follow their example. Look for them. There are a lot of impressive Christians, but the genuine ones reflect an awesome

fear and reverence for the Lord; it is the motive for their obedience.

- Our commitment is unchanging, even if it brings hurt to us. God honors the one who is steadfast, unwavering, not easily influenced and persuaded by others—one who is willing to suffer and make sacrifices to walk faithfully with the Lord.

There are a lot of impressive Christians, but the genuine ones reflect an awesome fear and reverence for the Lord.

There are also five negative characteristics that will not be the practice of one who dwells with the Lord. These are obviously contrary to God's nature and therefore are inconsistent with abiding in His presence.

- We do not slander or speak evil of anyone else.
- We do not do anything that would harm and wrong someone.
- We do not take up a reproach, even when someone has abused or hurt us.
- We do not misuse our money but practice good stewardship; we are not motivated in trying to get excessive gain or profit.
- We will not take a bribe against the innocent; this may not be money, but we avoid taking advantage of another person to enhance our reputation or status.

PRAYER: *Lord, I desire to dwell in Your presence. You are holy, and I am unworthy, but You are my righteousness. Help me to walk with integrity, do that which is righteous, and speak truth in my heart that my relationship with You will never be shaken.*

Abiding in God's Presence

Key Verse: I have set the LORD continually before me; because He is at my right hand, I will not be shaken. (Psalm 16:8)

Practicing the presence of Jesus is the key to walking in faith and victory. Praising the Lord and thanking Him in all things seems to create a sense of His presence. Days that are a joy and pleasure are those when He seems to be sitting beside me at my desk, walking down the sidewalk beside me, or participating unseen in my conversations and meetings. Nothing can shake us—no temptation, no sudden disappointment, criticism, or trial—when we are focused on Christ. It puts everything in perspective.

We must recognize that we have no goodness apart from Him. God is our refuge, but He provides us the blessing of fellowship with His saints, fellow believers, while on earth. That fellowship is our delight, and we have no tendency to place our attention and affections on other gods. While we would not even be inclined to idol worship, which we observe in many parts of the world, we recognize that to compromise (barter) and be drawn to the gods of wealth, status, reputation, or popularity brings only sorrow.

> **Practicing the presence of Jesus is the key to walking in faith and victory.**

The Lord also is the One who has blessed us with a good heritage. We see so many who have not had the privilege of a Christian home and godly parents. Their lives are confused and directionless; they have not had the influence of God's Word to nurture a foundation of spiritual values. We have to be overwhelmed with gratitude for God's blessings of our heritage. Circumstances throughout our lives have fallen into place because God determined our lot; He had a purpose for us and has given us a heritage to bless us that we might rejoice and glorify Him in our lives.

We can be confident of God's counsel and guidance. When we practice His presence and set Him before us constantly, even in the night He *"instructs our minds"* (v. 7). We can rest secure in Him because He will not forsake us or abandon us. Our salvation is secure not because of our goodness but because of the nature of the One who saves us and because of His faithfulness. Therefore we need not fear hell or eternal punishment, and we can dwell securely and confidently in the flesh, that is, in this life. He is unfolding and revealing the *"path of life"* (v. 11), the decisions we need to make, and the direction He has determined in His timing. That should not be our concern, however, for our desire should be only to enjoy His presence. Not only does that make our heart glad, but we find that in His presence is fullness of joy, fulfillment in life, and pleasures forever.

PRAYER: *Lord, You are my goodness; there is nothing worthy in me apart from You. You have blessed me with a wonderful heritage, and everything is coming together in my life just as You purposed it. Your desire is that I experience the fullness of joy that comes from an awareness of Your presence. You are my refuge. You counsel and guide me. Help me to stay focused on You and know that You are always with me.*

Assurance of God's Protection

Key Verse: My steps have held fast to Thy paths.
My feet have not slipped. (Psalm 17:5)

We will always be disillusioned if we presume that we will be treated with justice in this world. There is the perception that if we speak truth, avoid mistreating others, do good, and keep our hearts pure, then God will prosper and bless us. But the reality is that we will always be subjected to those who abuse us. We will find it is not uncommon to be swindled and taken advantage of by dishonest business practices and those who are driven only by selfish gain. We must live in a world that does not fear God or respect one another. So even deliberate attacks go with the territory!

The psalmist speaks of *"those who rise up against [him]"* (v. 7) and *"surround [him] . . . [with an] unfeeling heart"* (vv. 9–10), insensitive and uncaring. They speak out of pride and arrogance with intent to *"cast us down to the ground"* (v. 11), whether in actual harm, financial loss, or to despoil our reputation. Our enemies are people of the world who behave like a lion lurking in hiding places. We can usually stand against blatant evil, but it is more difficult to avoid that which is subtle and devious and blindsides us from unexpected sources.

> *We can usually stand against blatant evil, but it is more difficult to avoid that which is subtle and devious.*

Our appeal is appropriately to the Lord as we are usually helpless against such attacks. Although we have done nothing wrong, have not violated God's laws, and have not even spoken words that are deceitful or inappropriate, this is not the basis of our appeal. We may have walked faithfully in accord with God's will, *"held fast to [His] paths"* (v. 5), and affirmed that our *"feet have not slipped"* (v. 5); in fact, God has tried our hearts and not found anything wrong. But our appeal is not on the basis of what we have done or deserve but on God's character and assurance of His faithfulness.

He will heed our cry, will answer us, and *"incline [His] ear to [hear us]"* (v. 6) because we are assured of His presence and that He judges with equity. He is always with us and knows what we are going through. He is the *"Savior of those who take refuge at [His] right hand"* (v. 7). He is a refuge for those who instinctively turn to Him for vindication and do not take it upon themselves to react vindictively or to defend themselves. We come to Him knowing that He will show His loving-kindness and hide us in the shadow of His wings. Sin and injustice are contrary to His nature, and He will deliver our soul from the hand of the wicked.

Vindication may not be immediate, but we walk in faithfulness—never taking the battle upon ourselves—confident that God in His mercy will respond to our need and appeal. The key is keeping our eyes on Him, beholding His presence and remaining confident that we will see Him act in righteousness.

PRAYER: *Lord, the battles and personal attacks seem to be constant. I don't deserve Your favor, but I am confident You hear my prayer, know my needs, and heed my pleas. Help me to walk with integrity according to Your will. Keep my heart pure, my eyes upon You, and my faith strong that I may be worthy of Your favor and deliverance.*

God Provides Confidence of Victory

*Key Verse: The LORD is my rock and my fortress and
my deliverer, my God, my rock, in whom I take refuge; my shield
and the horn of my salvation, my stronghold. (Psalm 18:2)*

This is a beautiful expression of comprehensive praise and worship based on the opening statement, *"I love Thee, O LORD"* (v. 1). I love You because . . . You save me from my enemies when I call upon You. I love You because . . . when I am distressed and face the threat of death You hear my cry for help. I love You because . . . when the whole world is in turmoil and chaos, You draw me out, deliver me, and delight in me. I love You because . . . You reward me according to my righteousness, You enlighten my way, You are a shield of refuge, You deliver me from the contentions of the people, and on and on!

What a sense of victory He gives when we meditate on all the Lord has done for us! When we think of His power, His character, His grace, His holiness, and all that He does for us, our confidence and joy should overcome any threat or discouragement. Even the prospects of death, natural disasters, and the storms of life do not shake us, for the Lord is our rock, our fortress, and our deliverer. He is our shield, our refuge, and our salvation.

We can be assured that He will reward us for our righteousness, for keeping our hands pure, and for not engaging in sinful deeds. But it is not because of our own holiness; He is the One who guides us, protects us from evil and harm, and makes our way blameless. There is no one like the Lord. He blesses us and, like the deer, sets our feet on high places, aloof from the filth and hardships of the world to claim the victory and enjoy fellowship with Him.

> *When we think of God's power,*
> *character, grace, and holiness, our*
> *confidence and joy should overcome*
> *any threat or discouragement.*

He *"light[s] my lamp"* and *"illumines [our] darkness"* (v. 28), enlightening our understanding and showing us the way. In His strength we overcome. He trains our hands for battle; in His power we can *"run upon a troop; and . . . leap over a wall"* (v. 29). In His strength we can stand against a multitude and overcome any obstacle. He will protect us against our enemies and bring down those who hate us. He delivers us from contentions of the people. He upholds us and sustains us with His powerful *"right hand"* of authority and power. If we are exalted and raised to places of leadership, as was David, it is only because God has placed us there. The only barrier is our own pride and haughtiness in thinking we are self-sufficient, we can do it ourselves, and we are blessed because of what we have done. We are assured of victory; therefore we should give thanks to God, testify of His love and greatness among the nations, and sing praises to His name.

PRAYER: *Lord, it seems I am always under attack, if not by adversaries and critics, by circumstances that tend to rob me of my joy and victory. Help me not to rely on my own strength but to call upon You because You are my rock, my fortress, and my deliverer. You are my shield and my strength. I have no righteousness of my own, but You enable me to dwell in the high place of Your presence and holiness. You show me Your will and guide me in Your way that I may be pure and blameless. Even when I am lifted up over others, keep me humble. Help me always to recognize that You have blessed me and equipped me with strength to glorify You and testify of Your goodness and mercy.*

Psalm 19

Response to God's Majesty

*Key Verse: Let the words of my mouth and the meditation
of my heart be acceptable in Thy sight, O LORD, my rock
and my Redeemer. (Psalm 19:14)*

God's existence is revealed by the grandeur and glory
of His creation. The precise functioning of the way
nature fits together, the way days and nights and
seasons flow in orderly sequence and sustain life, is evident
throughout the world. There is no place, no people or language that does not have testimony and witness of a divine
Creator and the One who is sovereign over the universe. But
the physical, natural world is only a parallel or example of
the moral nature of God that governs all things and by which
God has chosen to bless mankind. Unfortunately these principles are largely ignored by society in its humanistic tendency to choose one's own concept of what is right or wrong.
But they are essential if an individual is to find blessing and
fulfillment in life. The psalmist continues a beautiful poetic
description in enumerating these comprehensive and distinc-
tive guides that make everything fit together spiritually and
practically.

1. The **law** of the Lord is **perfect**; following it is what
   restores us to fellowship with the Father and keeps
   our soul in tune with Him.
2. The **testimony** of the Lord is **sure**. Following it gives us
   wisdom for the choices and decisions we make; it is
   not complicated but available to the simple.
3. The **precepts** of the Lord are **right**; understanding these
   principles and values and applying them will bring a
   life filled with joy.
4. The **commandments** of the Lord are **pure**; they are
   not designed to be burdensome or punitive but to
   enlighten our understanding for expected behavior
   and integrity.

5. The **fear** of the Lord is **clean;** perseverance in a holy and righteous life without wavering comes from a reverence for the Lord. Living in awe of Him, His glory and presence, is a deterrent from anything sinful and impure.
6. The **judgments** of the Lord are **righteous;** they are not to be feared but desired because they convict us and restore us. They can be counted on to be just and redemptive. God does not simply ignore us, therefore they are of more value than gold and more precious than the most delicious delicacy is to the flesh.

Because God has revealed His law, precepts, and commands, we can know how to live and be assured of reward in following them.

Because God has revealed His law, precepts, commands, and judgments, we can know how to live and be assured of great reward in following them; they serve as a warning for what we should avoid and the consequences of choosing a way contrary to how God has instructed us. However, there is a danger of presumptuous sin. We are not capable of discerning our own errors and can easily presume to be walking in righteousness while living according to fleshly and self-serving desires. That is why not only outward behavior but also the meditations of our hearts, expressed in the words of our mouth, need to be acceptable to God.

PRAYER: *Lord, the glory of the universe, Your creation, is an awesome reminder of Your power and authority. I long to walk in obedience and fellowship with You. Thank You for giving Your law to guide me, but it is my heart that You see and judge. May my thoughts and meditations be pure and reflected in my words and conversation. Convict me of ways contrary to Your will, cleanse me of error, and guard me from presumptuous sins.*

Answered Prayer in the
Name of the Lord

*Key Verse: May He grant you your heart's desire,
and fulfill all your counsel! (Psalm 20:4)*

Because the Bible is fully inspired by God, I have always seen the prayers in Paul's epistles or elsewhere as revealing God's heart and what He wants for us. To see this beautiful Psalm of petition in that regard is reassuring in the scope of blessing which God wants to pour out upon us.

In our times of trouble, God will answer us and set us securely on high, that is, in His presence. He will lift our spirits above the turmoil and confusion of the daily battle. Our help and strength do not come from horses and chariots—things that represent the strength and power of the world such as wealth, financial support, organizations, or public favor. In fact, these will all eventually be bowed down and fall. But our support comes from God. The name of the Lord is our strength, our source of blessings, and the only thing in which we can boast. How do we access that help? By seeking refuge in the sanctuary of His presence. It comes from those quiet times of fellowship with Him in which all of the noise, busyness, and concerns of daily life are shut out. And God will accept all that we offer to Him—our heart, our affections, and our life. We cannot expect literal offerings to be acceptable if we have not given ourselves fully to Him.

**Life has meaning only as it is
consistent with God's will.**

We need to remember that we are not alone in the battle. There is a vast array of fellow pilgrims. God has given us a family and community of faith that shares in the joy of our victories; they bear our burdens with us and hurt when we hurt but are also blessed when we are blessed. Banners (v. 5) portray the image of warriors going to battle led by the flags of their king, representing the cause for which they are fighting and giving their lives. God gives us a banner, a cause to which we are to devote our lives. In the name of the Lord and for His glory, we discern our life's purpose. Life has meaning only as it is consistent with God's will.

When we come to Him, gain strength from His sanctuary—that secret place of fellowship with Him—find security in His name, and devote our lives to His cause and purpose, then we can be assured that our petitions will be answered. We have access to the saving deeds of His right hand of authority that is above all dominion and power. And He ultimately grants us our heart's desire and fulfills our counsel. What is our heart's desire? It should be only to know Him in all of His fullness! When we are focused totally on God and His glory, we will not be sidetracked by self-serving, personal desires. God can readily answer our prayers and work through us—in our decisions and the circumstances around us—to see that our life's purpose is fulfilled.

PRAYER: *Lord, there is such a natural tendency to rely on things that represent power and status in the world, but help me to realize that my only strength and security are in Your name. You are my confidence and the source of all I need. You will fulfill Your purpose and guide me by Your counsel only when my delight and heart's desire are for You and You alone.*

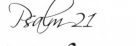
Psalm 21

God's Anointing for Leadership

Key Verse: O LORD, in Thy strength the king will be glad, and in Thy salvation how greatly he will rejoice! (Psalm 21:1)

This unique Psalm is focused on David and his position as king. God had greatly blessed him and given him his heart's desire and every request of his lips. He had given him wealth and authority, *"splendor and majesty,"* (v. 5) and lengthened his days. But what is significant is that even in his exalted position David recognized that all that he had came from God. Whatever he was, it was because of God's blessings; and whatever he did, it was because God enabled him. For anyone who gains a position of recognition or authority over others or simply prospers materially, it is difficult to remain humble and avoid taking some credit for what has been attained.

When I became president of the International Mission Board, I was overwhelmed by the responsibility. Though I had exhibited leadership skills in other roles, leading a global organization with a large, complex staff was far beyond my realm of experience. As I stood in the door of the office of the president, literally trembling, someone put his hand on my shoulder and said, "It's overwhelming, isn't it? But you need to understand, an anointing goes with that chair" (nodding toward the impressive, executive chair behind the desk). I discovered that God, indeed, does not lift one to a level of leadership without giving His Spirit to provide all that is needed. But I also discovered that access to those blessings comes from maintaining a sense of inadequacy and brokenness. I learned to discern that the constant criticism, mistakes, and sense of failure were necessary to keep me on my knees, ever dependent on the Lord and never prideful or presumptive about my own ability. It was not about exalting David, but the role of the king was to serve others and to bless his people that they would praise the Lord.

> *God does not lift one to a level of leader-*
> *ship without giving His Spirit to provide*
> *all that is needed.*

The strength of the Lord makes us glad, and in His salvation we rejoice! If God gives us what our hearts desire and grants our requests, it is not because we deserve them, but it is His nature to bless us with good things. God's desire is for us to be joyful and to experience an abiding gladness that comes from His presence and fellowship with Him; it is not because of the wealth, splendor, and comforts of a nice lifestyle or from extended life and health. He overcomes those who come against us and assures us that those who oppose us will not succeed. We need to discover, like David, that we can endure any trial and withstand opposition without being shaken because of God's loving-kindness and because we trust in Him, not because of our own strength and ability.

PRAYER: *Lord, I don't deserve the recognition and position of responsibility and authority You have given me. I am inadequate for leading others. But I'm thankful that You have assured me of strength and wisdom. You are the One who blesses me with joy and the comforts of life. You are the One who overcomes my enemies that I might not be shaken. Lord, I trust in You and Your loving-kindness; my joy comes from abiding in Your presence. I serve You and fulfill my responsibilities, not for my own glory and recognition but for Your glory and praise.*

Suffering for the Sake of the Kingdom

*Key Verse: All the ends of the earth will remember and
turn to the LORD, and all the families of the nations
will worship before Thee. For the kingdom is the LORD's
and He rules over the nations. (Psalm 22:27–28)*

Many of the Psalms reflect a time of turmoil and conflict in which the writer is overwhelmed by adversity, injustice, and persecution; but perhaps none
exceed this one in the desperation of feeling forsaken even by
God. He speaks of crying out day and night and receiving no
rest or respite. He reminds God that in the past His people
trusted in Him, and He delivered them, but he continues to
be a reproach, despised and slandered. Yet his hope is based
on the fact that God made him and he belongs to God. The
holiness of God is never questioned, and the thread of hope
to which he holds is the fact that God resides in the praises of
His people.

> **Whatever happens, even suffering
> and rejection, is for a higher purpose;
> God has not abandoned me.**

While the psalmist is crying out in a dilemma that is current, this is a prophetic passage revealing the crucifixion of
our Lord in graphic detail. We read, *"I am poured out
like water, and all my bones are out of joint (v. 14). . . .
They pierced my hands and my feet. I can count all my
bones* (vv. 16–17; none was broken as is typical of a crucifixion). . . . *They divide my garments among them, and for my
clothing they cast lots"* (v. 18). All of these matched precisely
the events of the crucifixion. As I read the first verse, the
thought occurred to me that perhaps when Jesus cried out on

the cross, *"My God, My God, why hast Thou forsaken Me?"* (Mark 15:34), it was not an expression of feeling abandoned by the Father as He took upon Himself the sins of the world as we have traditionally thought. Whenever Jesus encountered temptation, He used the power and truth of God's Word to counter the attacks of Satan. Spiritual warfare reached a pinnacle of intensity when Jesus went to the cross to conquer sin and death. It is not unlikely His thoughts went to Psalm 22, and He gained strength and assurance in being reminded that all that was happening to Him was programmed by the Father. God was on His throne and simply fulfilling His eternal purpose to provide redemption for a lost world.

Rather than rejection and abandonment, Jesus began to quote this passage of the Old Testament as an affirmation of the victory that was assured. He began, *"My God, my God, why hast Thou forsaken me"* (v. 1), but in the dryness of His mouth and searing lungs being stretched breathless by the pain and torture of the cross, He was not able to speak the verses that followed. In His mind He was claiming verse 3, that God continued to be enthroned in the praises of His people. And rapidly His thoughts ran to verses 27–28. Why was all this happening to Him? Why was it necessary to suffer such an agonizing death? So that one day *"all the ends of the earth will remember* (what He has done for them) *and turn to the LORD, and all the families of the nations will worship before Thee. For the kingdom is the LORD's and He rules over the nations."*

PRAYER: *Lord, help me be mindful that whatever happens to me, even the suffering and rejection I may have to endure, is for a higher purpose. You have not abandoned me or relinquished Your throne; I will always praise You, for You manifest Your presence and reside in the praises of Your people. Help me endure whatever comes for the sake of Your glory among the nations.*

Psalm 23

Assurance of God's Care

*Key Verse: The LORD is my shepherd,
I shall not want. (Psalm 23:1)*

What could be said about this beautiful and familiar "shepherd Psalm"? Many devotional books have been written on these verses; no other Scripture passage is quoted so often. There is a danger in that which is most familiar losing its meaningfulness to us. But there is, indeed, a wealth of blessing and application in this graphic image of the shepherd loving and caring for his sheep.

Like a shepherd, the Lord is our provision and protection. Apart from Him there is nothing that we need or desire. He provides for us not only adequately but in abundance, like a shepherd who leads his flock to the pastures of green grass. He leads us out of the turbulent waters of turmoil and stress of daily life to quiet our hearts and to drink of the peaceful, quiet water of His presence. He restores us when we come to the end of ourselves, realizing we cannot do it ourselves, and causing us to turn to Him. When we are willing to follow in submission to His will, He is faithful to guide our lives and will always lead us according to a righteous and holy life, to do what is right and that which glorifies Him.

> **Walking daily in a trust relationship
> with the Lord is the source of blessings
> that overflow in abundance.**

Not only does He feed and nurture us, care for us and lead us, but He also protects us when we go through times of need. I have observed that the reality of one's faith is evident in times of adversity and affliction. When a severe accident takes the life of a loved one, or one is diagnosed with a terminal illness, becoming distraught and reacting with anxiety or bitterness reflects a shallow and perfunctory faith. But one who has a genuine, intimate relationship with the Lord can walk through the *"valley of the shadow of death"* (v. 4) without fear. Even in the presence of personal attacks, ridicule, and confrontation with those who would cause us harm, our confidence is in the fact that the Lord is with us. He will protect us by the anointing of His hand upon us and will even flaunt His blessings as a testimony to our enemies.

Walking daily in a trust relationship with the Lord is the source of blessings that overflow in abundance. We can be confident His mercy and goodness will go with us all the days of our life. He will never leave us or forsake us. Our eternal security is guaranteed. We will dwell with Him forever, not because of our own goodness and righteousness but because we are His sheep and our trust is in Him.

PRAYER: *Lord, like sheep I tend to wander off and follow my own path of self-will, thinking I am adequate for whatever I may face in life. I confess that I need You to guide me and protect me from trials and concerns that attack me each day. I long for the peace that only You can provide from the pressures and stress of life. I need to be assured of Your hand upon me when the temptations and the enemy of my own fleshly nature tend to control my desires and my affections. You are my shepherd; You care for me and want only what is best. Help me to follow as Your sheep in submission and trust.*

In the Presence of the King of Glory

Key Verse: He who has clean hands and a pure heart, who has not lifted up his soul to falsehood, and has not sworn deceitfully. He shall receive a blessing from the LORD and righteousness from the God of his salvation. (Psalm 24:4–5)

Occasionally the poetic expression of a Psalm is built around a single graphic image and analogy. Picture a medieval castle with banners flying from the ramparts and shouting subjects lining the walls as they welcome their king returning victoriously from battle. The drawbridge is lowered over the protective moat that surrounds the castle, the orders are given, and the heavy, fortified gate begins to be raised for the king and his entourage to enter in all their glorious splendor. He will once again take his seat on the throne and rule his kingdom.

The day will come when Jesus Christ, our victorious Lord and King, will claim the nations as His kingdom. The world that He created out of nothing and the lands He formed from the seas will one day belong to Him. All that is within the world that He created will belong to Him. He is the King of glory; He is the Lord, strong and mighty, Sovereign over the nations, and the Father has given to Him *"all authority . . . in heaven and on earth"* (Matt. 28:18).

> **It is not enough to do good things and live a righteous life. God expects us to have pure motives and a sincere heart.**

But there is also a personal reference here to His lordship over our lives. Have we opened the doors of our hearts to welcome Him and enthrone Him as Ruler and King with authority over all that we do? The question is asked, *"Who may ascend into the hill of the Lord? And who may stand in His holy place?"* (v. 3). Who may accompany Him into that glorious, eternal kingdom and dwell in His presence? The answer is twofold with an additional twofold explanation: only a person who has clean hands and a pure heart. It is not enough just to do good things and live a righteous life. *"Man looks at the outward appearance, but the* LORD *looks at the heart"* (1 Sam. 16:7). God expects us to have pure motives that are not self-serving and a sincere heart in doing good. This will be characterized by one who does not lie and is not deceitful. Unfortunately, many who would never tell a lie to others often practice self-deceit in presuming to be righteous on their own rather than realizing righteousness comes from God; we must recognize that we receive blessing and salvation only from Him.

So, like the gates of that ancient citadel, lift up your head to praise and exalt the King of glory; open the door of your heart to welcome Him, dwell in His presence, and enthrone Him as Lord. Allow His righteousness to produce a pure heart and clean life that will enable you to enjoy the blessings of His salvation.

PRAYER: *Lord, how I long to ascend into the hill of the Lord and dwell in Your holy presence. I welcome You into my heart and enthrone You in my life. I pray that You would be glorified as I live a clean life and serve You with a pure heart. You are the Lord of hosts, strong and mighty; I confess You as the King of glory, my Master and Lord.*

The Implications of Fearing God

Key Verse: Who is the man who fears the LORD? He will instruct him in the way he should choose. (Psalm 25:12)

I have often struggled to define what it means to "fear God." This is a prominent theme throughout the Bible, especially in the Psalms. It obviously does not mean simply to be afraid of God, though that should not be absent in the awe and reverence we hold for the One who is all powerful—the dispenser of justice, who represents the highest power and moral standard in the universe. The closest I can come in my understanding is the relationship I had with my parents as a child. My obedience to what they told me to do and conforming to their expectations for my behavior was not entirely out of fear of being punished; it also was out of my respect and love for them. It was due to recognition of a submissive relationship and that I was under their authority.

We are told three important things about what we are to do because of our relationship with God and who He is. (1) We are to trust in Him. (2) We are to wait upon Him—a word that is often translated "hope." We believe His promises and that all He has assured us of belongs to us, even though it may not yet be evident because we hope or wait on Him. (3) And we are to fear the Lord. Then we are given assurance of some amazing blessings and truths.

> **We must earnestly desire to know
> His ways, walk in His paths, and
> abide in His truth.**

- God will instruct us in His way, the way He has chosen for us.
- Our soul will abide in prosperity. *"Beloved, I pray that in all respects you may prosper and be in good health, just as your soul prospers"* (3 John 2).
- Our descendants will inherit the land—they will not lose what we pass on to them, not just in material wealth, but in our spiritual legacy.
- God will reveal His secrets. We will have an intimacy in which we know the heart of God. (What an awesome privilege!)
- We will know God's covenant, His purpose for us personally and how He is working out His divine plan that we might walk within it.
- Our eyes will continually, always, be focused on Him and following His will.

But all of this is contingent on a submissive relationship to God, as described in the beginning of this Psalm. We must come into His presence and lift our soul to Him. We must trust only in Him. We must earnestly desire to know His ways, walk in His paths and abide in His truth. We must recognize that He is our salvation. It is only because of His compassion and loving-kindness that our enemies are overcome and our sins are forgiven.

PRAYER: *Lord, I come into Your presence and humbly lift my soul, waiting expectantly for You. I bow in awe and fear, for You are my salvation; You do not remember the sins of my youth because You are loving and merciful and compassionate. Show me Your way, teach me Your truths, and reveal the secrets of Your heart that my soul may prosper and my descendants may inherit the blessings of those who wait for You.*

A Life Worthy of Vindication

Key Verse: O LORD, I love the habitation of Thy house, and the place where Thy glory dwells. (Psalm 26:8)

Living for the Lord and doing everything right does not mean the absence of problems or that we will be exempt from adversity. While the natural reaction is to try to deal with opposition and the issues that come against us, our only hope is in the Lord and the conviction that He is just and will vindicate us. However, we cannot be presumptuous regarding His grace and intervention. Our appeal is contingent on how we live and the integrity of our heart. We cannot be indifferent in our behavior, indulge in things of the world, compromise our values, do whatever we choose, and still expect to benefit from God's loving-kindness and mercy.

> *We cannot be indifferent in our behavior, do whatever we choose, and still expect to benefit from God's loving-kindness.*

The model for how we are to live is an extensive list that is quite practical. This is what God expects of us:

- Walking (living) with integrity—absolute honesty and transparency in all actions and relationships with no hypocrisy or hidden motives.
- Trusting in the Lord without wavering; no circumstance or trial can cause us to doubt God's purpose and lordship in our lives.
- Being willing for God to examine and judge not just our behavior and actions but the innermost thoughts of our heart and mind—our feelings and attitudes.

- Walking in God's truth, that is, obedience to His Word and what He has said, confident of His faithfulness in all He has promised.
- Keeping the fact of His loving-kindness before us—aware that our relationship with Him is totally dependent on His undeserved grace and mercy.
- Avoiding identification with those who are deceitful and hypocritical and association with friends or groups that practice evil.
- Being faithful in worship—coming to the altar of the Lord in consistent devotion, not simply to have our needs met but out of thanksgiving and praise for the Lord.
- Bearing faithful testimony in declaring to others the wonders and glory of the Lord.
- Desiring above all things to dwell in God's presence and revel in the blessing of His glory.

I have long ago come to the conclusion that the only thing that will enable us to live a holy life for the glory of God is to have a heart for God. The only way to avoid yielding to the subtle temptations that constantly and unceasingly confront us in this world is to be desperate to know Him in all of His fullness. Our greatest desire is to be in the place of His habitation. We want His presence to be manifested in our heart so that His glory is reflected in us.

PRAYER: *Lord, test me, try me, examine my heart and my mind that I might walk with integrity in Your truth. My desire is to worship You and to experience Your presence at church but not only there. May my home, my office, my car, hotel rooms, and airplanes also be the place of Your habitation and Your glory.*

Psalm 27

Seeking God's Face

Key Verse: One thing I have asked from the LORD, *that I shall seek: that I may dwell in the house of the* LORD *all the days of my life, to behold the beauty of the* LORD, *and to meditate in His temple. (Psalm 27:4)*

There is no need for us ever to be overcome by fear because the Lord is our light, our salvation, and our defense. Our security and confidence are in Him. Anxiety usually comes with the fear of the unknown and of what might happen; it is obscure and cloaked in darkness, but the light of God's truth delivers us. Though critics attack us when we have to stand against public opinion, and circumstances overwhelm us like a *"host encamped against us,"* there is no need to fear, for our confidence is in the Lord.

Our prayers are typically focused on asking God to do something as we petition Him regarding our needs or intercede for others. We want to see His hand at work on our behalf; we ask for a demonstration of His power and faithfulness to respond to our supplications. However, our desire should not be for His hands or activity, but for His face. He desires for us to seek Him for who He is, not because of what He can do for us. He wants us to behold His glory and holiness. The desire of our heart should be to see Him and to know Him.

Our desire should not be for God's hands and activity but for His face, to behold His glory and holiness.

Someone has observed that we make requests of God because of His faithfulness—what He has promised; we thank God because of His goodness—what He does; we praise God because of His greatness—who He is, and we worship God because of His holiness—the nature of His character. Coming into His presence reflects the submissiveness of our relationship to Him. Bible reading and prayer are essential to living in confidence and freedom from fear. But appropriating the blessings of a victorious life does not come from simply practicing the disciplines of piety. It comes from the motives of one's heart and a desire above all else to dwell in God's presence. Our heart should be desperate to live in unceasing fellowship with the Father in which the beauty and glory of His nature are constantly before us.

When we have a view of life filtered through the perspective of His abiding presence, the adversaries of temptation and enemies of carnal attractions are overcome. We will not fear but walk in confidence, for God lifts us up. He is gracious to us. He will not abandon us or forsake us. He hides us in the secret place of His presence where we find protection and salvation. We will find ourselves in despair unless we truly believe in His goodness and faithfulness and take courage in the hope we have in Him. We must learn to seek Him by faith and claim the blessing and hope that comes from an intimate relationship with Him.

PRAYER: *Lord, give me a desire, above all else, to seek Your face and to know You in all Your fullness, to dwell in the place of habitation where You manifest Your presence. Give me patience to seek You and wait upon You, to be strong and take courage, confident that You will overcome my enemies and I will see Your goodness, not just in the afterlife but here and now!*

Psalm 28

God Hears When We Call

Key Verse: The LORD is my strength and my shield;
my heart trusts in Him, and I am helped; therefore my heart
exults, and with my song I shall thank Him. (Psalm 28:7)

Who has not experienced occasions when we feel that our prayers go unanswered and with skepticism wonder if we are not just going through the motion of repetitive, meaningless litany in our prayers? Does God really hear us? In His power and providence, does He not do whatever He determines regardless of our petitions?

If God does not hear when we call, we are utterly hopeless, like all who will simply die and go to the grave without our prayers making any difference. If God does not hear our prayers, then we are no different from the hypocrites who speak of peace and good deeds but do iniquity because of the evil in their hearts. They will receive a just judgment from the Lord, but so will we if the Lord does not heed our prayers of confession and repentance and pleas for His grace and mercy.

But the Lord is our rock, a solid foundation in whom we can trust. He is our strength and our shield. We don't have to depend on our own ability, which will always be weak and inadequate. We don't have to defend ourselves, using our own strength in trying to resist temptation and the enemies that threaten to destroy our peace and well-being. We have the privilege of coming before the throne of God to appropriate all that God has promised and provided for us. Prayer is that channel of access; when we come to Him believing, truly trusting in Him, we receive the help we need.

We can be assured that the Lord cares
for us and is available to respond to our
cry for help and to meet our every need.

Isaiah 65:24 says, *"It will also come to pass that before they call, I will answer; and while they are still speaking, I will hear."* God appeals to us in Jeremiah 33:3, *"Call to Me, and I will answer you, and I will tell you great and mighty things, which you do not know."* We can be assured that the Lord cares for us and is constantly available to respond to our cry for help and to meet our every need. We are His anointed, and He has promised to bless His inheritance. He will be our Shepherd who guides us, protects us, and provides for us. He will carry us in His arms because He loves us and we belong to Him, unlike the evildoers who do not regard the works of the Lord.

Therefore, we are to come before Him with supplication, laying all our needs at His feet. And because we come with the assurance of answered prayer, we come exulting in Him and thanking Him. This confidence and faith put a song in our heart—an attitude of joy and praise.

PRAYER: *Lord, You are my rock and my shield. I always find help when I trust in You. I need Your strength for the tasks You set before me today; I want to walk in righteousness, obedient to Your will and the way You have determined for me. Never let me doubt Your availability and response to my prayers. I come to You in faith, trusting You for help. I come thanking You and praising You for Your blessings and the assurance that You hear and answer my prayers.*

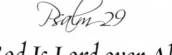

God Is Lord over All

*Key Verse: Ascribe to the LORD the glory due to His name;
worship the LORD in holy array. (Psalm 29:2)*

Jesus is Lord whether people acknowledge Him as Lord or
not. He is sovereign over the nations even though they do
not recognize Him and worship Him. His lordship, majesty, and power are not contingent on our confession and
giving Him permission to carry out His purpose and will.
However, the key to experiencing the fullness and potential of
His power and purpose is our confession and submission to
His lordship. We are to come into His presence and acknowledge His glory. We are to ascribe in our understanding and
confession the strength and power that is His. In worship we
are to attribute to Him the glory that is due and of which He
alone is worthy.

When we come into His presence, confessing Him as
Lord—acknowledging Him as Ruler of our lives—we can
come only arrayed in holiness. This relationship with God, in
recognizing who He is, will be a deterrent to sin and self-
centered behavior. We will have the experience of Isaiah
6:1–4 in which He had a vision of God sitting on His throne,
high and exalted. The hosts of heaven were declaring His
holiness, and the whole earth was filled with His glory. The
response was to recognize his own unworthiness, his unclean-
ness and sin and to receive the purifying cleansing that only
God's Holy Spirit could bring into his life.

> *The key to experiencing the fullness of
> His power and purpose is our confession
> and submission to His lordship.*

Having acknowledged and ascribed to the Lord the holiness and power that characterizes His lordship, we recognize His authority over all creation, an authority that is manifested simply by the spoken Word of God. This passage takes us back to the creation account in Genesis 1 when God spoke and the world came into being. His "voice," the authority to command the forces of nature, controls the universe. The natural order that holds things together is due to His power and purpose. The cedars of Lebanon were one of the most impressive aspects of nature in the ancient world, perhaps like the California redwoods. There is no more intimidating force of nature than the vastness of the ocean and its swells—stirring powerful waves that break upon the shore. The course of the stars, Sirion like a wild ox, the mating instincts of animals, and the destructive power of fire or storms that sweep the wilderness are all in response to His voice. His eternal, irrevocable, predetermined will and purpose are always being fulfilled in the world.

Whether one is admiring the grandeur of the Grand Canyon or a majestic mountain panorama, sitting by a quiet stream, or reveling in the beauty of green grass and spring flowers, God has created a world that is His temple. It is His dwelling place and declares His glory. He is eternal and unchanging; He is king forever, and this Lord is the One who blesses us, His people, with strength and peace.

PRAYER: *Lord, help me to see You in the world around me. Never let me lose a sense of awe at the natural world and the fact that it reflects Your glory. You are the Lord of my life, but may each moment be a conscious process of acknowledging Your lordship, Your power, and Your glory and coming before You in submission to Your holiness.*

God Lifts Us Up in Time of Need

Key Verse: For His anger is but for a moment, His favor is for a lifetime; weeping may last for the night, but a shout of joy comes in the morning. (Psalm 30:5)

To *exalt* means to praise, to glorify, and to give honor, but it also implies to fill with delight and pride. *Exult* means to rejoice greatly and be jubilant as in triumph. The psalmist often uses these terms to describe what happens when we come into God's presence and relate appropriately to Him. Here another similar term is used, *extol*, which means to praise and laud in the highest terms! What is it that elicits this kind of response? It is an awareness that God lifts us up out of our troubles.

When we cry for help in times of need, He hears us and heals us. We do not know the specific situation described by the psalmist, but it appears that he was on the brink of death. It could have been, like many go through today, a debilitating or terminal illness in which there is no hope and death seems to be inevitable. Or it may have been such a difficult time of criticism and attack by his enemies that the situation seemed hopeless; nevertheless, there was no light at the end of the tunnel. But God had delivered him, kept him alive, and his soul did not descend to the place of death. This was certainly a cause for rejoicing, singing praise to the Lord, and giving thanks to His name.

> **Whether due to God's discipline or trials that are common to life, times of darkness, weeping, and grief are always temporary.**

The reference to God's anger indicates that suffering may have been due to the psalmist's own sin, and this was the consequence of retribution and God's discipline. Sometimes our trials and times of darkness and depression are due to our own choices and actions. The punishment and grief that result from failure to walk in holiness, righteousness, and obedience to God's will are inevitable. But sometimes they are simply due to living in a fallen world. Nevertheless, whether being subjected to God's discipline or the trials and suffering that are common to life, those times of darkness, weeping, grief, and feeling out of fellowship with Him are always temporary. The light of the morning sunrise always dispels the darkness of the night, and when the light of God's presence shines upon us, the joy returns. We can be secure knowing that His favor is permanent; it is for a lifetime and cannot be shaken.

There will be times when we feel we could die and may want to. Death may seem to hold the only relief we can see. But God gives us life in order to praise Him. He would be deprived of our praise in this world if we went to the grave! Therefore we extol Him, for He turns our darkness to light, our weeping into joy, our grief into dancing and celebration. Though we may necessarily go through times of remorse and repentance for our sin and mistakes, He clothes us with gladness! He doesn't do that for our blessing and benefit but for us to praise Him and in our innermost soul give thanks to Him forever.

PRAYER: *Lord, thank You for the confidence that You take every sad and grievous experience and turn it into joy and gladness. Even Your judgment is short-lived and passes quickly that I might be restored to give praise to Your name. You deliver me from the pit of depression and preserve my life so I can give thanks to Your holy name.*

Deliverance in Times of Distress

*Key Verse: How great is Thy goodness, which Thou hast
stored up for those who fear Thee, which Thou hast wrought
for those who take refuge in Thee. (Psalm 31:19)*

We often go through times of distress when it seems
nothing seems to be working out. When our plans
go awry and dreams are shattered, a valley of
depression often follows in which all hope and joy are gone.
It is intensified when a sense of failure or times of affliction
are accompanied by others' rejection. The reaction to a gro-
tesquely deformed burn victim comes to mind as I read this
passage or the attitude many feel and express toward a girl
with loose morals who is found to be pregnant out of wedlock. It may be the repulsion others feel toward a drunkard
whose life has been dissipated by sin and iniquity. Nevertheless,
the image is of one who has become a reproach and object
of dread to his neighbors. Everyone seems to be against him;
the gossip and slander literally take away his will to live.
Our petty problems that leave us despondent would pale in
comparison to the troubles and afflictions described by the
psalmist.

Yet, in the pits of despair, he doesn't lose his confidence
in the Lord as his security and hope of deliverance. God is
his refuge, a source of comfort, his rock, the foundation that
is unshakable—his fortress and place of protection. He continues to trust in the Lord, confessing, *"Thou art my God"*
(v. 14). In spite of all that he is going through, he recognizes
that his *"times are in Thy hand"* (v. 15). God is in control
and will deliver him from his enemies and the circumstances
that beset him. When he pleads for God's face to shine upon
him and to save him, the appeal is based on knowledge of
God's mercy and loving-kindness, not the psalmist's own
merit. The plea is for deliverance, but it is for God's name
sake, that His truth and integrity would be vindicated and

God would be glorified. He asks God to lead him, guide him, and rescue him that he would never be ashamed, regardless of what he is called on to suffer.

> ### God has stored up goodness for those who fear Him and take refuge in Him.

In conclusion we find a beautiful expression of what it means to trust in the Lord. It is a confidence that God has stored up goodness for those who fear Him and take refuge in Him. Though everyone seems to be against us, our relationship with God is as if He has allowed us into a secret place of intimacy in His presence where He shelters us from all the strife, the talk, the criticism, and rejection of others. When we seem cut off from any source of support, when no one understands and we are subjected to conspiracies that would undercut our reputation, God protects us, preserves us and recompenses us for all we suffer. So the final admonition is to love the Lord, be strong, take courage, and hope in Him!

PRAYER: *Lord, I am so often attacked and criticized; it seems the conspiracies and slander to undercut my work and reputation never cease. Thank You for guiding me and delivering me for Your sake and that Your purpose would be fulfilled. Help me never to be ashamed as I look to You as my stronghold. Thank You for bringing me into the secret place of Your presence and pouring Your goodness into my life in times of strife and conflict. I acknowledge my times are in Your hands and You will preserve the faithful. I love You and take courage because my hope and confidence are in You.*

The Blessing of Forgiven Sin

*Key Verse: I will instruct you and teach you in the
way which you should go; I will counsel you
with My eye upon you. (Psalm 32:8)*

This Psalm of penitence is at the heart of our Christian experience and relationship with God. The fact of God's grace is truly amazing. Because of what Christ did for us on the cross, all our transgressions of God's law are forgiven when we come to Him in faith! He has covered our sins and no longer holds us accountable for them. But we who are blessed by experiencing forgiveness and God's salvation cannot be guilty of deceit; rather than pretending to be righteous, we must acknowledge our sin and the need to receive God's cleansing.

Therefore, it is essential to acknowledge and confess our sin. Failure to do so and *"[to keep] silent about my sin"* (v. 3) will actually have a painful affect physically. The psalmist describes this as his body wasting away, groaning all day long, and his vitality drained away as with a fever. It will also overwhelm us as a flood of circumstances; we are unable to cope with the pressures of life because we are out of fellowship with God. We will find assurance of God's will elusive as we are unable to know the way He is leading, and our own decisions simply seem to lead to problems. Living in the self-deceit of unconfessed sin is like an unbridled horse or mule; one does not tend to come near to God because of his own rebellious self-will.

> God's desire is not only to forgive
> our sin; He wants us to live with a
> sense of cleansing and wholeness.

We must recognize God's desire and readiness always to forgive not only our sin but also the guilt of our sin. He wants us to live with a sense of cleansing and wholeness. He does not want us to carry the burden of guilt for our failure while just accepting theoretically the fact of God's grace. Verse 5 is one of the most important principles to be found in Scripture. Do not hide your iniquity; acknowledge your sin to God and confess your sin. First John 1:9 says, *"If we confess our sins, He is faithful and righteous to forgive us our sins and to cleanse us from all unrighteousness."*

The bonus of confessed sin is what is beautiful! Our fellowship with God is restored. He becomes our "hiding place" and preserves us from trouble. He instructs us and teaches us in the way we should go, and He counsels us—guides our decisions—with His eye upon us. The Lord's loving-kindness will surround us with *"songs of deliverance"* (v. 7) and there is a joy that puts a song in our hearts. As a forgiven sinner who receives such an outpouring of blessings from the Lord— blessings that come from acknowledging and confessing sin—we should rejoice and literally shout for joy. He has made us righteous and enables us to be pure and upright, not only in our behavior but in our heart.

PRAYER: *Lord, thank You for forgiving my sin, for every transgression of Your law, and for the times I have been disobedient to Your will. Don't allow my pride, my ego, and my fleshly nature to keep me from acknowledging and confessing my sin. Reveal every sin that I might experience cleansing and be made righteous in Christ. Restore me to fellowship with You and guide me and instruct me. Give me a submissive heart to follow Your counsel and Your will. Let me know the joy of being a forgiven sinner.*

Psalm 33

God's Providence over All

Key Verse: Let all the earth fear the LORD; let all the inhabitants of the world stand in awe of Him. (Psalm 33:8)

The glory of the Lord is recognized and expressed by His praise, His providence, His power, His plan, and His protection. As observed in so many Psalms, the writer is overwhelmed by God's goodness and faithfulness. His heart erupts in spontaneous **praise** and admonition to others, even the whole earth, to sing praise to Him. The joy of our hearts should be expressed in song and instruments. This is appropriate because His Word is upright and His work is done in faithfulness. He loves righteousness and justice, and the earth is full of His loving-kindness.

God is praised because of His **power** over all the realm of nature. He created the world simply by His spoken Word and breathed into man the breath of life. The whole world should be in awe of Him and fear Him because His glory has been revealed. This expresses God's heart and desire and, therefore, is the impetus for our mission task.

The **providence** and sovereignty of God are evident as we are told in verses 10 and 11, *"The LORD nullifies the counsel of the nations; He frustrates the plans of the peoples. The counsel of the LORD stands forever."* While it may not be evident in the events that surround us, God is carrying out His **plan** in our lives and in the world from generation to generation. God has chosen those who respond to Him in faith to receive His inheritance and blessing. He sees from heaven the works and understanding of men and shapes their hearts. We can know Him only because of the initiative He has taken in mercy and loving-kindness to reveal Himself through Jesus Christ and to call us to Himself. Our hope for success and a victorious life is in Him, not in our own strength or physical might described in the metaphor of horses, the strength of a warrior or a mighty army.

> *While it may not be evident, God is carrying out His plan in our lives and in the world from generation to generation.*

God's plan will prevail over nations and in our lives, for His eye is upon us. When we fear God and stand in awe of Him—recognizing His power and providence and responding to Him in praise—He is able to guide and direct our paths. He keeps us aligned with His plan and purpose for our lives because our hope is in His loving-kindness.

But also, He is our **protection**, delivering us from death, sustaining us in times of hardship and need. He is our help and shield, protecting us against temptation and danger, but only as we trust in Him and rejoice in Him. We are aware of God's providence and power and experience His plan and protection only to the degree that we recognize His loving-kindness and place our hope in Him. That awareness is reflected in a relationship of fear and awe and a heart that expresses praise and worship to the Lord.

PRAYER: *Lord, You are sovereign over all the earth. Give me the faith to see world events and things affecting my life from Your perspective. May Your plan and purpose in my life supersede my own. Help me always to stand in awe of Your power and providence. Keep Your eye upon me, and may my hope be only in You and in Your loving-kindness.*

Psalm 34

Fear the Lord and Praise Him

Key Verse: O taste and see that the LORD is good; how blessed is the man who takes refuge in Him! (Psalm 34:8)

It is important to keep everything in perspective, especially when we are overwhelmed by pressures or temptations or go through times of need. The key is to bless the Lord and praise Him at all times, in spite of our trials and circumstances, always seeking to magnify and exalt the name of the Lord. That keeps us from becoming self-centered and succumbing to the pride of self-sufficiency. Even the righteous will experience affliction, go through times of fear, and suffer deprivation. But there is assurance that the Lord always delivers us. We must seek the Lord, confident that He desires to bless us and will answer when we call.

This perspective reminds us again who we are relative to God. We are to stand in fear and awe of Him, recognizing His Almighty power and providence. As those who fear the Lord, we are given two amazing promises.

1. We are assured of His **protection** and fortified by His presence. *"The angel of the Lord encamps around those who fear Him and rescues them"* (v. 7).
2. We are assured of His **provision**. *"For to those who fear Him, there is no want . . . they who seek the LORD shall not be in want of any good thing"* (vv. 9–10).

It is awesome to keep the image in our minds of a host of angels encamped around us, not allowing fear, anxiety, physical wants, or a broken spirit to conquer us. Yes, we will come under attack, but we are surrounded by God's presence, and He will deliver us. He desires to give us every good thing, but we can receive those blessings only when we are humbled and boast in Him alone.

> *If we desire a victorious and fulfilling life, we must learn to fear the Lord.*

If we desire to receive that victorious and fulfilling life, and the blessing of a long and fruitful life, then we must learn to fear the Lord. What are the behaviors of those who learn to live in that relationship and perspective?

- Keeping their tongues from evil.
- Avoiding speaking deceit.
- Turning away from evil and doing good.
- Pursuing peace in all relationships.

What a beautiful promise that the Lord hears our cries! He saves us from all our troubles. He is near when we are brokenhearted. When our spirits are crushed with disappointments and discouragement, He delivers us. The keys are living in righteousness because of our fear and reverence for Him and praising Him at all times.

PRAYER: *Lord, may my praise not ever become routine or only in isolated times of worship, but be the continual expression of my heart and my mouth. Teach me to fear You and seek You that I might experience the fullness of life You desire for me. Thank You for delivering me from affliction, healing my broken heart, saving me when my spirit is crushed, and surrounding me with Your protection. All that I know of You is only a taste of Your goodness, but I take refuge in You and magnify Your name.*

Psalm 35

Dealing with Betrayal and Slander

Key Verse: Let them shout for joy and rejoice, who favor my vin-dication; and let them say continually, "The LORD be magnified, who delights in the prosperity of His servant." (Psalm 35:27)

A Christian should expect opposition from the world. A missionary, or one who is conscientious about wit-nessing to the lost, should expect to be maligned and ridiculed. My greatest disillusionment, however, has been the opposition and conflict among those who know and serve the Lord. The greatest hurt has come from the betrayal of a colleague or being maligned by those who had given a pre-tense of friendship and support.

I have readily identified with the psalmist in reacting against those who humiliated and devised evil against me. Some fought against me, sought to undercut my leadership and destroy my reputation. Others maligned and slandered me without cause. They rejoiced when I stumbled and devised deceitful words, spreading malicious rumors and digging a pit to entrap me. Their attacks were seldom out front in the open but always devious and in darkness. So how do you react when people treat you that way, especially those who are supposedly your friends?

> *In the midst of personal attacks and slanderous gossip, we are to praise the Lord and declare His righteousness.*

The important principle reflected in this passage is not to take it upon yourself to respond but to relinquish it to the Lord. That is why the psalmist appeals to God to contend with those who oppose him. He asks God to rise up against those who pursue him and cause them to be ashamed and dishonored. Let them be caught in their own trap. Often it seems that the Lord is unconcerned; the attacks and the affliction continue until we cry out, *"Lord, how long wilt Thou look on? Rescue my soul from their ravages"* (v. 17). But notice several guides relative to our own attitude and response.

- We are to humble ourselves and subject ourselves to God's judgment, confident He will vindicate us according to our righteousness; therefore, be sure to stand for that which is right and walk in integrity rather than reacting in kind.
- We are to pray for those who abuse us as if they were our friend or brother; lift them to the Lord and ask Him to bless them and change their hearts.
- We are to recognize that God will exercise judgment and bring vindication not for our sake but for the sake of justice and that He might receive the praise.
- We are to believe that God does not want us to experience distress and be victimized by those who slander and humiliate us in order to magnify themselves, but He delights in our prosperity that He might be magnified in our deliverance.

Job 4:6 says, *"Is not your fear of God your confidence, and the integrity of your ways your hope?"* Even in the midst of personal attacks, betrayal of friends, and being the object of slanderous gossip, we are to praise the Lord and declare His righteousness.

PRAYER: *Lord, in the midst of criticism and personal attacks, help me not to respond in anger and counterattacks but with grace. You have said, "Vindication is mine." Help me to leave it with You and praise You, even in times of pain and rejection.*

God's Limitless Mercy Overcomes Sin

*Key Verse: Thy lovingkindness, O LORD, extends to the
heavens, Thy faithfulness reaches to the skies.
Thy righteousness is like the mountains of God;
Thy judgments are like a great deep. (Psalm 36:5–6)*

When sin is described in the horrible reality of wickedness, depravity, and rebellion against God, it makes God's mercy and loving-kindness that much more meaningful. Much is said in the Psalms about the fear of God. Recognizing His lordship and the exalted nature of His holiness and power should elicit an awesome fear and respect that would be a deterrent to ever acting contrary to His holiness and righteous ways. But a sinner is one in whom *"there is no fear of God before his eyes"* (v. 1).

The awful power of sin is portrayed. Its self-centered arrogance literally puts one in bondage to destructive behavior and judgment. Transgressing and violating God's laws are appealing to the ungodly. They are flattered by their own independence. There is no wisdom in those who choose sin, nor is there any goodness. Foolishly they give themselves to wickedness and practice deceit, taking pride in their iniquity. They are so inclined to evil that while lying in bed their thoughts contemplate and plan a path of sin.

> **We are constantly inclined to
> sin. That is why God's loving-
> kindness is so precious.**

Whether that portrays our heart, our past life, or an occasional indulgence in self-gratifying thoughts and actions contrary to God's will, it reflects how wonderful God's mercy is. His loving-kindness extends farther than the heavens and His faithfulness higher than the skies, which means they are limitless. His righteousness rises like a huge mountain, and His judgments of forgiveness and mercy are deep beyond discernment like the depths of the ocean.

We are constantly inclined to sin; it is our nature. That is why God's loving-kindness is so precious. It is why we can have refuge from sin and temptation only in His presence and the shadow of His wings. The images that contrast our salvation are all here. Because He is light, we are able to move from darkness to light. We are able to drink of the fountain of His grace in abundance. It is only because of His righteousness that we are able to become upright, even within our hearts. Dwelling in His house, His presence allows us to experience the abundant, unceasing flow of His grace and mercy so that we never succumb to the pride that would lead us to sin. He drives away the wicked who would influence us and draw us away and allows us to see the end result when the wicked have fallen and will be judged.

PRAYER: *Lord, when You describe the nature of sin and its awful power in our lives, I recognize that it is a picture of my life. It reflects not only who I was before I knew Christ Jesus; it is even now the inclination of my self-centered pride. Thank You that I can take refuge in the shadow of Your wings and that Your loving-kindness is greater and extends farther and deeper than all my sin. I am not worthy of Your mercy, but I drink from the abundant flow of the fountain of Your grace and rejoice to know You and walk in the light of Your presence.*

Psalm 37:1-9

Steps for Overcoming Anxiety

*Key Verse: Delight yourself in the LORD; and He will give
you the desires of your heart. (Psalm 37:4)*

When things do not go our way and anxieties begin to
accumulate, we typically lose our perspective and
confidence in the Lord and in the future. Peace in
our hearts gives way to fretting and stewing over our helplessness to change our circumstances or events that cause us
concern. While fear is usually focused on a clearly seen object
or threat, anxiety is a fear that is not clearly identified because
it is caused by the unknown and the uncertainty of what
might happen. Such an attitude is usually caused by the dangers, temptations, and influences that are a reality in our
fallen world. But we are told not to be concerned or envious,
seeking comfort and security in those values that conflict
with God's righteousness. They will fade away; they are not
permanent, and the rest of this Psalm portrays the contrast
between those who belong to God and those who do not.

Here, however, in the opening verses, we are given several clear and simple admonitions for how we are to respond
to anxiety and the result of responding appropriately.

- Trust in the LORD. . . . [It leads to doing] good. (v. 3)
- Delight yourself in the LORD. . . . He will give you the
  desires of your heart. (v. 4)
- Commit your way to the LORD. . . . He will do it. (v. 5)
- Rest in the LORD. . . . Cease from anger and forsake
  wrath. (vv. 7–8)
- Wait patiently for Him. . . . [You] will inherit the
  land—the blessing. (vv. 7, 9)

> *When we take delight in the Lord*
> *and discover the joy of resting in*
> *Him, we find that He alone is*
> *the desire of our hearts!*

I have often heard my wife tell about a time when she was pouring out her heart in concern for our children when they went off to college. She was overwhelmed with anxiety as they were totally away from her control and ability to advise them and care for them. She said that it seemed God spoke to her and said, "You are not praying; you're fretting!" When we come into God's presence and bring our concerns and supplications, we do so in faith, trusting Him and relinquishing them to Him. There's not much we can do about the future and what might happen, so we are to focus on doing good. *"Dwell in the land and cultivate faithfulness"* (v. 3). We are to live our lives where God has placed us and concentrate on our faithfulness, being obedient in what we can be responsible for. We are to commit our ways to the Lord, confident that He will take care of whatever needs to be done. This is the beautiful promise of Proverbs 3:5–6, *"Trust in the LORD with all your heart, and do not lean on your own understanding. In all your ways acknowledge Him, and He will make your paths straight."*

Delighting ourselves in the Lord is not a way to get what we want because it is not about us, our needs, and our wants. When we take delight in the Lord and discover the joy of resting in Him, we find that He alone is the desire of our hearts!

PRAYER: *Lord, don't let my lack of faith allow me to succumb to anxiety and fear. When I am threatened or concerned, may it lead me to trust in You and to commit my way to You. May my only desire be for You and to delight in Your presence.*

Psalm 37:10-40

Contrast between the Righteous and the Wicked

Key Verse: The steps of a man are established by the LORD; and He delights in his way. (Psalm 37:23)

As one grows in the Lord, the contrast with people in the world becomes more obvious. We are inundated with the images and appeals of materialistic values in our consumer society. The deceptive message that happiness comes with prosperity, with accumulating possessions and comforts, and with indulging in sexually gratifying pleasures should be readily rejected. But there is a subtle tendency to be envious of those who seem, without restraint, to enjoy a worldly lifestyle and ignore God in their self-centered pursuits.

We are reminded of how God considers the righteous in contrast to the wicked, and the outcome of each course of life is clearly portrayed. The wicked, or simply those who do not respect God and acknowledge His lordship in their lives, will one day be cut off and cease to exist. In fact, God laughs at their arrogance and pride for He knows what is coming. Their derision and condescending attitudes toward the righteous will be the sword that will pierce their own heart in judgment. They will one day vanish like smoke.

> *There is a subtle tendency to be envious of those who seem to enjoy a worldly lifestyle and ignore God in their self-centered pursuits.*

The irreligious and skeptics may seem to have the upper hand and dominant influence in society, but God has provided an eternal inheritance for those who humble themselves and trust in Him. These are those who will not be ashamed, for they have not yielded to temptation to sin in the midst of evil days. They are satisfied with a little rather than desiring wealth and abundance that comes from compromising with the world. They are gracious and give to others rather than selfishly accumulating wealth for themselves. They have experienced God's faithfulness and grace in being lifted up when they have stumbled and fallen. They know that God is on His throne, directing their steps and taking joy in a life that is lived in obedience for His glory. They are confident they will never be forsaken, and even in times of famine God provides for their needs.

The admonition is to depart from evil, avoid it, and do good. Assurance is given that the Lord is just, and those who belong to Him and are faithful will be preserved forever. But it is not only a future inheritance; as we go through this life, God gives us wisdom and discernment to speak justice. The law of God is not just a guide for our actions; it is planted firmly within our hearts. It shapes our values and is the compelling motive for our behavior. Therefore, our steps do not slip. Our salvation is from the Lord. If we wait for the Lord, and our hope is in Him, even in the midst of the wicked asserting themselves all around us, He will deliver us. He assures us of prosperity when we take refuge in Him and walk in the way He has set for us.

PRAYER: *Lord, You have had Your hand upon me since I was young. Thank You for keeping me from being enticed by the ways of the world. It is distressing to see how a sinful and materialistic world is so dominant. Keep me from being tempted by anything that does not glorify You. Direct my steps in a way that allows You to delight in my life. Give me confidence in Your provision. Enable me to be satisfied only by that which is righteous, even if it is little, for I look forward to the inheritance You have prepared.*

The Effects of Sin in Our Lives

Key Verse: Do not forsake me, O LORD; O my God,
do not be far from me! Make haste to help me, O Lord,
my salvation! (Psalm 38:21–22)

Sin is unnatural for a Christian. Yet it is not uncommon for us to yield to temptation and to be drawn away from the Lord by self-serving desires and carnal influences. The tendency is to rationalize and justify our behavior or attitudes—reacting spitefully when someone maligns us or takes advantage of us, indulging in sexually explicit lusts, and giving place to anger that attacks and tears down one we should love. Marital infidelity is rampant; many carry the guilt of past mistakes or struggle with lifestyle habits in conflict with the holiness and purity to which God has called us.

There is no doubt regarding the convicting power of God in response to our sin. This is because we have been united with Christ, and any attitude or behavior that is contrary to what Jesus would do becomes apparent to us. Over the years God has nurtured me in a pattern of earnestly seeking Him, asking Him to reveal any sin in my heart or anything I have done that is displeasing to Him or hurtful to others. His revelation and insights lead me to confession and a beautiful experience of receiving assurance of forgiveness and cleansing. However, conviction often requires us to confess to others and make restitution. It also enables us to grow and overcome the subsequent power of sin.

Many carry the guilt of past mistakes
or struggle with lifestyle habits in
conflict with the holiness and purity
to which God has called us.

But to live with the awareness and consequences of one's sin is a horrible existence. I am reminded of times as a child when I disobeyed my parents. There was always a tendency to hope they did not find out. That usually resulted in trying to hide my actions and further deception. The anxiety that grew from this deception made me so miserable that it was almost a relief when they found out and punished me. This Psalm describes the agony of one distressed because of sin. There is an awareness of severed fellowship with the Father, and the psalmist acknowledges he is deserving of God's wrath and the indignation of His anger. The burden of our iniquities has an affect on our physical well-being; it is a feeling of arrows piercing our body or being pressed down. When we tolerate sin, we feel crushed, our heart is agitated, and the joy is gone, displaced by mourning and sighs of helplessness.

Sin affects our relationship with others—with family, colleagues, and loved ones—because it is impossible to relate to them with integrity and transparency. Enemies of our spiritual walk seize the opportunity to lure us by their snares to doubt God's goodness and lead us on a path that leads to destruction. The light goes out of our eyes; that is, we lose perspective in life and cannot discern the Lord's will, make wise decisions, or envision the hope that God has placed within us because God seems far away.

Of course the answer is to hope in the Lord. The only solution is to come humbly to the Lord, pleading with Him not to forsake us as we deserve. We must realize He is not far from us; He is our salvation, and He will hasten to forgive and to help us.

PRAYER: *Lord, convict me of my sin—not just my actions but attitudes that separate me from You. Forgive and cleanse me that I may be restored to the joy of Your salvation.*

The Transient Nature of Life

Key Verse: *"Lord, make me know my end, and what is the extent of my days, let me know how transient I am."* (Psalm 39:4)

L ife is extremely short! One of the most important lessons we can learn as an impetus to walk with the Lord and stay focused on things of eternal value is to realize how quickly this life will be over. My self-image has always been far more youthful than the reality of my age. Thoughts have always been focused on the future and what I will do someday. With retirement in view, my perspective has suddenly changed to realize how little time is left to accomplish whatever God intends for me to contribute in this life. We cannot presume upon the future. The untimely death of peers is a reminder that we never know how much time we will have and that whatever we do must be now, in the present. James 4:14 says that life is like a vapor that appears for a little while and then vanishes away. Psalm 90:12 tells us, *"Teach us to number our days that we may present to Thee a heart of wisdom."*

> **We cannot presume upon the future. Whatever we do must be now, in the present.**

It is good to put the things that concern us in proper perspective. Realizing how short life is will help us invest each moment and each day in that which serves the Lord and His purpose. We become so caught up in petty controversies that are actually rather trivial and will not even be an issue a few days later. The time consumed and attention given to shopping, making decisions regarding clothes, the decoration of our house, and accumulating and caring for possessions are insignificant compared to spiritual realities. What will happen to all the wealth we acquire? Why do comforts and material things become such an obsession beyond that which is necessary? From the day we are born, even though we go through years of growth and maturing, we are in the process of dying and moving toward our eternal reward.

We are told to recognize that whatever we accomplish is because of what the Lord has chosen to do in our life. Therefore we do not boast or take pride in conceited claims of what we have done. Putting life in perspective will not only cause us to guard our ways, to live with integrity and walk in purity, but it will cause us to guard our words as well. Our greatest tendency is to sin with our tongue, especially when the wicked or others come against us. We can identify with the feeling of the psalmist when he said, *"My heart was hot within me . . . the fire burned; then I spoke with my tongue!"* (v. 3). Jesus said that we will give an account for every idle word. We need to learn to muzzle our mouth and bite our lips; it is just not worth it to say things that are hurtful or to criticize and put down others, no matter how we can justify it because of what they have done. It is better to be as one who is deaf and dumb and keep silent.

Once again this perspective of life compels us to turn to the Lord that He might hear our cry and deliver us from our transgressions, for our hope is in Him.

PRAYER: *Lord, I tend to get so caught up in the agendas and issues of daily life. Trivial controversies and disagreements put a strain on relationships with those who are closest to me. Help me guard my heart and my words and keep life in eternal perspective.*

Steps to Restoration

*Key Verse: Many, O LORD my God, are the wonders which
Thou hast done, and Thy thoughts toward us; there is none to
compare with Thee; if I would declare and speak of them,
they would be too numerous to count. (Psalm 40:5)*

This is a graphic portrayal of what the Lord does for us. Picture the contrast of struggling to move in a slimy, muddy pit with walking on a solid rock. It is the difference between groveling in the guilt of sin and failure—discouraged, having lost heart—and experiencing a sense of victory in which there is a song in our hearts.

The situation is one in which we often find ourselves. There is a sense of failure, and the spiritual warfare is intense as *"evils beyond number have surrounded me* (v. 12)." Iniquities have overtaken us; not only are we not capable of living righteously; we are no longer even able to see and discern what is right. We have lost heart because others seek our hurt.

But in this situation the Lord hears our cry; He lifts us up and restores us to a firm foundation. He puts a song in our hearts. Evidence of being out of fellowship with the Lord and away from His will is when there is no longer a song of praise going through our minds! It is awesome to realize that God actually thinks about us. When we are going through times of despair, we usually forget the wonders He has done for us—they cannot be numbered! He does not withhold compassion from us, but His mercies preserve us, for He is our help and our deliverer.

---

*Evidence of being out of fellowship with
the Lord is when there is no longer a
song of praise going through our minds!*

What must we do to claim this victory and be restored to the solid rock of faith? We are to wait patiently, trusting in Him, confident that He hears our cry. We are not to rely upon religious ritual, but we are to come to Him. As the psalmist said in verse 7, *"Behold, I come."* It is not in what we do but a matter of a personal relationship with God. The result is delighting to do His will; that becomes the joy and desire of our life. It is not a matter of legalistically trying to obey His law but hiding His law within our hearts; it becomes a part of our very being. We do not just keep the testimony of God's goodness and righteousness within us, but we speak of His faithfulness and salvation. We proclaim the good news of His mercy and righteousness to others. We do not resort to pride or falsehood but put our trust in Him.

We can be confident of God's compassion and His loving-kindness. He is not magnified when we struggle with sin and go through periods of distress. His purpose in allowing us to experience failure and go through times of struggle is so that we will turn to Him, and He will be glorified in responding to our trust in Him and delivering us.

PRAYER: *Lord, it is awesome to realize that Your thoughts of me and all that You have done for me are too numerous to count. Thank You for hearing my cry in times of despair and when I find myself under attack or pulled into the filth and slime of sin. May Your law be firmly in my heart; my only desire is to do Your will. Thank You for giving me a song in my heart that I might proclaim Your righteousness and magnify Your name.*

Psalm 41

Sensitive Response to Those in Need

Key Verse: As for me, Thou dost uphold me in my integrity, and Thou dost set me in Thy presence forever. (Psalm 41:12)

Too often we presume that a relationship with the Lord is characterized by personal piety and a focus on worshipping and exalting Him. But we should not forget that being properly related to the Lord, and walking in fear of Him will manifest itself in how we relate to others, especially those in need. The story of the Good Samaritan reminds us of the danger of fulfilling our religious duties while ignoring the human need around us—the suffering, distraught, lonely, and the lost who need a word of witness. James 1:27 says, *"This is pure and undefiled religion in the sight of our God and Father, to visit orphans and widows in their distress, and to keep oneself unstained by the world."*

We are told that the one who considers, is aware of, and responds to the helpless or the poor is the one who is blessed. God delivers us from trouble when we give ourselves to others. He protects us and does not allow us to be overcome by our enemies. When we are sick and in need, He sustains us by His grace and restores us to health. Jesus modeled compassion to the oppressed, the poor, and the broken and expects us to walk in His steps. Focusing on ourselves, our own needs and comforts, is a manifestation of the fleshly nature, not the Spirit of God. This is why He told the rich young ruler to sell all that he had and give to the poor; until he gave himself and what he had to others, his life was all focused on his self-centered nature. We are not properly related to God until we are sensitive and responsive to the needs of others. Blessing others and ministering to them is the key to being blessed ourselves.

> *Being properly related to the Lord mani-*
> *fests itself in how we relate to others,*
> *especially those in need.*

Loving God and doing good, however, does not exempt us from slander and opposition. There are those who misunderstand our motives and speak evil against us. Those whose hearts are pure and seek to serve God in the kind of world in which we live will always be the subject of gossip. Rumormongers will spread lies seeking to bring harm or to discredit our reputation. And what is most painful is that they are usually those closest to us. When a close friend or brother, with whom we work or attend church, talks about us and maligns us, our natural tendency is to rise up against him.

But we need to seek God's grace and walk in integrity. We can be assured God is pleased with us when we do not succumb to selfish motives. Our enemies will not prevail, and their criticism and attacks will do us no harm. There are two keys to claiming victory in these situations. One is trusting God to enable us to maintain our integrity; the other is being conscious of abiding in God's presence. When we are aware He is with us, we are blessed and confident He will sustain us.

PRAYER: *Lord, I admit that I get so busy in my responsibilities of serving You that I overlook the prolific needs all around me in the world. I am even insensitive to the hurts and concerns of colleagues with whom I relate. Open my eyes to others. May Your Spirit guide me to respond with compassion toward those in need. And when others criticize and malign me, help me to maintain my integrity and be aware of Your presence.*

Desperate for God

*Key Verse: As the deer pants for the water brooks,
so my soul pants for Thee, O God. My soul thirsts
for God, for the living God. (Psalm 42:1–2)*

The most important characteristic in our relationship with God is to have a heart that desires Him. Being obedient to His will and becoming the kind of person whose life glorifies God comes from finding pleasure in Him above all else. A chorus we often sing repeats the refrain, "I'm desperate for you. . . . This is the air I breathe. . . . Lord, I'm desperate for you." Several years ago one of our mission volunteers was kidnapped; he was tied up, and his captors threatened to kill him. After eventually being released, he related how desperate he was to be set free and said, "God seemed to say to me, 'You should be this desperate to know Me!'"

We know what it is to be like a thirsty deer, panting for water. Maybe we have been running or working on a hot day, our mouth is dry and parched, and we desperately crave a drink of water. That should reflect our desire for God and desire to experience the reality of His presence in our lives. In my life and ministry I have always had a longing for something to happen that could not be explained by my own work, personality, programs, and efforts—something that has no explanation except the touch of God's Spirit! Those times when we don't have a sense of God's constant presence are characterized by loneliness, helplessness, and despair. Having a heart for God and His righteousness is really the only thing that will keep us from yielding to temptation and being vulnerable to sin. There is no abiding joy and spontaneous praise apart from an awareness that He is dwelling within us, providing a constant flow of His all-sufficient grace, filling our hearts with His love, and anointing us with His power.

> *The most important characteristic in our relationship with God is to have a heart that takes pleasure in Him above all else.*

The psalmist mentions the times in the past when he experienced the joy of worship and being in fellowship with God, just as we can remember those times when we felt a personal intimacy with God and authentic worship experiences. When we no longer have a manifestation of that divine relationship, it is no wonder our soul would be in despair and downcast. We feel dejected and forgotten by God. It is terrible not to have access to the spiritual resources we need to cope with the stress and pressures of life and to be totally dependent on our own limited strength. Situations oppress us like a horde of enemies coming against us, set on defeating and overwhelming us.

The key is to keep our hope steadfast and to keep praising the Lord until we become conscious of the flow of His loving-kindness sustaining us in every situation throughout the day. His presence becomes like a song in the night, bringing peace and blessing.

PRAYER: *Lord, I want to know You and the fullness of Your presence. There is not a moment that I do not need Your grace and loving-kindness. I am helpless without Your strength. I am overwhelmed by pressures and responsibilities, vulnerable to temptation, and inclined to futile, self-serving motives when on my own. Give me a heart that is desperate for You. Manifest Your presence in my life that I might have a heart of praise and hope in You.*

Psalm 43

Allowing Conflict to Bring Us to God

Key Verse: Why are you in despair, O my soul? And why are you disturbed within me? Hope in God, for I shall again praise Him, the help of my countenance, and my God. (Psalm 43:5)

I don't know if David was going through a time of defeat and oppression by his external enemies and the nations surrounding Israel or if he was just feeling the pressures of leadership in which Israel was in rebellion and expressing disrespect for his authority.

I would wish that the only adversities I had to deal with in leading the IMB and our international mission efforts were religious opposition in Muslim countries or government restrictions and bureaucracy overseas. However, the most painful and severe opposition usually comes from within. People do not have a natural tendency to be submissive and follow leadership. Confrontation can get pretty brutal as staff and missionaries react to issues that threaten their own self-interests. Even outside the organization, much of the communication from churches and among our denominational constituency is not affirmation and support but criticism and condemnation. Rather than a gracious, developmental approach to seek to understand decisions and actions, others presume there are ill motives and readily attack the character and competence of those in places of leadership.

In times of despair, the answer is to turn to God, praising Him in all things and in all circumstances.

When the opposition becomes intense, my own exasperation leads me to the conclusion that I don't have to put up with this! When people do not treat you justly and are actually deceitful in spreading distorted information, there is a tendency to feel that God has rejected you; He has not been faithful in doing His part to protect you from the oppression of the enemy. But an important lesson to learn is not to defend yourself but relinquish the issue to God and trust Him to vindicate you.

I have learned that times of confrontation and opposition—when your own people appear to undercut your leadership—are usually times when communication has not been adequate. It usually indicates I have not had the wisdom to be sensitive to what others think and feel and have even acted in the flesh. The decision may have been the right one, but it was not enacted with discernment of the way God would have led. That's why prayer in such a situation leads us to God's light and truth. When we are overwhelmed by opposition and are victims of injustice, we need to seek God's dwelling place. It is a time we need to fall on our knees in worship rather than seeking to unravel the problem or to defend our own credibility and authority—*"Then I will go to the altar of God"* (v. 4). It is there our joy and confidence will be restored. Once again the principle is reinforced: in times of despair and when our soul is unsettled, the answer is to turn to God and express our hope in Him by praising Him in all things and in all circumstances.

PRAYER: *Lord, help me not to blame You when I encounter challenges and feel despondent due to lack of respect and support. When I have lost the joy and experience inner turmoil because of being misunderstood and mistreated by others, let that be a trigger to bring me back to You, humbly seeking Your wisdom and leadership, allowing You to teach me discernment and leaving vindication in Your hands.*

Psalm 44

The Lord Has Proven His Faithfulness

Key Verse: Our heart has not turned back, and our steps have not deviated from Thy way. (Psalm 44:18)

It strengthens our faith to be reminded of how God has worked in the past among His people. The strong traditions and stories about how God intervened on behalf of the children of Israel had been passed down and were well known. We hear testimonies from others about how God has done miraculous deeds, and we are encouraged. The psalmist recognized that Israel did not win their battles by their own sword, but it was God. Note the three things acknowledged about the victories God had provided (v. 3):

- His right hand was the symbol of His authority.
- His arm represented His strength and power.
- The light of His presence provided wisdom and guidance.

But often it seems as if these victories and manifestations of power are ancient history or something that happens in the lives of others while we still struggle with defeat. We try to acknowledge Him as king and confess that in His name we can claim the victory. We must not trust in our weapons of the flesh or take pride in our own ability. We should boast only in the Lord, reflecting our confidence and faith by giving thanks to His name. Yet we go through times when we feel He has rejected us and allowed us to be overwhelmed by our adversaries, whether actual opposition from people or situations. We feel the reproach of others and seem to be objects of ridicule among those in the world because of our allegiance to God and our choice to believe in Him.

> *Often it seems manifestations of power*
> *are ancient history or something*
> *that happens to others while we*
> *still struggle with defeat.*

We may feel humiliated because of our faith and go through times when the victory is not evident. Although it appears God has rejected us, we must not forget Him and our covenant of faith to trust in Him. We must never let the affections of our heart turn back or allow our steps to deviate from following God and living according to His righteousness. God knows the secrets of our heart, and we dare not allow ourselves to be attracted to anything that infringes on His lordship or cease to confess and call upon His name. We may feel like the psalmist, that in our affliction and oppression God has hidden His face from us; our soul has sunk down to the earth—it couldn't get any worse—and we are being killed all day long. We must never forget that God is our help, but our plea is not for our own desire for relief and blessing; it is for the sake of His loving-kindness. We rely on Him because of His faithfulness, and it is for His glory.

Habakkuk 3:17–19 expresses this so graphically, *"Though the fig tree should not blossom, and there be no fruit on the vines, though the yield of the olive should fail, and the fields produce no food, though the flock should be cut off from the fold, and there be no cattle in the stalls, yet I will exult in the Lord, I will rejoice in the God of my salvation. The Lord God is my strength."*

PRAYER: *Lord, You are my strength. Regardless of what I have to go through, I will not forget You, resort to my own efforts, or deviate from Your way. The struggle is real, but I can trust You to lead me by Your light and truth, and I will praise You in all situations.*

A Submissive Relationship to God

Key Verse: Thou hast loved righteousness, and hated wickedness; therefore God, Thy God, has anointed Thee with the oil of joy above Thy fellows. (Psalm 45:7)

The majesty of the Lord is something we seldom truly comprehend. It usually elicited spontaneous praise and poetic descriptions by the psalmist and an attempt to capture God's awesome character and sovereignty in an expression of allegory. God's splendor and majesty are described in terms of victorious power. He is the representation of truth and righteousness. His right hand of authority elicits submission and meekness from those who follow Him. His arrows of conviction pierce the hearts of His enemies— those not in submission to His lordship. And His scepter, the symbol of His rule as King, represents absolute moral purity and uprightness.

One has no choice except to yield in submission and come before Him as a loyal subject. An effective leader is a model to his followers and influences and inspires them for the sake of a desired result; those who belong to God, like Him, love righteousness and hate wickedness. We enter into a relationship with Him in which our worship and adoration are a natural and appropriate response not only to His being God but *"my God."* It is a personal and intimate experience that results in our being *"anointed . . . with the oil of joy"* (v. 7) above others. It is a relationship that causes us to forget worldly attractions, material wealth, and the acclaim of colleagues and friends. Instead, we find total pleasure in God's presence and serving Him.

Fullness of joy comes only through a submissive relationship with Christ in which we find total satisfaction in Him.

A question worthy of assessment is whether or not we have that kind of relationship with God. Do I have that anointing of joy? Jesus said in John 15:11, *"These things I have spoken to you, that My joy may be in you, and that your joy may be made full."* Such fullness of joy doesn't come through circumstances, wealth, the absence of problems, and everything going our way. It comes only through a submissive relationship with Christ in which we find total satisfaction in Him. Being in the presence of the King can only mean being overcome with gladness and rejoicing. So, if we are not experiencing that abiding joy and a heart that is filled with praise and thanksgiving, does it not say something about our relationship with God?

We should not fail to note the influence of one's submission to the majesty and authority of His lordship. It will be passed on to subsequent generations as sons replace their fathers so that all generations remember and honor the name of the Lord. And it will also result in widespread witness and missions impact of "the peoples" knowing and giving thanks to the Lord.

PRAYER: *Lord, so often my soul is distraught, and anxieties rob me of the joy I sometimes have in You. I find myself wanting to be set free from the constant problems and challenges so that I can have a heart that is glad and an attitude of praise; but I realize even that desire is for the sake of my own blessing and benefit. My only desire should be for You, to be in Your presence and experience the fullness of Your joy. So I come to You with my heart overflowing with Your goodness and grace.*

Psalm 46

Finding a Refuge in God

Key Verse: "Cease striving and know that I am God;
I will be exalted among the nations, I will
be exalted in the earth." (Psalm 46:10)

We are constantly overwhelmed by the demands of life; turmoil and stress are normal. How many times do we want to stop the world and get off? The more work we do, the more responsibilities seem to pile up. Worries and conflicts continue to accumulate. God is saying to us, "Just stop! Be still; quit trying to organize your life and striving to deal with it in your own strength and efforts." When life seems out of control, the to-do lists never get done, and concerns about illness, financial security, and external dangers destroy our sense of peace, we need to be reminded that God is what we need! He is always present and available in our time of need, but we have to pause and redirect our thinking from our own struggles to recognize His sufficiency. We must realize that He is sovereign over all the world, and if He can be exalted among the nations, surely He should be exalted in our lives.

A refuge is a place of safety and protection; it is a place to hide from the storm or to escape the threats of an enemy. The fact that God is powerful is not just a general fact of reality—He is *our* strength! Seldom do we comprehend all that God has provided us in terms of blessing, peace, joy, and strength. We don't experience it because we seldom come to Him and rely upon Him. We must appropriate His power through faith. We don't have to wait until we come to the end of our rope, but we claim it by first acknowledging our own helplessness and weakness. Paul discovered this in 2 Corinthians 12:9 when Christ said to him, *"'My grace is sufficient for you, for power is perfected in weakness.'"* Paul responded by saying, *"Most gladly, therefore, I will rather boast about my weaknesses, that the power of Christ may dwell in me."*

> *Whatever we confront, whether personal pressures and stress or a world in turmoil, we must never forget that God is with us.*

I have never felt so insecure as in the time of an earthquake in Indonesia. You think having your feet on solid ground is security, but when that ground starts bucking and waving, there is no place that's secure. The awesome forces of nature can wreck havoc as earthquakes destroy cities and ocean storms create destructive tidal waves, but the dwelling place of God cannot be shaken. Nations are stirred in an uproar of war and violence, and kingdoms are destroyed, but they cannot affect the stronghold that is our God. Whatever we confront, whether personal pressures and stress or a world that is in turmoil, we must never forget that God is with us. Our need is to know Him, to quit trying to solve our problems ourselves, and to rest in Him. He will make the internal wars and conflicts cease; He will remove the threats just as *"He breaks the bow and cuts the spear in two"* (v. 9), and He will be our constant help in times of trouble.

PRAYER: *Lord, You are my refuge and strength in times of need. I tend to be so busy that it is hard to be still and just rest in Your presence. I'm guilty of striving in my own strength. Teach me to slow down, to stop and know You more intimately. You will be exalted in all the earth only when I, and Your people, truly know You and abide in You. I will not fear, regardless of the threats or calamity that come when my plans go awry and everything seems out of control, for You are my refuge and help. Thank You for being there—ever-present, unshakable, and my strength in times of weakness.*

Psalm 47

Responding to God's Greatness

*Key Verse: Clap your hands, all peoples; shout to God
with the voice of joy. For the LORD Most High is to be feared,
a great King over all the earth. (Psalm 47:1–2)*

How we deal with life actually reflects our concept of God. If we truly recognize Him as King over all the earth and acknowledge His power and sovereignty, nothing can shake our confidence and faith in Him. Being aware of His power and authority elicits an attitude of fear and respect; this will be reflected by submission and obedience to His lordship. To grasp the glory and grandeur of His nature means unrestrained expressions of praise and adoration.

Years ago I read a popular book, *Your God Is Too Small.* It characterized how most people viewed God as "the Man upstairs," a butler always available to provide for our every whim and need, or someone we ignore except in times of trouble. Some view Him as an angry disciplinarian, just waiting to punish us when we do something wrong. Others worship Him but only as a sentimental tradition or as an emotional crutch. However, when we recognize that He is the Lord Most High and King over all the earth, there is no moment in time or situation in life in which He is not exerting His lordship. We can ignore Him and be disobedient to Him, but He is still Lord. In 1999, when the sovereignty of Hong Kong, then a British territory, was reverting to mainland China, someone asked one of our missionaries what was going to happen when the change occurred. His reply was that the sovereignty of Hong Kong would be unchanged, for God is still sovereign over the nations! In spite of the evil and war and chaos in our world, God has not relinquished His throne—*"[He] reigns over the nations"* (v. 8).

> ## We can ignore Him and be disobedient to Him, but He is still Lord.

The psalmist portrays an image of a grand procession of the king with his entourage entering the palace and ascending to the throne, the seat of power and authority. There are banners waving and the fanfare of the trumpets acclaiming His glory. It was significant that God programmed such a scene when Jesus entered Jerusalem prior to His crucifixion. When the religious leaders were disturbed by the praise of the crowds acknowledging Him as the Messiah, which they thought to be blasphemous, Jesus said if they were to remain silent, the very rocks would cry out. God is truly worthy of our praise. In fact, when we begin to comprehend His greatness and His glory, emotions are stirred until we have to clap our hands and shout with joy. If we are not sensing that kind of feeling with each thought of our Lord, could it be that something is amiss in our understanding of who He is? If we are overcome by life and find ourselves discouraged and despondent, could it be that practically we feel abandoned because God is no longer on the throne of our life? But He is exalted and in ultimate control; our only response is to praise and worship Him, giving Him the glory due His name.

PRAYER: *Lord, so often my prayers focus on my own needs when I should just praise You and celebrate Your greatness and glory. All the evil and trouble going on in the world, and even the petty problems in my own life, make it appear that You have relinquished Your throne and are no longer in control. But You are truly King over all the earth! I want to know You, to comprehend Your glory and power, and to praise You.*

Jerusalem—Symbol of God's Glory

*Key Verse: As is Thy name, O God, so is Thy praise
to the ends of the earth. (Psalm 48:10)*

Jerusalem was built to be the city of God. On Mount Zion
it was visible from the plains and all the valleys surrounding it. One had to go "up to Jerusalem" to travel there.
The centerpiece of the city was the temple, which represented
the presence of God in the midst of His people. The massive
fortifications of the walls and the ramparts were impressive
and would defy any adversary from ever thinking of challenging the rule and dominion of the kingdom of Israel as
represented by this city.

The city was a focus of pride for the people. It represented their security and the glory of their kingdom. It was a
reminder to the nations around of how God had manifested
His power and blessing in subduing the peoples and prospering the nation of Israel. But the city was simply a symbol and
representation of God's glory. It wasn't these buildings and
edifices but God Himself that is exalted in the whole earth.
His power and authority strike fear in the hearts of those
who do not follow in obedience to His will. This is the God
who breaks up ships by the wind and storms and destroys
armies.

He is also the God who is filled with loving-kindness.
And that is where the thoughts of His people go when they
worship Him. In spite of His awesome power, we know Him
because of His gentle and loving nature that provides mercy
when we come into His presence. His right hand of authority
judges in righteousness. We can be assured that He reigns
forever, and although He is Lord over all the earth, He will
guide us faithfully throughout this life.

> *Those of us who have come to know God and experienced His loving-kindness cannot help but tell others about it.*

Those who had the privilege of going to Jerusalem would return to their country or their village and try to describe the grandeur to their children. It is like one who had the rare privilege of traveling overseas and would come back telling about seeing the Eiffel Tower, the pyramids, or Buckingham Palace. The stories would continue to be passed on. In a similar way, those of us who have come to know God and have experienced His loving-kindness cannot help but tell others about it. When we have been given the privilege of comprehending His glory and have known His guidance as He revealed His will and directed our paths, we are compelled to pass on the testimony of His faithfulness to our children. When we have had an opportunity to discern His glory and miraculous power, we should declare to the nations that God would be praised to the ends of the earth. Like the city of Jerusalem, beautiful and elevated on Mount Zion, so is the name of the Lord. It is the name above all names and greatly to be praised.

PRAYER: *Lord, Your greatness is beyond comprehension. Jerusalem in ancient times so stood out among all the other cities and kingdoms; it was a symbol of Your exalted nature, lifted up above all the earth. It was beautiful, bringing joy and delight to the nations. May You be so lifted up and exalted in my life that Your praise would be the focus of all I do. Help me to be faithful in declaring Your glory so that future generations and all the ends of the earth will praise Your name.*

Psalm 49

The Futility of Wealth and Status

*Key Verse: For the redemption of his soul is costly,
and he should cease trying forever—that he should live
on eternally; that he should not undergo decay. (Psalm 49:8–9)*

It is so hard to put the things of this life in proper perspective relative to eternity. This world is where we live, and society—the context of our existence—influences us to focus exclusively on the values of the world. Advertisements and credit card promotions persuade us to succumb to consumer indulgence; "buy now, pay later" appeals entice us to increasing indebtedness in order to get more. Our lifestyle tends to be totally devoted to fulfilling our needs and desires, providing a comfortable lifestyle and accumulating wealth that will at least provide security in our later years. Status and wealth are the marks of success, according to the world.

But those who trust in riches and wealth, accumulate houses and land, and receive the acclaim of the world will die and lose it all. When we die, this body and all the materialism surrounding it will perish; the destiny of this existence is no different than that of the beasts that perish—nothing is left. Many seem to think that their accomplishments and success will assure them of a legacy. Their names may continue on buildings, businesses, and financial institutions; but there is nothing one can do to redeem one's own soul. All our good deeds, money, and philanthropy cannot counter the guilt of sin and provide salvation and eternal security. One may gain the whole world but lose his own soul. Nothing can keep our bodies from eventually decaying, and it takes something other than what we can do ourselves to guarantee eternal life.

> *All our good deeds, money, and philanthropy cannot counter the guilt of sin and provide salvation and eternal security.*

We must never forget the costly price of redemption. God Himself had to become a man and die; He had to suffer the rejection of men and the cruel brutality and shame of the cross to pay the penalty for our sins. It was the shed blood of the sinless Son of God that purchased our redemption, not anything that we have done. And because of our faith and confidence in what Christ has done for us, when we die, our spirits do not go to some nebulous netherworld (Sheol), but God will receive us. He is our security and our hope.

This life is relatively short. How foolish for people to give themselves entirely to temporal values and worldly accomplishments. We should not be jealous of those with wealth or status, nor should we be alarmed when we go through times of adversity or suffer because of the iniquity and evil intent of others. We need to heed the wisdom God gives us and gain understanding that we can see all that is in this life from His perspective.

PRAYER: *Lord, may I never take for granted Your salvation or forget how costly the redemption of my soul was. The death of Christ on the cross, and the shedding of His blood, was the terribly high price for the sins of the world. Keep me from being attracted to the self-centered and materialistic values of this world. Never let me succumb to pride over my own accomplishments and status as if they mean anything, for You are my hope and my security.*

Psalm 50

God's Only Need Is Worship
and Praise

*Key Verse: "He who offers a sacrifice of thanksgiving
honors Me; and to him who orders his way aright I shall
show the salvation of God." (Psalm 50:23)*

As I commemorated my tenth anniversary as president of the International Mission Board, there were many thoughts and memories about what I had experienced during those challenging years. Being in a position to get a global overview of what God was doing all over the world had given me a distinct and dominant impression, above all else, of God's providence. He is working to fulfill His purpose. He doesn't need me or my church or denomination; His mission will be fulfilled. But it would be tragic if I failed to be obedient and forfeited the privilege of being a part of what He is doing.

God doesn't need anything because He is God. So often we serve Him as if He would, in some way, be deficient if we did not do what we were supposed to do. We usually give our offerings with an attitude that they are needed for God's kingdom work, but the reality is that we return our offerings to Him (1) because they belong to Him and (2) because we are grateful that He has allowed us to receive and use His resources. This Psalm expresses this awesome concept as God declares, *"For the world is Mine, and all it contains!"* (v. 12). He owns the cattle on a thousand hills; every beast and bird and everything that moves belong to Him. He has no need of anything. He explains that His people did not bring sacrifices because of His need but in order to honor Him. His sovereignty over all the earth is reflected as all creation declares His nature—His power and authority and righteousness. Heaven and earth respond to His summons to judge His people. Our relationship with Him should be in recognition of His lordship, His ownership, and His right to rule our lives. Our worship and all we do should be to honor and exalt Him.

> *The person who is thanking God out of a heart of gratitude is the one to whom God reveals the assurance of salvation and guides.*

Why does He respond when we call upon Him and rescue us out of our troubles? It is not for our sake, because we deserve it, or because He is obligated to help us; it is for His sake, that He might receive honor and glory. Yet we come before Him and plead for mercy and for help in difficult situations as if we can take His intervention for granted. We fail to humbly reflect a thankful heart and gratitude that would honor Him. We go on living just like those in the world, ignoring a disciplined and holy way of life that honors God. It is not necessarily the one who attends church faithfully and strives to please God by good works who honors God but whoever *"offers a sacrifice of thanksgiving"* (v. 23). Hebrews 13:15 says, *"Through Him then, let us continually offer up a sacrifice of praise to God, that is, the fruit of our lips that give thanks to His name."* The person who is constantly thanking God out of a heart of gratitude, humbly recognizing his unworthiness of God's blessings, is the one to whom God reveals the assurance of salvation and guides in his daily walk.

PRAYER: *Lord, I get so concerned about trivial things and my own needs. Help me to comprehend Your greatness, to realize everything belongs to You, and that You have access to all the resources in the world. Thank You for providing what I need. May I use it for Your glory and recognize that I am only a steward with the privilege of returning as an offering that honors You, as I give with a thankful heart.*

Psalm 51:1-9

Conviction, Confession, and Cleansing

Key Verse: *Be gracious to me, O God, according to Thy
lovingkindness; according to the greatness of Thy
compassion blot out my transgressions. (Psalm 51:1)*

This penitent Psalm of David reveals how we should
respond when we become aware of having sinned.
It is a response of conviction, confession, and cleansing. One of the tragedies of not knowing God is the lack of
conviction regarding what is right and wrong. Sometimes
there is a tinge of conscience because of cultural condition-
ing regarding acceptable and unacceptable behavior, but a
nonbeliever can continue in self-serving and worldly attitudes and actions because there is no relationship with
God.

Fortunately for the Christian, the Holy Spirit has been
given to live within us, and one of His roles is to convict us of
sin and unrighteousness. He guides us in that which would
please and honor God and reveals to us when we go astray
and are out of God's will. When David was confronted by his
sin, the conviction he felt was not just guilt because of what
he had done; it affected his relationship with God, who is
holy and righteous. He readily confessed his sin. He did not
try to assess blame or justify what he had done but readily
took responsibility for it. In confession he acknowledged his
need for God's mercy. He was not deserving of forgiveness
and knew it would be based only on God's compassion. In
recognizing God's holiness, he realized he was worthy of His
judgment. His plea is for God to have mercy on him, blot out
his transgressions, wash him thoroughly from iniquity, and
cleanse him from sin. But notice also what happens when one
who knows God sins.

> *God's Spirit convicts us of sin in order to lead us to repentance and confession—a joyous experience.*

- We are aware of our sin; it is constantly before us. We can't get away from the guilt of having done wrong and that which is displeasing to God.
- We realize it is against God and His holiness that we have sinned.
- We recognize we have a basic sin nature with which we were born; when we don't rely on God's truth, it is our inclination to sin.

The beautiful conclusion of coming under conviction and confessing our sin is the assurance of cleansing. God does not keep holding our failure over our head and putting us on a guilt trip. Romans 8:1 says, *"There is therefore now no condemnation for those who are in Christ Jesus."* When God's Spirit convicts us of sin, it is in order to lead us to repentance and confession, which results in forgiveness, cleansing, and restoration—a joyous experience. He washes us whiter than snow, blots out our iniquities, and restores the joy and gladness in our heart. We are assured that God hides His face from our iniquities; He no longer sees them. They are gone! But the real key is to understand that sin is not just our actions and words; it is a heart problem. Our need is for God to create a clean heart and renew a spirit that is steadfast in our devotion to Him. Our dependence must be on Him, and our desire must be for His holiness.

PRAYER: *Lord, never let me become insensitive to sin. Convict me and lead me to confess my sin that I may experience Your mercy in forgiveness and cleansing. It is easy to recognize things I do that are wrong, but convict me of those hidden sins that are not so obvious that I might walk in holiness and fellowship with You.*

Psalm 51:10-19

A Clean Heart and Effective Witness

*Key Verse: Create in me a clean heart, O God,
and renew a steadfast spirit within me. (Psalm 51:10)*

Continuing the theme of conviction, confession, and cleansing, we should realize as the psalmist that God's primary interest is not in our religious ritual and fulfilling the formalities of religious devotion. He is pleased when we are broken over our sin and our remorse leads us to come to Him for mercy. This indicates our reliance on Him, our confidence in His grace and faithfulness, and evidence that we are not basing our acceptance on pride and what we are able to do for ourselves.

There are several consequences of being forgiven, cleansed, and restored to fellowship with God. We are able to influence others in the way of righteousness and lead sinners to faith. We will overflow with an attitude of praise as our *"tongue will joyfully sing of Thy righteousness"* (v. 14). God will receive our offering of service and what we give to Him with a pure heart. But notice what needs to happen for this result to occur as reflected by the prayer of petition beyond the initial confession and plea for cleansing.

> **Without joy in our life it is impossible
> for us to influence and witness to
> others effectively.**

1. *"Restore to me the joy of Thy salvation"* (v. 12).
   When we sin, we do not lose our salvation, for salvation is of God, but we do lose the joy of our salvation. Without joy in our life that reflects the genuineness of our faith, it is impossible for us to influence and witness to others effectively.

2. *"Do not cast me away from Thy presence, and do not take Thy Holy Spirit from me"* (v. 11). People lose the joy of their salvation because they feel separated from God. When we feel we have lost fellowship with Him, He seems far away, and there is no evidence of the Holy Spirit in our lives; the joy is gone because we feel we are left on our own and are helpless.

3. *"Create in me a clean heart, O God, and renew a steadfast spirit within me"* (v. 10). Why do we feel God has abandoned us and do not sense His abiding presence? It is because of sin that has come into our hearts. It may not be a blatant, obvious sin such as David's sin of adultery, but when we allow attitudes of resentment, bitterness, jealousy, or unforgiveness into our heart, or entertain unwholesome thoughts that are not pleasing to God, the relationship that sustains us is no longer there. So once our sins are acknowledged and confessed, we need to seek a clean heart, for that is where it all started.

PRAYER: *Lord, I want to be used to witness and influence others by the example of a victorious life as well as authentic words of testimony. I want to live with a spontaneous attitude of praise. Cleanse my heart of sin and give me a disciplined spirit that will persevere in times of temptation. Let me always be aware of Your abiding presence, for that is what gives me the joy of knowing Your salvation and enables me to offer You the sacrifice and service that are pleasing to You.*

Domination of Evil in the World

*Key Verse: I will give Thee thanks forever, because Thou hast
done it, and I will wait on Thy name, for it is good,
in the presence of Thy godly ones. (Psalm 52:9)*

One of the most disturbing challenges to our faith is the blatant disregard for God in all elements of society. If we allow ourselves to dwell on the godless carnality in which we live, we begin to doubt the reality of God's power and providence. It seems our Christian witness is weak and ineffective in influencing our world for Christian principles. We wonder if God's kingdom of righteousness will prevail as assured in His Word when there is so much evidence to the contrary.

The open glorification of sex and sensual gratification in entertainment are flaunted with little restraint. Corporate scandals reflect that business and economic leaders have no moral compass beyond self-aggrandizement and accumulation of personal wealth. Politicians and government officials seem to have no hesitancy in mishandling the truth if it serves their purpose. The media put their spin on information to propagate postmodernism and relativism in which there are no absolute moral standards. The result is religious expression being declared illegal in the public marketplace and sanctity of human life abolished in the justification of abortion rights. Immoral relationships and an aberrant homosexual lifestyle have become acceptable, and even Christians choose to reject the authority of God's Word in believing and following whatever is convenient.

> ***Those who take refuge in God and
> trust Him for their salvation and
> security will have the last word.***

This is portrayed by the psalmist as those mighty men, people of influence, who appear to boast in evil. They take pride in their independence and arrogance. They are indifferent to those who are victimized by their self-serving ambitions and pursuit of power, whether the poor and neglected elements of society or individuals whose lives and careers have become the carnage of their deceit and lies. Families have been destroyed by indebtedness because they believed the lies of financial institutions to use credit to acquire all their desires of the "good life" now. Lives have been wrecked by the deceit of the government collaborating with the gambling industry to entice people to take risks under an illusion of instant wealth.

However, God will judge those who have ignored Him and practiced such worldly deceits. Those who take refuge in God and trust Him for their salvation and security will have the last word and will witness the demise of those inclined to evil and given to the pursuit of wealth at any cost. In contrast, we are to trust God's love and mercy continually. We are to give thanks in recognition that God is responsible for whatever we have become and accomplished. We are to associate only with those who are godly and wait, or hope, in the name of the Lord.

PRAYER: *Lord, I am constantly confronted with the godless, worldly values and influences that pervade our society. Help me not to be inclined to embrace and accept the false hopes and deceitful standards of success that abound around me but also not to be discouraged in the hope and assurance I have in You. You are my refuge; my trust will be in You forever, and I am confident I will see Your judgment on those who reject You.*

Psalm 53

The Total Depravity of Man

Key Verse: God has looked down from heaven upon the sons of men, to see if there is anyone who understands, who seeks after God. Every one of them has turned aside; together they have become corrupt; there is no one who does good, not even one. (Psalm 53:2–3)

Most people have a basic misconception regarding sin in thinking that we are sinners because we have committed sin and done wrong. However, the reality is that we commit sin because we are sinners. There is an inherent sin nature in each person that is called "Adamic sin" because we have all descended in the flesh from Adam, who rejected God and sinned. This is explained in Romans 5:12, *"Therefore, just as through one man sin entered into the world, and death through sin, and so death spread to all men, because all sinned."* This passage goes on to explain that, in the same way, life has been provided to all who believe through one Man, Jesus Christ, who became sin for us that we might live.

There is no exception to the sin nature. It is characteristic of everyone. It is evident from an infant focused only on its own needs, the selfish actions of a toddler, and rebellious behavior of a child. Sin is not an acquired behavior; it is our natural tendency. No one, apart from God's grace and the power of His Spirit, does good or seeks after God. Of course there is something in the spirit of man, created in the image of God, that has been described as "a God-shaped vacuum," which has resulted in all the perverted religious expressions throughout the world as men seek God. It is that lack of completion without God that the Holy Spirit uses to draw us to Him. But that can happen only when one comes to the conviction of sin, repents, and acknowledges the futility of one's own efforts to find God.

> *No one, apart from God's grace and the power of His Spirit, does good or seeks after God.*

Actually, our sin nature leads us to practically deny God, for to acknowledge Him requires us to recognize His moral nature and therefore our accountability for deeds which are contrary to His righteousness. Hence, it is more convenient, although foolish, to simply deny His existence. There is no exception. Man is wicked, depraved, corrupt, and does not seek God; he commits injustices, has turned aside to his own will, and does not do good. This passage is quoted in Romans where Paul concludes, *"All have sinned and fall short of the glory of God"* (Rom. 3:23).

In conclusion, the appeal is that all would come under conviction, be aware of their sin, and be put to shame, that salvation might come from the Lord, and God's people would be restored. God is our only hope. Salvation brings joy and gladness because we do not deserve it and are not able to earn it; we experience it only because of God's mercy through what Jesus Christ has done for us in taking our sin upon Himself on the cross.

PRAYER: *Lord, never let me take pride in my own goodness or be deceived to think I am anything but a sinner in Your sight. Were it not for Your love and mercy, I, like others, would still be captive to that old sin nature that is corrupt and not even capable of doing good. Thank You for giving me a new nature in Jesus Christ.*

Psalm 54

Responding to Criticism

*Key Verse: Behold, God is my helper; the Lord is the
sustainer of my soul. (Psalm 54:4)*

This Psalm seems to continue the previous one as it
begins with the plea to *"Save me, O God, by Thy
name"* (v. 1). In our sin nature our only hope of being
saved is God and the righteousness and loving-kindness represented by His name. However, it is not only a desire for
salvation but that God would *"vindicate me, help me and
sustain me"* (vv. 1, 4). Apparently adversaries had arisen. The
psalmist was experiencing opposition from those who were
not focused on God and who even sought his life.

I could readily identify with the supplication expressed
here as, at the time of meditating on this Psalm, there were
those coming against me, challenging my integrity, and
inflicting injustices. While they may not have been seeking
my life, they were definitely seeking to destroy my reputation and credibility and undercut my leadership. There is a
natural tendency to respond in kind, to take these people to
task, and take vengeance in response to their actions. But
I am reminded that I must always respond with grace and
leave vindication to the Lord. Jesus set the example for us as
described in 1 Peter 2:21–23, *"For you have been called for
this purpose, since Christ also suffered for you, leaving you
an example for you to follow in His steps, who committed
no sin, nor was any deceit found in His mouth; and while
being reviled, He did not revile in return; while suffering, He
uttered no threats, but kept entrusting Himself to Him who
judges righteously."* God said in Hebrews 10:30, *"Vengeance
is Mine, I will repay."*

> *We must always trust God to bring*
> *about justice rather than seeking to*
> *exact retribution ourselves.*

We must always trust God to bring about justice rather than seeking to exact retribution ourselves. He will exhibit His faithfulness in repaying evil. It may not be immediate but in His time and in His own way. Therefore we must keep trusting ourselves to Him, confident that He will hear our prayer and supplication. He will help us, not necessarily through vindicating us before our enemies, but in giving us strength and the ability to withstand the criticism and personal attacks with patience and grace. He will sustain us and keep us from returning evil for evil. He is the One who guards our soul when our natural reaction would be to defend ourselves and attack those who abuse us.

If God is our help and sustainer, the One who saves and vindicates us, what then is our part that gives us assurance we will one day look with satisfaction on our enemies? We are to (1) sacrifice our rights, die to self, and put our life and reputation on the altar, and (2) we are to give thanks to the Lord. It is in praise and giving thanks that we express our faith and confidence in God and that He will work, even when there is not yet any evidence of His intervention. Praise makes us aware of His presence and allows Him to take control of our emotions and guide our actions and response.

PRAYER: *Lord, it is so hard not to respond to the criticism and injustice of others by being defensive and attacking them. I need Your help to sustain me, knowing vindication is Your responsibility, not mine. Help me to lay it all on the altar, sacrifice my pride and reputation, and never cease to give thanks to You.*

Psalm 55

Relinquishing Our Burdens

Key Verse: Cast your burden upon the LORD, *and He will sustain you; He will never allow the righteous to be shaken. (Psalm 55:22)*

Everyone seeks to cope with the demands and pressures of life, but those in a place of leadership are especially vulnerable because of the burden of responsibilities. Whether a pastor, always in the forefront and held accountable for the success of the church, a businessman whose board scrutinizes the bottom line of profits and market share, or the leader of a mission organization, the stress is never ending. A leader is a lightning rod for criticism and complaints, if not from one side, then the other. It is a no-win situation. It is especially painful when the attacks become personal and seem to be motivated by ill motives or a grudge, and one's adversaries seem intent on undermining one's credibility.

When the worries and anxiety seem overwhelming, resulting in sleepless nights, and the distractions sidetrack the vision, one just wants to fly away like a dove and find a place of solace and rest apart from the rat race. Many times I have been tempted to relinquish the leadership role in which I found myself. How attractive it has been to think of just going back to church planting in some remote and isolated location, doing what God originally called me to do, or opting for early retirement, away from the public eye and the target of detractors. I have often come to the point of saying, "I don't have to put up with this! I'm out of here!" And God would quietly reply, "Yes, you do. I have called you and placed you where you are." And I realized I had no choice but willful and joyful obedience, whatever the cost.

*Our confidence is in God and knowing
that He will give us peace in the midst
of battles that bring discouragement
and self-doubt.*

What is especially painful is when friends and colleagues are the ones who let you down and betray you. The attacks are easy to handle when they come from someone you don't even know, or generic criticism toward the organization. But when one of your own is the source of malicious rumors or allows you to become the scapegoat for what he should have been responsible for, the pain is greater. In times such as this, we come to God, pleading for Him to hear our prayer, not to hide from our supplication but to give heed and answer. Our confidence is in God and knowing that He hears and responds—whether morning, noon, or night—and will give us peace in the midst of the battles and strife that bring discouragement and self-doubts.

This brings us to one of the most beautiful and precious promises in the Bible in verse 22. It is not in fighting the battle ourselves but in relinquishing our burdens to the Lord that we receive assurance He will sustain us. God will deal with those who are dishonest and abusive, but He will never allow the righteous to be shaken. Our only responsibility is to trust Him and continue in righteousness and integrity, never allowing the attacks to cause us to respond with weapons of the flesh in vindication and anger.

PRAYER: *Lord, I am always burdened about something. I just want to get away and escape the burden of responsibility and constant attacks that go with my role. Help me to trust in You and relinquish every care and concern in confidence You will sustain me.*

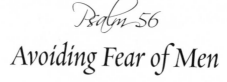

Psalm 56

Avoiding Fear of Men

Key Verse: In God I have put my trust, I shall not be afraid. What can man do to me? (Psalm 56:11)

There is a cliché that says, "I love mankind; it's people that I can't stand." A pastor was quoted as saying, in reference to a church that was going through problems, "The church would be a wonderful place were it not for the people." Relationships are a challenge. It is difficult to bridge differences, to communicate and relate to various personalities, and to show respect and understanding when conflicts arise. Someone has said that Paul's thorn in the flesh was not a physical ailment but a companion who was difficult to get along with. The most painful and threatening experiences are when we come under attack by those who spread gossip, slander our motives, and seek to destroy our credibility and reputation.

We are instructed to confront and settle differences with a brother, to be transparent and always seek reconciliation, but unfortunately there are those who are devious in speaking behind our backs. They twist our words, always looking for an opportunity to entrap us, undercut our leadership, and attack our integrity. However, because of our pride, we usually fear what people can do to us and our reputation. Fear doesn't come from God but from allowing our minds to conjure up images of what might happen and what people may think of us. When God is the focus of our life and devotion, we are not threatened by what may happen to us. When our trust and confidence are in Him, fear of what mere man can do to harm us is greatly diminished.

> **When God is the focus of our life
> and devotion, we are not threatened
> by what may happen to us.**

In fact, we are reminded of the relative power of the alternative. Will we trust Almighty God, sovereign over the universe who indwells us through Jesus Christ in all power and authority, or will we allow our minds to fear mortal men? To choose the latter is to forget that God is for us and to ignore all the promises of His Word that give us assurance of His love and care and protection. Therefore, our trust must always be in God and His Word. How do we do that in the face of opposition and personal attacks by others? It is through an attitude of praise, thanking God for the truth of His Word, and reminding ourselves that His vows and promises are binding.

God knows the turmoil and doubts we go through. While traveling in Iran, we saw tear bottles. These were bottles that fit the eye socket in which the wives of crusaders would catch their tears during the years their husbands were gone in battle so they would know how much they were missed. God knows our every heartache; He records all our tears and will redeem and comfort us. He is the One who delivers our soul from death, keeps our feet from stumbling, and enables us to walk before Him in the light.

PRAYER: *Lord, I feel so many people are against me. They distort my words and intentions and seem devious in seeking to undercut my reputation and leadership. Help me trust in You and know that You are for me. No one can harm me apart from Your will and purpose. Deliver my soul from pride, do not let me succumb to fear, and keep my feet from stumbling as I walk in the light and truth of Your Word and promises.*

God's Grace in Times of Affliction

Key Verse: I will give thanks to Thee, O Lord, among the peoples; I will sing praises to Thee among the nations. (Psalm 57:9)

It is amazing that we would expect the world to treat us with respect and justice. Those who do not know God have no hesitation in taking advantage of others or inflicting harm for the sake of their own self-gain. We will be attacked and victimized by unscrupulous business practices, flawed contracts with unseen contingency clauses, or colleagues who will blame us for that for which they were responsible. When we think we deserve better, we should remind ourselves that we really don't! Whatever good we receive and the blessings in our life are because of God's graciousness. We are never to think that we can accomplish anything in ourselves. Whatever is good and whatever we are able to do is because of God. He is our refuge from the storms, the attacks, and the conflicts we encounter in the normal course of life.

This passage brings to mind the storm shelters in my grandmother's rural community. The storm shelter was a room-sized pit dug in the ground and covered over like a mound of dirt. She and her neighbors had seen the destructive power of tornadoes and when storms would come, they would retreat to this shelter until the storm passed. God is like that storm shelter. He is our refuge. Like seeking a shade tree for respite on a hot, sunny day, we escape the heat of trials and troubles under the shadow of His wings. In His presence we experience loving-kindness and mercy instead of the insensitive personal attacks of the sons of men. We are able to rest secure in His truth when we are taunted by the sarcasm and cutting remarks of those who would ridicule our faith and our desire to live a righteous and disciplined life. In Him we are confident He will bring reproach on those who do us harm and will see that they are caught in their own trap of deceit.

> *Begin each day by "awakening the dawn" with a heart of praise giving glory to God.*

How does one keep a steadfast heart and stay focused on God's grace and loving-kindness when encountering the treachery of attacks and deceit? By praising the Lord and focusing on His glory. We are told in Colossians 3:2, *"Set your mind on the things above, not on the things that are on earth."* Instead of being distracted by all we encounter in the world, be reminded that God is exalted above the heavens, and His glory is over all the earth. One takes refuge in Him by standing firm in His mercy and truth. An attitude that puts everything in proper perspective is an attitude of praise. Begin each day by *"awaken[ing] the dawn"* (v. 8) with a heart of praise giving glory to God.

Another key to keeping one's heart steadfast is to be proactive in serving the Lord, witnessing and being engaged in His mission. When we are *"giving thanks among the peoples"* and *"praising Him among the nations"* (v. 9), we are not dwelling on ourselves and our own troubles and afflictions. God has been gracious to us not for our own benefit but for His glory and that we might be faithful in fulfilling His mission.

PRAYER: *Lord, You are my refuge when I am attacked and there are those who maliciously trample upon me. Be gracious beyond what I deserve that I might sing Your praises and You would be exalted among the nations. Help me begin each day with an attitude of praise that I might not be distracted by the criticism and troubles I might encounter today.*

Confidence in God's Ultimate Judgment

Key Verse: And men will say, "Surely there is a reward for the righteous; surely there is a God who judges on earth!" (Psalm 58:11)

Powerful metaphors are used to show the inherent wickedness of the unrighteous and once again to reflect on our sin nature from birth. We do not choose to sin; it is the natural tendency of human nature. We have to choose not to sin, and in doing so we are aware of our inability to live a righteous life apart from God's sovereign grace and intervention. The nature of sin just leads us deeper and deeper into its bondage. Like a conscience that has been numbed because it has been ignored, a sinner is like a deaf cobra that does not hear or heed the voice of the charmer. Being indifferent to God's call to righteousness puts us under bondage. It is as if we are under a spell; wickedness becomes easier and easier, and the pangs of conscience become nonexistent.

The primary message is a plea for God's vengeance. We who have been subjected to the unrighteousness and violence that is so prevalent in the world can only turn to the confidence that God will punish in no uncertain terms those who do wrong. We want assurance that He will intervene and reward the righteous and judge the wicked. The problem is that we want to see it immediately. We pray for God to help us, to deliver us from our problems or from the pain inflicted by an abusive relationship, and we want Him to do it now. We pray with expectation that God will deliver us and judge those who mistreat us today, immediately. And when there is no evidence of His intervention, we begin to doubt His sovereignty, question His goodness or wonder if He even cares.

> *The blessing of experiencing God's grace
> in times of suffering is to be preferred
> over relief and deliverance.*

However, our timing is seldom God's. He left the children of Israel in bondage in Egypt for more than four hundred years. They wandered in the wilderness for forty years before being blessed with the prosperity of the Promised Land. Had God relinquished His throne or compromised His moral nature? Not by any means! But His purpose is something greater than relieving us of suffering or mistreatment. He has a plan and purpose that will be fulfilled in His time, and it may not even be in our lifetime. Christians in China and Muslim countries suffer the abuse of persecution of evil regimes and never see deliverance in their lifetime. But one day those who do evil against God's anointed will be punished. The righteous will be rewarded because *"there is a God who judges on earth"* (v. 11). Such was the experience of Paul; though God did not deliver him from his thorn in the flesh, He provided grace to endure. The blessing of experiencing God's grace in times of suffering is to be preferred over relief and deliverance.

When we don't see God acting on our behalf, we must not succumb to doubt and lose heart and certainly must not become vindictive and assume the vengeance that is God's prerogative alone. Sometimes our comfort and assurance are only in the promise that the wicked will be destroyed and that we will one day see the righteous rewarded.

PRAYER: *Lord, it is so difficult to go day after day and year after year suffering abuse and mistreatment at the hands of others. We live in a sinful world and long to see Your judgment prevail. Don't let me lose heart but remain confident that justice will come. Help me to realize that Your grace is a blessing far greater than relief from trials.*

Psalm 59

A Secure Stronghold

Key Verse: But as for me, I shall sing of Thy strength;
yes, I shall joyfully sing of Thy lovingkindness in
the morning, for Thou hast been my stronghold,
and a refuge in the day of my distress. (Psalm 59:16)

The psalmist once again pleads with God to intervene and deliver him from his adversaries. The sequence expressed is to pray, to wait, and to praise. This frequent reference to opposition seems to affirm that if we seek to serve God and be faithful, we will come under attack— whether by actual enemies, by temptation, or because of trying circumstances. The appeal for deliverance is a request to be *"set on high,"* aloof from the battle, to a place where we find security.

It is important to determine why we suffer affliction and trials. Often it is because of our own sin or the consequences of our mistakes or lack of discipline. Having examined his heart and his life, the psalmist determines that what he is experiencing is not because of his transgression or guilt but because of godless, vicious men. However, in contrast to similar passages where the opposition is clearly personal, here it appears to be the nations that are coming against Israel and God's people, but the application is the same.

> **One who seeks to serve God and be**
> **faithful will come under attack by**
> **actual enemies, temptation, or trying**
> **circumstances.**

We should first examine our hearts to discover if there is any sin that would result in our suffering the consequences and trials we encounter. Our appeal, however, is not justified by our innocence but only because of God's strength and our confidence in His loving-kindness. Deliverance, then, is not on our behalf but for His sake, that *"men may know that God rules . . . to the ends of the earth"* (v. 13). It is for His glory and to affirm His lordship. Though the psalmist asks that they be destroyed, he is literally asking that they be brought to an end. Earlier he appeals that they not be slain but scattered. If our enemies were destroyed, we would quickly forget about them and become presumptuous about our triumphant life. But having been brought down and scattered, they are a continual reminder that God is our stronghold and our shield.

So rather than trying to overcome the situations and attacks of others, we are to pray and turn to God for deliverance. Then we are to wait and watch in confidence that, as our stronghold, He will enable us to look triumphantly over our foes. Finally, we are to sing, an expression of praise, because God is our stronghold and our fortress. He is our refuge and strength. In times of distress we claim the victory that will be provided when we begin each morning with a song of joy because of His loving-kindness and mercies. As we are told in Lamentations 3:22–23, *"The LORD's loving-kindnesses indeed never cease, for His compassions never fail. They are new every morning; great is Thy faithfulness."*

PRAYER: *Lord, the reason I come to You for deliverance from oppression is not for my own comfort but that others would know You are sovereign and You are my stronghold and security. Regardless of my suffering and distress, help me to sing joyfully of Your loving-kindness; in fact, let me begin each day with a song of joy that gives me assurance of Your faithfulness throughout the day, whatever I may encounter.*

Psalm 60

God Is the Source of Courage

Key Verse: Through God we shall do valiantly, and it is
He who will tread down our adversaries. (Psalm 60:12)

When we are going through troubled times and diffi-
culties, there is a natural tendency to feel that God
has rejected us. We easily succumb to the subtle
temptation that was common to Jewish perceptions that when
things go well, it is because we are good and God is blessing
us, and when things go wrong, it is because we have failed
and God is punishing us. This "cause and effect" philosophy,
however, is contrary to God's nature and purpose in our lives.
He doesn't guarantee the absence of hardship and, in fact,
often allows it because of a greater good He has in mind.

When we are reveling in our own misery and misfortune,
what God does is remind us of His sovereignty. When the
psalmist was having a pity party and complaining how
God had rejected and broken His people, notice how God
responded. He said, "Look at the tribes and peoples that surround you. I am the one that established the boundaries
of Shechem and gave the allotment of land to the valley of
Succoth. Gilead and Manasseh are mine. Ephraim, Judah,
Moab, and Edom are simply instruments in my hand." Our
own troubles appear so small when we put them in the perspective of God's sovereignty over the nations. When I get
discouraged because the world is sinking in depravity, and
problems seem to deter our mission task from moving forward, I can hear God saying, "Egypt, Libya, and the Sudan
belong to me; China, Afghanistan, and Russia are mere instruments in my hand."

> *God will not allow us to experience deliv-*
> *erance by our own hand, lest in our pride*
> *we take the glory that is due only Him.*

God wants to remind us that we will not overcome and win the victory in our own strength or by our own means. We must look for Him to lead the way and give us help when we encounter the adversary, whether personally or as the people of God. He will not allow us to experience deliverance by our own hand, lest in our pride we take the glory that is due only Him. But when we come to Him, acknowledge His power and sovereignty, and rest in Him, He will give us courage and valor to face the enemy and our trials, and He will *"tread down our adversaries"* (v. 12).

But something else that God does is give us a cause, a mission, a purpose in life. He gives *"a banner to those who fear Thee"* (v. 4). Picture medieval knights riding into battle carrying the banner of their king. Their banner signifies to whom they belong. It identifies them with the cause for which they are fighting. The one to whom the Lord gives His banner is the one who fears Him. Throughout the Psalms we see that the fear of the Lord is the compelling characteristic that draws us close to Him and that keeps us from sin. That deep respect and awe of Him is what assures God that He will get the glory. It enables Him to bless and prosper those who fear Him and walk in His truth.

PRAYER: *Lord, give me Your banner and a compelling purpose in life that demonstrates I belong to You. Help me serve You faithfully and in obedience out of an awesome and genuine respect and fear. Let me serve You valiantly according to Your will because I know the battle is Yours, and You who will overcome my enemies.*

A Rock and a Refuge

*Key Verse: For Thou hast heard my vows,
O God; Thou hast given me the inheritance of those
who fear Thy name. (Psalm 61:5)*

There is no distance so remote or depth of despair that God does not hear us and heed our prayer. Years of missionary experience overseas and global travel have carried me to destinations that some would describe as "God-forsaken" places. Serving in these remote locations, often where the power of evil is so apparent, it is not uncommon to lose heart and become discouraged. But God is ever present and hears our cry *"from the end of the earth"* (v. 2). He lifts us up and places us on the security of a solid rock of refuge.

I recall when our family spent several months in Bangalore, India. Behind the guesthouse where we lived was a rock quarry. The kids would play on the massive rock structures of that granite mountain, hiding in the crevices or climbing to the top of an outcropping and lording it over their play-mates because they had attained the highest pinnacle. That's what God does for us when the discouragement of a faint heart simply drives us to Him and we rely on Him.

> **God is ever present and hears our cry.
> He lifts us up and places us on the
> security of a solid rock.**

- He lifts us above our problems and doubts.
- He places us securely on a rock foundation that is a refuge from troubles.
- He becomes our tower of defense against our enemies.
- He provides a dwelling place and shelter in His presence forever.

Why do we have assurance of this response and provision of God when we pray and cry to Him in our time of need?

- Because He knows we have made a commitment of faith—a vow to believe and trust in Him.
- Because of our confidence in the inheritance of salvation and blessing that He gives to those who fear His name.
- Because we know the years of our life are in His hand; He preserves and prolongs them as He has promised.
- Because we have an eternal security and will dwell with Him forever.
- Because He continually pours out mercy and lovingkindness according to our need and provides His truth to guide and sustain us.

But primarily it is so that we will sing praise to His name forever. We must never forget that all God does for us is not because of our need or because we deserve His grace. He doesn't provide escape from troubles and a refuge of peace and blessing simply for our benefit; it is so that we would praise and glorify Him. Our vows, or commitment, to live for Him is for the purpose of glorifying Him in our life, for He is worthy of all praise and honor. So the primary issue is whether or not we are true to our commitment each day.

PRAYER: *Lord, thank You for the assurance that You hear my cry and know my need wherever I am, and that You provide a refuge under the shadow of Your wings. Lead me always to fear Your name and stand confidently on that rock that is a tower of strength against anything that would threaten my faith and keep me from praising You.*

Responding to Personal Attacks

Key Verse: My soul, wait in silence for God only, for my hope is from Him. He only is my rock and my salvation, my stronghold; I shall not be shaken. (Psalm 62:5–6)

B eing in what is considered a position of status from a human perspective, I constantly have had to deal with personal attacks, betrayal of trust, and elements that seem intent on "thrusting me down from my position." My character and integrity have been assailed. I have been the victim of malicious rumors and falsehoods that seem to take on a life of their own. Certainly I have not been without flaws, and mistakes in judgment have justified much of the criticism. I have discovered the issue is not whether or not I will be subjected to personal attacks or whether my leadership credibility will be undercut—that goes with the position. The issue is how I will respond.

God is my only security. As long as I am trusting in Him, He is my salvation not only from sin but also from unjust attacks. Because He is a rock and a stronghold, as long as I resort to His strength as my refuge and comfort, I will not be shaken. But the most important advice here is to *"wait in silence for God only"* (v. 5). There is a natural tendency to become defensive and to counterattack by criticizing those who come against me, especially if they are spreading falsehoods. However, choosing to engage an adversary simply intensifies and prolongs the battle. It gives even greater attention to the gossip and slander. To respond with grace, or not to respond, results in the issues quickly being dissipated.

> *When we find ourselves under attack, we don't have to fight the battle. React with Christlike grace, and He will vindicate us.*

How does one take abuse and remain silent, patiently waiting on God to deal with the matter? By remembering that He is our hope. It is almost as if the psalmist could not express this sufficiently as he describes God as our rock, our salvation, our stronghold, our strength, and our refuge. We don't have to fight the battle. Let His glory rest on us and be seen in us—react with Christlike grace, and He will vindicate us. When we find ourselves under attack unjustly, we are not to respond to our adversaries but are to pour out our heart to the Lord. We are to *"trust in Him at all times"* (v. 8).

Someone has said in these situations we are to wait on the Lord silently, expectantly, and continually. Even when we talk about our problems, we are focusing on ourselves and keeping the issues at the forefront of our consciousness, usually resulting in feelings of anger or anxiety rather than a peace that comes from relinquishing them to the Lord. It is hard not to try to take control and deal with the problem instead of waiting patiently, trusting in the Lord. We are reminded that status, whether men of low degree or of rank, is just an illusion. Riches are something not worth pursuing. Power belongs to the Lord, and what a marvelous characteristic that His power is combined with the compassion and mercy of His loving-kindness.

PRAYER: *Lord, there will always be those who assail me and seek to bring me down, but they are nothing compared to You. Keep me from being defensive and fighting the battle myself, but lead me always to respond with Christlike grace and rest in You. Help me never to set my heart on status or riches, for You are my rock and my salvation. You are my stronghold, and I will trust You alone.*

Thirsting for God

*Key Verse: God, Thou art my God; I shall seek Thee
earnestly; my soul thirsts for Thee, my flesh yearns for Thee,
in a dry and weary land where there is no water. (Psalm 63:1)*

One of the most important conditions of a Spirit-filled
life is to have a deep yearning and desire for God.
Throughout my ministry I have had a longing to be
used in a way that can only be described by God's power. We
can accomplish a great deal through our own efforts and
hard work. The clever implementation of programs and mission strategies can produce results, but there is no greater
satisfaction than to see the hand of God intervening in such a
way that only He can get the credit for what is done.

We often go through times of dryness in our spiritual life
when there is no sense of God's presence. We grow weary
working harder and harder, but our busyness produces no
evidence of God's blessings. In a world that is blatantly ignoring God and His values, we long to see His power and glory
manifested, even in judgment if not in revival. I have been
through times of personal struggle, fighting temptation and
discouragement, and watching others fall into sin. I am convinced the only deterrent to becoming vulnerable to sin and
spiritual failure is to have a heart that is desperate for God.
The person who thirsts for God and desires to experience His
power and holiness will never feed the seeds of lust and self-
gratification. The one who considers God's mercy and loving-
kindness more precious than life itself will not indulge sin or a
self-centered lifestyle but will devote himself fully to being the
kind of person in whom God can entrust His power.

> **The only deterrent to becoming vulnera-
> ble to sin and spiritual failure is to have
> a heart that is desperate for God.**

Spiritual mediocrity is sometimes more devastating than occasional lapses into sin. To live day after day, year after year, going through the motions, engaged in the perfunctory practice of prayer and Bible reading and faithfully attending church without any manifestation of God's anointing is sad, indeed. God knows our heart. There can be no pretense when we come into His presence. He discerns whether or not that passion and thirst for Him is there, and He always responds.

It is a precious experience to be aware of His presence continually, even as we lie in bed at night. We can walk in victory when we are consciously clinging to Him, confident He is the One that upholds us. It is a relationship that begins with a confession that He is our God and Lord of our life. We find a song of praise is constantly on our lips; and, whether literally or figuratively, our hands are lifted in submission to bless Him and receive all that He has for us as we come into His presence in humble surrender. Jesus said, *"If any man is thirsty, let him come to Me and drink. . . . 'From his innermost being shall flow rivers of living water'"* (John 7:37–38).

PRAYER: *Lord, may I never cease to long for You and yearn to see Your power manifested in my life. So often I feel spiritually dry and distant from Your presence. I live in a world that does not know You, a weary land that needs to see Your power and Your glory. You are my God! I lift my hands in submission and surrender to Your will. Your lovingkindness is more than life to me, and I will constantly give You praise.*

Dealing with Devious Attacks

Key Verse: Then all men will fear, and will declare the work of God, and will consider what He has done. (Psalm 64:9)

In this prayer of supplication, David expresses confidence that God will prevail and will defeat the enemies who conspire against him. However, his appeal is not so much for deliverance, as he is confident of that, but for protection from fear of the enemy. It is usually easy to deal with a problem or challenge when it is obvious and clearly understood. We will readily resist temptation when confronted with something that is blatantly wrong. But the subtle undercurrents of gossip and being blindsided by the unexpected bring turmoil in our life. Anxiety arises out of an unknown threat and fear of what might happen. We can usually deal with an objective fear, but uneasiness occurs in a situation and relationship that we cannot put our finger on, and that doesn't give us a handle to deal with it. The rumors and dread of what might happen rob us of peace and a sense of well-being.

When we lived in Bangkok, there was an escalation of terrorist threats in which Americans were rumored to be targeted. The American embassy and the International School were barricaded. We were told to stay home and avoid any kind of public assembly. An oppressive fear swept the expatriate community. It occurred to me that terrorists did not have to attack and bomb us; they accomplished their purpose by simply creating an atmosphere of fear that paralyzed our normal activities. David had enemies; that was reality. But he prayed that he would not succumb to the dread and fear of his enemies.

> *The most painful attacks are words that are unjust and lay a snare to destroy our reputation or malign our motives.*

People will talk behind our backs. We will always be subject to gossip and to those who would use slanderous rumors to attack us. The most painful and grievous weapons are words that are unjust and lay a snare to destroy our reputations or malign our motives. It is difficult to counter them because we don't know their source. They come from *"the secret counsel of evildoers"* (v. 2) that *"[lay] snares secretly"* (v. 5) and *"shoot from concealment at the blameless"* (v. 4). In the strength of the Lord, like David, we can deal with an enemy that is seen, but our complaint is about the subtle and devious conspiracies that cannot be confronted. Our confidence and freedom from fear come in knowing God will cause them to stumble and will use their own lies against them.

We are reminded that when God does deliver us from fear and from our enemies, it is not just for our sake but that others will see what God has done. They will know that His hand and integrity overcome evil. The result will be that everyone will fear the Lord, and those who are righteous and upright in heart will glory in the Lord and always find refuge in Him.

PRAYER: *Lord, I usually lose my sense of peace and well-being, not from challenging situations but from rumors and anxiety over what is being said about me. Show Yourself strong in overcoming any who have evil intent toward me. Help me to take refuge in You and maintain an upright heart that others would see Your works and glorify You.*

The Joy of God's Presence

Key Verse: O Thou who doest hear prayer,
to Thee all men come. (Psalm 65:2)

God's sovereignty and reign over all the earth are evident to all. When we comprehend that God is the Maker and Ruler over all creation, there is no other response except to stand in awe, praising Him and giving ourselves in humble submission to His authority.

He established the mountains by this strength. If He can calm the roaring waves of the sea, He can bring peace in the midst of tumult, conflicts, and confusion among the peoples throughout the earth. He is so glorified by the majesty of His creation that the dawn and sunset are like a shout of joy. God is the one who enriches the soil, waters the crops, and prospers the harvest. The rivers that course through the valleys, the rain that waters the earth, the pastures, and hills that sustain the cattle are all the work of His hands. This should bring joy to our lives and is intended to draw all men to trust Him and honor Him, even to the ends of the earth.

But there is a personal blessing and benefit for those who do come before Him, acknowledge His lordship, and worship Him. God hears their prayers. Even when iniquity comes into our lives, God forgives us. It is not a matter of living above sin. We are vulnerable to temptation. There will be times when we do wrong and transgress God's laws. But He is not only sovereign over the earth, He is a personal God who hears our prayer and responds with grace and forgiveness, restoring us to fellowship with Him.

*If there were no assurance of the
forgiveness of sin or eternal life,
I would still trust Christ because of
the blessing of knowing Him.*

The greatest blessing we experience is the privilege of dwelling in His presence. When He calls us to repentance and faith in Jesus Christ, it is not just for salvation from sin or so we can be assured of going to heaven. We enter into a relationship of having been reconciled to God. We dwell in His courts; the reality of His daily presence in our lives is satisfying as we experience His grace and goodness. Jesus told His disciples in John 14:17 that the One they knew and was with them (Jesus) would be in them in the person of the Holy Spirit. Paul explained it in Colossians 1:27 as, *"Christ in you, the hope of glory."* I'm not sure at what point I came to realize that this was the essence of the Christian life. If there were no assurance of the forgiveness of sin or eternal life in heaven, I would still trust Christ and believe in Him because of the blessing of knowing Him and living in Him each day.

We need to realize that the purpose for which He forgives our sins is to draw us to Himself. He wants to bless us with an abundant life that is filled with joy and praise. He desires for us to be restored to the image of Christ; it was necessary for God to save us in order for us to be restored to Christlikeness. Eternal life in heaven is simply the bonus of being in Christ. The One who redeems us and draws us to Himself in righteousness offers this awesome experience to all who would trust Him, even to the ends of the earth.

PRAYER: *Lord, never let me lose a sense of awe at Your creation. I praise You that as sovereign over the universe You have chosen to draw me into Your presence to experience Your goodness. May I always be conscious of the awesome privilege of intimate fellowship with You day by day. Use my witness that all men, to the ends of the earth, might come to You.*

Living to the Praise of God's Glory

Key Verse: If I regard wickedness in my heart, the Lord will not hear; but certainly God has heard; He has given heed to the voice of my prayer. (Psalm 66:18–19)

Several parallel themes emerged as I read and meditated on this Psalm—see and sing, trials and trust, hear and fear. This was a message and admonition to Israel, but it is also instruction to us personally. However, it is not only for us but for all the earth.

When we see the awesome works of God and how He intervenes in human history—and in personal events to give us life and bless us—it should elicit songs of praise and shouts of joy. God's people reflected on how He had brought them out of Egypt miraculously, preserved them in the wilderness and enabled them to cross over the Jordan River into the Promised Land. It demonstrated the power of His majesty and that He rules the world. This was not just a testimony to Israel but to other nations who observed His mighty works, because God's intent was that all the earth would recognize and praise Him.

We need to recognize how God is constantly working in our own life. There are many nominal Christians whose commitment is only a pretense, like the nations surrounding Israel that feigned obedience to God. Many, not in outward rebellion but with a subtle attitude of self-centeredness and self-sufficiency, exalt themselves. Marks of authentic faith among those who have seen and experienced the glory of God's grace are an abiding joy and a heart of praise that are seen and are evident to others. That will always be our most effective witness, to the nations as well as to our family, neighbors, and colleagues.

> *We go through trials so that God can
> purify us and bring us to the place
> of more abundant blessing.*

The psalmist seems to attribute his trials to God, just as we often blame God when we go through adversity and hardship. However, we must recognize that God in His sovereignty does allow us to encounter oppressive burdens and to be trampled down by others who abuse us and take advantage of us in order to punish us. We go through the trials of "fire and water," but it is so that God can purify us and refine us as silver and bring us to the place of a more abundant blessing. We should recognize that He is always with us, has promised to preserve our life, and *"does not allow our feet to slip"* (v. 9). Therefore we should use these experiences to simply renew our trust and commitment to Him.

Finally, we are invited to come and hear what God has done. Those who stand in reverence and fear of God will be sensitive to how His providence is being worked out in all the experiences common to life and will praise and extol Him. We do not hear God and are not able to put the trials of life into perspective if we are holding on to sin in our hearts. It is not necessarily the outward, blatant deeds of wickedness but attitudes of anger, bitterness, or self-sufficiency that make us insensitive to God. Sin causes us to lose sight of His faithfulness and all that He has done for us. But those who fear God know that God hears and heeds their prayer and does not withhold His loving-kindness.

PRAYER: *Lord, I do not want my relationship with You to be blocked by any wickedness in my heart. Convict me of sin. I am confident of Your loving-kindness and yearn for Your forgiveness and total cleansing because I fear You and want my life to bless Your name. Help me to see Your sovereignty at work in my life that I might sing Your praise and trust You in every trial.*

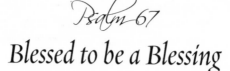

Blessed to be a Blessing

Key Verse: God be gracious to us and bless us, and cause His face to shine upon us—that Thy way may be known on the earth, Thy salvation among all nations. (Psalm 67:1–2)

The prayer for God's blessing in verse 1 is often the essence of our prayers. Whether explicit or implied, we want God to bless us, to prosper us, to favor us, to guide and protect us. This verse is often used for a benediction in our worship services; we then say "Amen," and go home. But the next verse clarifies why God would choose to bless His people. It is only so that they will make His way known on the earth and His salvation among all peoples.

God did not choose Israel and bless them because they deserved His blessing but in order that they would serve Him and fulfill His mission. Why should God be gracious to us and care for us? Why would He protect us from harm and prosper us materially? It is not for our benefit but for the sake of bearing testimony of His way, an example of holiness and godly living among those around us and as a witness to the ends of the earth. We certainly don't deserve God's blessings and shouldn't expect them if we are not living for Him and are not faithfully devoted to fulfilling His mission. A prominent pastor whose church had moved into a beautiful, new sanctuary put this in perspective when he said, "It is not a matter of how many we seat but how many we send. Our worship center should be our global outreach center. The only reason God has so richly blessed us is that we might be equipped to fulfill His mission in the world."

> ## *We don't deserve God's blessings and shouldn't expect them if we are not living for Him and devoted to fulfilling His mission.*

What is it that God wants all the earth to know about "His way"? He wants them to know that He is Savior, Sovereign, and the Source of all blessing. He said in Isaiah 45:22, *"Turn to Me, and be saved, all the ends of the earth; for I am God, and there is no other."* He wants them to realize that He is the One who judges the peoples and guides the nations on the earth. In His providence and sovereignty God is controlling human events and the destiny of the nations. And He wants them to know that the earth yields its produce—their crops and cattle multiply—because He is the One who sends the sun and rain and has designed the natural order of the universe for our benefit.

But all of this is for the primary purpose that all the peoples of the earth would praise the Lord. *"Let the nations be glad and sing for joy"* (v. 4). God's ultimate purpose is to be exalted and praised by all the peoples of the earth, for He alone is worthy of worship and honor and praise. His desire is that all the nations, those suffering oppression and in bondage to sin and spiritual darkness, would be set free to be glad and sing for joy. But that comes only through knowing His way and experiencing His salvation. How can that happen? It will come about only through our witness and faithfulness in fulfilling God's mission. That is why He has blessed us and been gracious to us. It is why His face shines upon us with favor—not for our benefit but *"God blesses us, that all the ends of the earth may fear Him"* (v. 7).

PRAYER: *Lord, I am constantly praying for Your blessings on my life. May the grace and favor You give me be only for the purpose of proclaiming Your salvation to the nations. Let me never take Your blessings for granted but use them to become a blessing to the nations that they might know You and praise Your name.*

When God Arises!

Key Verse: Blessed be the Lord, who daily bears our burden, the God who is our salvation. (Psalm 68:19)

L **et God arise!"** That should be the passion, the desire, and the cry of our hearts, that God would arise and manifest Himself and His power among us. How we need God to arise and intervene in our nation and throughout the world! We need God to arise and restore our families. We need Him to assert Himself and His lordship in our lives that we might walk in holiness and live in a way that glorifies Him. Three general themes are reflected when God arises and manifests His presence and power.

1. He rebukes the rebellious. When God arises, His enemies will be scattered. Those who stand in opposition to Him will flee and be driven away as smoke. He will judge those who, in their arrogance and conceit, have exalted themselves and ignored God's claim over their lives. He will shatter them because of their evil deeds.

2. He rewards the righteous. When God arises, those who love the Lord will rejoice and sing praises, for He is their righteousness. He will reward them for their faithfulness and devotion, leading them in blessing and prosperity. He gives strength and power to His people and to those who acknowledge and ascribe the strength and glory that are due His name.

3. He restores the rejected. When God arises and reveals Himself, those who are the outcast, rejected, and despised will be those to whom He responds and with grace restores to a place of favor. He becomes an advocate for the widow, a father of the orphan; He provides a home for the lonely and leads the prisoner to prosperity. He is a God of deliverance who daily bears our burdens.

> *We need God to arise and assert His lordship in our lives that we might walk in holiness and live in a way that glorifies Him.*

How awesome to think that every day God is taking our burdens upon Himself. He did not just save us from sin by His one-time death on the cross; God *is* our salvation. Constantly, every day, He is saving us from that which would discourage us, the temptations that would defile us, and the doubts that threaten to erode our faith. He bears the stress of a schedule that is out of control, the burden of a dysfunctional family, and the discouragement of a debilitating illness or a strained relationship.

When we stop and meditate on all the wondrous works of God, as the psalmist did, we are reminded of His strength and power and majesty. He brought His people through the wilderness, brought rain to the parched land, scattered the forces of opposition, and revealed His holiness at Mount Sinai. When God arises, His strength and presence are like myriads of chariots. He rides upon the highest heavens, and all the kingdoms of the earth will recognize His power and sing praise to His name.

PRAYER: *Lord, thank You for the assurance that You are not only my salvation but that You bear all my burdens every day. I can trust You to deal with my adversaries; therefore, I will rejoice in Your name and sing praises to You. With the psalmist I declare, "Let God arise," that Your power and providence may be seen in our world today.*

Responding to Persecution

*Key Verse: But as for me, my prayer is to Thee, O LORD, at an
acceptable time; O God, in the greatness of Thy lovingkindness,
answer me with Thy saving truth. (Psalm 69:13)*

I can always identify personally with the psalmist when he
bemoans adversaries who seem to *"hate me without a
cause"* (v. 4) and create distress. But this passage brought
to mind the many believers who are subjected to persecution
by both family and government authorities. All over the
world victims cry out against injustice and discrimination.
They are abused physically and subjected to economic deprivation. They are overwhelmed by a flood of ridicule and
ostracism with no one to come to their defense and rescue
them. Their *"eyes fail"* (v. 3) as they seek to envision and
wait for deliverance, which never seems to come.

They endure suffering because they are consumed by zeal
for the Lord's house. Their lives are totally surrendered to
advancing God's kingdom; they are obsessed with remaining
faithful for the sake of His church. Their passion is not to be
delivered or to be relieved of suffering, though they pray for
it, but that they would not deny their faith and bring shame
to their witness. There are many testimonies of how those
who seek God have found Him due to the faithfulness in suffering by those who have discovered there is a cause worth
dying for. One of the ancient church fathers, Tertullian,
observed that the blood of martyrs is the seed of the church.

> *One's testimony of faithfulness in
> the midst of suffering is what distin-
> guishes an authentic Christian
> and draws others to the truth.*

Ezekiel 36:23 says, *"'Then the nations will know that I am the LORD,' declares the Lord GOD, 'when I prove myself holy among you in their sight.'"* One's testimony of holiness and faithfulness, even in the midst of suffering, is what distinguishes an authentic Christian testimony and draws others to the conviction of the truth. The psalmist acknowledges that God sees his folly and knows all his failings, but his appeal is that it would not be allowed to bring shame to the Lord and be a deterrent to others coming to know Him. Why should we expect others to be drawn to Christ if the witness of our life is no different from others in the world? Do those who would seek God see the reality of our faith in the way we bear reproach and suffering? Adversity is often our greatest opportunity to testify to the victory that we have in a living Savior!

Our concern should not be for the Lord to deliver us from trouble, restore our comfort zone, and give us a life of ease without any trials or opposition but that we would remain faithful and not bring shame to Him. Our appeal to God is our confidence in His loving-kindness, the greatness of His compassion, and that He does hear our prayer and answer at an acceptable time. In our affliction and pain we know that God has set us *"securely on high,"* so we continue to praise Him and magnify His name. Coming before Him in humility and with thanksgiving is the key to victory, and it is more pleasing to God than a sacrifice or religious ritual.

PRAYER: *Lord, forgive me for getting so upset with the trivial inconveniences I have to suffer when many are persecuted for their faith. I pray that my attitude and behavior, especially in the midst of trials and affliction, would never bring shame to You but others would see Christ in me and be drawn to You by the faithfulness of my testimony, even in suffering.*

Psalm 70

The Value of Enduring Suffering

Key Verse: Let all who seek Thee rejoice and be glad in Thee; and let those who love Thy salvation say continually, "Let God be magnified." (Psalm 70:4)

Patience and long-suffering are spiritual gifts. It is not our natural tendency to endure suffering or inconvenience. We are even impatient to see God's will played out in our lives. The values of our world entice us to demand instant gratification, immediate solutions. Even when we submit to God's will, we want to know where it is leading. When we pray, God sometimes answers yes, and sometimes no, but usually the response is not instantaneous. This is because He wants us to trust in Him and not to become presumptuous in thinking all we have to do is pray, and He is obligated to respond immediately. God knows the greater value of building our faith through having to wait without losing hope.

Romans 5:3–5 tells us, *"We also exult in our tribulations, knowing that tribulation brings about perseverance; and perseverance, proven character; and proven character, hope; and hope does not disappoint, because the love of God has been poured out within our hearts through the Holy Spirit who was given to us."* The book of James echoes this same truth in chapter 1, *"Consider it all joy, my brethren, when you encounter various trials, knowing that the testing of your faith produces endurance. And let endurance have its perfect result, that you may be perfect and complete, lacking in nothing"* (vv. 2–4). *"Blessed is a man who perseveres under trial; for once he has been approved, he will receive the crown of life, which the Lord has promised to those who love Him"* (v. 12). James goes on to explain that God does not tempt us and bring these trials upon us. They are common to life in this world, but God does use them to perfect and strengthen our faith that we might be complete in Him and gain a greater reward.

> *Praising God in all things and in all situations is the key to persevering and claiming victory over adversity and suffering.*

The psalmist prayed that God would bring shame upon those who afflicted him with injustices and that He would humiliate and turn back those who sought his life or at least maligned his reputation and deliberately tried to hurt him. Certainly those who are persecuted and tortured pray for deliverance and God's judgment and vindication on their tormentors. But their victory and ability to endure are in praying for strength to persevere and endure the suffering that is inflicted upon them. They can endure because their greatest value, even beyond their own well-being, is the salvation that comes from God. In seeking Him, even in the midst of suffering, they can rejoice and be glad.

Praising God in all things and in all situations is the key to persevering and claiming victory over adversity and suffering. Even when we do not experience immediate deliverance and relief, we can still rejoice because of our confidence that the Lord is our help. Our faith is strengthened by patient endurance and perseverance in trials.

PRAYER: *Lord, help me to guard my heart when I encounter personal attacks and those who seek to undercut my leadership and discredit my work. You are my help and deliverer to turn back their attacks and cause them to be dishonored. Help me to learn patience and persevere that I might grow in my faith, delight in Your salvation, and magnify Your name.*

A Refuge throughout Life

*Key Verse: Be Thou to me a rock of habitation, to which I may
continually come; Thou hast given commandment to save me,
for Thou art my rock and my fortress. (Psalm 71:3)*

God is our security in all situations and our salvation in
times of need and trouble. He is our rock and our
fortress. Our desire should always be to dwell in Him,
for we have no protection in our own strength from the influence of the wicked or from being overcome by situations that
discourage and defeat us. When we are conscious of being
safe and secure in Him, we will not take pride in our own
ability, our status, or what we ourselves have accomplished.
Our natural response is to praise God continually. We recognize there is no one like Him whose righteousness is all
encompassing, *"reach[ing] to the heavens"* (v. 19). When He
is our refuge and place of habitation, *"[our] mouth is filled
with [His] praise, and with [His] glory all day long"* (v. 8).

> **When we are conscious of being safe
> and secure in Him, we will not take
> pride in our own ability, our status,
> or what we have accomplished.**

---

1. He saved us in the past. God took us from the womb,
and His hand has been upon us since birth. When we think
of how we have been nurtured in the faith and have the privilege of being saved and knowing God from an early age,
when so many do not have that opportunity, it is evidence of
God's blessings. So many live in cultures where they are
deprived of knowing the way to God, or in families that did
not nurture them in a commitment to God's will. When we

are reminded that God chose us and has guided our life from our youth, it should elicit a heart of praise toward Him.

2. He sustains us in the present. Because God is our refuge and place of habitation, He is never far from us and is always available when we need help. When enemies speak against us and problems make us feel forsaken, we marvel at how God rescues us out of the hand of the wicked and keeps us from yielding to temptation. He always inclines His ear to hear our prayer and enables us to walk in righteousness, avoiding desires and actions through which we would be ashamed. Therefore, our praise is to be continual.

3. He secures us in the future. As we anticipate old age, God will not cast us off. When our own strength begins to fail and we are *"old and gray"* (v. 18), He will not forsake us. Even when we face trouble and distress, we are reminded of God's faithfulness in the past. He is our hope, and we can be confident He will revive us again. When we look back over a lifetime of experiencing God's mighty deeds and all that He has taught us, we become aware of our responsibility to declare a testimony of His strength and righteousness to successive generations and praise Him even more and more.

God, being our refuge, our rock, and our fortress throughout our lifetime causes us to live a life that is *"to the praise of [His] glory"* (Eph. 1:6). When we dwell in Him, our lips will always be shouting for joy and singing His praise. Our tongue will be a testimony of His righteousness and faithfulness continually.

PRAYER: *Lord, You are my refuge; Your righteousness will deliver and rescue me. You are my rock and my fortress to which I can come at all times. You have demonstrated Your power and faithfulness in the past and the present, and I can trust You for the future. You will hear my prayer and save me, for my hope and my confidence are in You.*

Psalm 72

The Role of Godly Leadership

Key Verse: Blessed be the LORD God, the God
of Israel, who alone works wonders. And blessed be
His glorious name forever; and may the whole
earth be filled with His glory. (Psalm 72:18–19)

This is a Psalm beseeching blessings on the king. It has an application to anyone in a position of leadership and reflects (1) a responsibility, (2) a resource, and (3) a result. Whether one is the king of Israel, a pastor, or simply holds a leadership role or position of respect and authority within an organization, one is to be an instrument of God to serve others and to fulfill God's purpose.

There is the **responsibility** to follow God's judgments and appropriate His wisdom that decisions might always be just and according to His righteousness. A leader is to be concerned for the peace and welfare of those under his authority, bringing justice to the afflicted and vindication on behalf of those who are needy and oppressed. He is to be a constant source of blessing like the showers that water the earth; he is to have compassion on the poor and rescue those who are victims of violence. He has a responsibility to rule or govern in a way that the righteous will flourish and peace will abound.

A leader's **resource** is the guidance, wisdom, and judgments that come from God and the prayers and blessings of His people. Since becoming president of the International Mission Board, I have been conscious of the massive prayer support that goes with my position. Seldom is there a day when something doesn't happen that reminds me there must be thousands of Southern Baptists and missionaries around the world who are praying for me. God will bless and prosper the leader devoted to Him, as He did the king of Israel with the gold of Sheba, but the assurance of spiritual blessings is the greater resource and far more needed than riches and wealth.

Leadership is a servant role to bless others. It is a role of responsibility through which God is to be glorified and His purpose fulfilled.

The **result** of God's blessings upon one in leadership is the successful fulfilling of God's purpose. It is like the abundance of fruit and grain that the earth produces. One's enemies and those in opposition will acquiesce in submission to his authority. One's name will be respected and become a legacy to generations that follow. But the primary result is the name of the Lord will be glorified.

The challenges of leadership are constant and often bring discouragement. It is good to be reminded that it is not about the one in position of authority, but it is about the people one leads. Leadership is a servant role to bless others. It is a role of responsibility through which God is to be glorified and His purpose fulfilled until ultimately *"the whole earth be filled with His glory!"* (v. 19).

PRAYER: *Lord, I cannot understand why I would be subjected to trials and challenges that seem to contradict Your sovereignty, but Your judgments are righteous. In my responsibilities of leadership, I need Your wisdom and guidance, but only that You would be glorified and Your purpose fulfilled. Help me to be a sensitive, servant leader and realize the responsibilities of my position include that of spiritual leadership.*

Avoiding Envy of Worldly Values

Key Verse: With Thy counsel Thou wilt guide me, and afterward receive me to glory. Whom have I in heaven but Thee? And besides Thee, I desire nothing on earth. (Psalm 73:24–25)

In spite of God's goodness to us, one of the most subtle and prevalent dangers is to envy those in the world who seem to have it so good in spite of the fact that God has no place in their life. We, like the psalmist, stumble when we find ourselves wishing we were free to indulge in the hedonistic pleasures that others seem to enjoy. We see promiscuous lifestyles portrayed on television; politicians and prominent sports figures seem to flaunt basic spiritual values of holiness and godliness without retribution. We observe that more and more people in society never go to church and have no evidence of spiritual piety, yet they seem to prosper with beautiful houses, expensive cars and boats, taking vacations to exotic places, and accumulating wealth. Envy begins to distort our perspective even in childhood and school when we want to be a part of the popular crowd—those who always wear the latest fashions and have the neatest toys. Those who are a part of elite cliques and indulge in drinking and partying without any apparent parental restraint are envied as the "in crowd" and those always having fun.

When it seems those who arrogantly ignore God are prospering, increasing in wealth, enjoying life, and able to indulge every self-centered whim and desire, it is easy to begin to feel sorry for ourselves. We wonder, "What is the use of trying to be faithful to God and living a holy life?" We feel our self-denial results only in being deprived of what others are free to enjoy and *"in vain I have kept my heart pure, and washed my hands in innocence"* (v. 13). Such attitudes should alert us to the fact that our *"feet [are] close to stumbling"* (v. 2) and our steps are about to slip.

> *There is nothing we should desire*
> *on earth except God who is eternal*
> *and the source of all we need.*

When we come into God's presence and into that secret place of worship and fellowship with Him, that is a sanctuary from the world, all of this comes into perspective. We know that judgment will come on those who ignore God, and they will be *"cast . . . down to destruction"* (v. 18). The day will come when they will be destroyed in a moment and swept away. We must never be deceived to think that the temporal, worldly pleasures in which so many indulge are worthwhile or allow our carnal nature, like a beast, to be attracted to them.

Realize that we have something far more valuable—a relationship with God in which He is with us continually; He holds us by the hand, keeping us from slipping or straying. He guides us with His counsel and assures us that we will be rewarded by being received into His glory. There is nothing we should desire on earth except God who is eternal and the source of all we need. Our flesh may fail and sometimes be jealous of others in the world, but God is our strength and our refuge from worldly desire.

PRAYER: *Lord, You are the desire of my life. All I have in You supersedes the physical pain and mental stress of resisting the comfortable and self-serving lifestyle of the world. Give me confidence each day of Your hand upon me, and guide me with Your counsel. Don't let me be deceived by the illusion of worldly success, for You are my sufficiency in this life and Your eternal glory my reward.*

Hope When Defeated and Forsaken

*Key Verse: How long, O God, will the adversary revile,
and the enemy spurn Thy name forever? (Psalm 74:10)*

Israel was in a time of defeat and had been devastated by the enemy. Destruction was rampant, and even holy things had been desecrated and destroyed. There was no prophet in the land, and it seemed that God had deserted them. It seems that this is a picture of the situation in our own country. What was once a nation that honored God and whose foundations were based on spiritual truths is now being overcome by godless humanism and postmodern philosophies that reject God. With respect for pluralism and self-centered diversity, our society denies the concept of moral absolutes and religious truth.

Worship has been marginalized, and the secular become predominant. Prayer and Christian witness is forbidden in the public marketplace as judicial authorities displace God for the sake of advocating libertarian human rights.

One only has to survey European countries to note the consequences of such trends. Churches and cathedrals that once acknowledged God's prominence in the lives of the people now stand empty or are turned into museums and restaurants. Religion is something irrelevant and given perfunctory assent only for the sake of traditional marriages and burials. Promiscuity is accepted as the common lifestyle in places like the Netherlands, France, and Scandinavia; and sanctity of life no longer exists as abortion and euthanasia are justified on the basis of convenience.

> *In times of darkness and spiritual
> oppression, we are to be reminded
> of God's covenant and His faithfulness
> to "plead His cause."*

A former generation of Christians in the Soviet Union and other communist countries probably felt the same way when the advocates of humanistic and totalitarian governments denied them their freedom of religious expression. It would have been natural to feel that God had rejected them when He did not intervene for generation after generation. In Israel the years had passed when there was no prophet proclaiming the Word of God and no miraculous manifestations of God's blessings. One of the tragic consequences of such apathy and decline is the absence of any spiritual guidance within society.

Sometimes we feel the same way personally when our lives become dry spiritually. The stress and concerns of life overwhelm us, and we no longer have that "secret place" where we meet God. The "sanctuary" of fellowship with Him, when He would speak into our lives, is gone. In desperation we cry out, "How long will God allow this situation in which He is deprived of His glory among the people?" The response is to affirm God's sovereignty, as His power over all things has been demonstrated throughout the earth. When His people are reviled, so is His name. In times of darkness and spiritual oppression, we are to be reminded of God's covenant and His faithfulness to *"plead [His] own cause"* (v. 22). We are to be assured that we, as those who are spiritually needy and afflicted, will arise and praise His name.

PRAYER: *Lord, how long must the nations live in darkness and the righteous suffer? Give me patience to persevere and confidence in Your sovereignty to vindicate the righteous. It seems that You have already abandoned our American society, but help me not to lose hope that You will plead Your cause and vindicate Your name.*

Certainty of God's Judgment

Key Verse: But God is the Judge; He puts down one,
and exalts another. (Psalm 75:7)

One's name is symbolic and represents all that a person is. To call one's name brings to mind the appearance of that person but not only what one looks like; one's name creates an image of his personality, his characteristics, and our relationship to him. Likewise, the name of the Lord represents who He is and all His attributes. Throughout the Scripture we are told the "name of the Lord" is power, salvation, a strong tower (protection and security). However, that does not mean the name itself but that the name represents the nature of God. Our hope and security is the fact that His name is always near. He is a God who is available; therefore, we are constantly thankful to Him that He is a God we can relate to. Because of that, we not only experience His wonderful works, but we declare them and give testimony of them to others.

But we are also reminded of the certainty of God's judgment. He is the One who has established the earth and determines the destiny of man. He is the One who rewards and lifts up the righteous and puts down and punishes the wicked. No one from the east or the west, or anywhere in the world, can exalt himself and assume God's place of judgment. Neither can anyone in *"insolent pride"* (v. 5) presume that he is aloof and exempt from God's hand of judgment, which will be poured out upon the wicked.

> *In view of the coming judgment in which*
> *this world will be destroyed, we need*
> *to be holy, humbly focusing on things*
> *of eternal significance.*

God has established the earth and *"firmly set its pillars"* (v. 3), and He is the only One who will determine when it will be destroyed in the time of judgment when *"the earth and all who dwell in it [will] melt"* (v. 3). Peter must have had this Psalm in mind when he wrote in 2 Peter 3:10–12, *"But the day of the Lord will come like a thief, in which the heavens will pass away with a roar and the elements will be destroyed with intense heat, and the earth and its works will be burned up. Since all these things are to be destroyed in this way, what sort of people ought you to be in holy conduct and godliness, looking for and hastening the coming of the day of God, on account of which the heavens will be destroyed by burning, and the elements will melt with intense heat!"* Obviously, in view of the coming judgment in which this world will be destroyed, we need to be holy, humbly focusing on things of eternal significance rather than boastful of this life.

There will be that final judgment when God separates the righteous and the wicked, and those who are redeemed will enter their eternal glory. However, we are told that we will all give an account for what we have done; our works will be judged not to determine our salvation but whether our reward is gained or lost. But God manifests His sovereignty in judgment in this life as well. He is the One determining who will prosper and be exalted and who will be put down. That doesn't leave any room for boasting and pride in what we accomplish or the status we attain. Knowing the reality of this fact should result in our *"singing praises to the God of Jacob . . . forever"* (v. 9).

PRAYER: *Lord, thank You for the assurance that one day You will judge the wicked and that I can trust You and wait upon Your appointed time. In spite of the apparent domination of an insolent and prideful world, I will praise You and declare Your works. I am grateful that I don't have to fear Your judgment, but help me to live a humble and holy life that reflects the salvation You have provided in Your providence by grace.*

Psalm 76

The Wrath of God's Moral Nature

*Key Verse: Thou, even Thou, art to be feared; and who may stand
in Thy presence when once Thou art angry? (Psalm 76:7)*

We are so blessed to experience the loving-kindness
and grace of God that we sometimes ignore the
reality of His wrath. It is always comforting to
think of Him caring for us with the tenderness and gentleness
of a shepherd. It gives us confidence to know that His mercy
is unending, and He readily forgives and restores us when we
come to Him in repentance, confessing our sin, whenever
we have failed. But it is easy to become complacent and presume upon His grace, neglecting to realize His moral nature
demands a wrathful response to sin and an independent spirit
among His people. He cannot ignore and tolerate an arrogance that takes lightly the responsibility to walk in holiness
and obedience to what He has commanded.

Often we read of God becoming angry and punishing His
people, Israel, when they sinned, rejected His will, and went
their own way. He was incensed with jealousy when they
chose to worship other gods. When they made the golden
calf in the wilderness at the time He was revealing His law to
guide them, God, in anger, decided to wipe them off the face
of the earth, until Moses intervened. When Moses made
excuses in failing to respond to God's call at the burning
bush, Exodus 4:14 says, *"Then the anger of the LORD burned
against Moses."* God is absolutely holy, and it would be a
violation of His nature to allow sin in His presence. His sovereignty demands absolute, unequivocal submission and obedience. For our affections and devotion to be given to
anything else is considered adulterous and worthy of God's
wrath.

God's sovereignty demands absolute obedience. For our devotion to be given to anything else is considered adulterous and worthy of God's wrath.

The psalmist reflects that God is known and exalted throughout the tribes of Israel and Judah. He is the One who has brought peace by establishing His presence in the midst of His people on Mount Zion. His majesty is exalted as He dwells in His tabernacle in Jerusalem, the city of peace. In demonstrating His power and majesty, a response of praise and worship is required. He is to be feared by all the kings of earth, for His wrath will be poured out on all those who fail to humble themselves before Him and bring gifts of devotion to Him.

Our fear of the Lord should be due to the awe and respect we have for Him as we comprehend His greatness. But it also should be due to our awareness of His wrath and the punishment that is inevitable for those who fail to live in a way that acknowledges His lordship and rule. Hebrews 10:26–31 reminds us, *"For if we go on sinning willfully after receiving the knowledge of the truth, there no longer remains a sacrifice for sins, but a certain terrifying expectation of judgment . . . the LORD will judge His people. It is a terrifying thing to fall into the hands of the living God."* The fear of the Lord should, therefore, result in our faithfulness in fulfilling our vows of commitment to Him.

PRAYER: *Lord, I do not serve You because I fear Your punishment, but Your wrath is justified when I sin against You and am disobedient to Your will. I want to be found faithful and walk in holiness because You are worthy of my devotion, and I love You.*

Putting Times of Despair in Perspective

Key Verse: Thou art the God who workest wonders; Thou hast made known Thy strength among the peoples. (Psalm 77:14)

Though often discouraged, I have seldom found myself in a pit of despair in which all hope was gone. There have been those times of being overwhelmed by problems and disappointments in which frustration and hopelessness dominated my emotions and outlook on life. My vision had crumbled, and all efforts to accomplish anything fulfilling proved futile. These were those times of culture shock and self-doubts that came in regular cycles on the mission field. There was little joy in life; facing the tasks of each new day was drudgery. Attempts to worship were just perfunctory, and prayer was nothing more than gripe sessions of pouring out my complaints to God. I felt abandoned by God, unloved by family, and unappreciated by colleagues and those I came to serve.

I have known those who have gone through times of chronic depression, in which hopelessness and despair sidetracked their ministry, put a burden on their family, and led to thoughts that life was not worth living. Sometimes it was due to an experience of grief or guilt from a moral failure, but more often it was just the inability to cope with the pressures of life. This must have been the situation with the psalmist as he expressed how this affected his faith and relationship with God.

- The Lord had rejected him forever.
- God will never be favorable toward him again.
- His loving-kindness had ceased.
- His promises had come to an end, unfulfilled.
- God had forgotten to be merciful and gracious.
- In anger He had withdrawn His compassion.

> *When hope grows faint, we should recount the times He has blessed us and we have found Him sufficient for our needs.*

The solution was not to dwell on one's circumstances but on the Lord's past deeds. When we are disturbed and hope grows faint, we are to be reminded that God will hear us in the day of trouble. We are not to lose sight of His sovereignty and are to remember His miracles and meditate on His works. We should recount the times He has blessed us and we have found Him sufficient for our needs. The solution is like the old hymn which says, "Count your many blessings; name them one by one." We are to think of His holiness and that His greatness and power are being demonstrated among the peoples throughout the earth. In other words, we are to get beyond the narrow focus of our personal problems and emotions to see things through a big picture perspective. God is at work in the world, and we are called to be His people and a part of what He is doing. If nothing else, we are to meditate on His redemption and the fact that we are children of God. We have been saved, and He will guide us like a shepherd faithfully leading His flock.

PRAYER: *Lord, thank You that You hear me in the days I am troubled when I lift my voice to You. You reach out to me whenever I seek You. You are faithful to manifest Your power in my times of need. I will remember the wonders You have wrought in my life and how You are at work in the world. I will worship You and rest secure in Your love.*

Psalm 78:1-8

Nurturing Successive Generations

Key Verse: We will . . . tell to the generation to come the praises of the LORD, and His strength and His wondrous works that He has done. (Psalm 78:4)

While we are responsible for being obedient to God's will, witnessing to a lost world, and being conscientious about our personal walk with the Lord, one of our most awesome responsibilities is to train and nurture our children in God's ways. It is sad that many children and young people are in families that faithfully attend church but have never come to an authentic, personal faith. They are taken to Sunday school, and the church crowd is their primary fellowship, yet they never see reality in their parents' faith in coping with adversity. They don't observe them demonstrating relationships of love and mutual submission where conflicts and arguments are unthinkable. They seldom see them pouring out their hearts for lost nations and sharing Christ with a neighbor. It is no wonder that worldviews expressed by a younger generation of Christians are no different than those expressed in the secular world.

It is not satisfactory for children to grow up simply following the faith of their parents. They must come to the place of recognizing their own need for a personal relationship with Jesus Christ. They need to embrace a commitment to His lordship that will be the predominant value of their life. That will happen only when they see the authenticity of their parents' faith, one that is lived out with consistent, daily relevance. Each successive generation of the nation of Israel seemed to flip-flop back and forth between times of faithfulness to God and His purpose and times of rejecting Him and succumbing to the influence of their pagan neighboring tribes. Therefore they were admonished to pass on the teachings of God to their children. Their offspring were to be well-informed and reminded of God's faithfulness and His wonderful works.

A pattern of worship and lifestyle of praise were to be ingrained in their lives.

> *Children will embrace a commitment to His lordship only when they see the authenticity of their parents' faith lived out with consistent daily relevance.*

It seems the members of each generation in our society are being more and more influenced by the world around us. They go through the motions of being faithful and active in church; they give lip service to beliefs they have been taught—parroting testimonies of others—but there is little evidence of moral conviction and the power of God in their lives. On the other hand, God seems to be raising up a remnant among a younger generation that has a heart for a lost world and is willing to give themselves with abandon to God's mission. What makes the difference? These are those who have been taught (1) to put their confidence in God, (2) to trust the power of God as demonstrated by His works in the past, (3) to follow the commandments of God and (4) walk in His truth. God will not be without a witness, but we have a responsibility to see that successive generations are faithful to be that witness and that they will have a faith to pass on to those who follow.

PRAYER: *Lord, I pray that I will never forget the wondrous works You have done and Your faithfulness and compassion in my own life. Help me to be faithful to testify to others and to live in such a way that my children and grandchildren will see evidence of Your goodness and power and follow my example of walking in Your truth.*

Psalm 78:9-72

A Continuing Pattern of Rebellion

Key Verse: But they deceived Him with their mouth, and lied to Him with their tongue. For their heart was not steadfast toward Him, nor were they faithful in His covenant. (Psalm 78:36-37)

It is shameful that we seem never to be satisfied in spite of God's abundant blessings. We pray for God to prosper us and provide our every whim and desire, yet it is not for the sake of His glory but for our comfort and pleasure. We arrogantly think that we deserve God's blessings and feel resentful when they seem to be withheld. God pours out His grace upon us, only for us to respond with sinful, self-serving indulgence in the things of the world. The resulting consequences of suffering and trouble make us aware of having strayed from God's favor, but our repentance is usually less than genuine and heartfelt.

Such is the pattern of Israel in this overview of history in which God delivered them from Egypt, manifested His power in bringing the plagues on their captors, provided manna in the wilderness, faithfully led them by the cloud and pillar of fire, yet they still rebelled. As referenced in the behavior of the tribe of Ephraim, *"They did not keep the covenant of God, and refused to walk in His law; and they forgot His deeds, and His miracles that He had shown them"* (vv. 10–11). Even when God *"divided the sea"* (v. 13) and *"gave them abundant drink"* (v. 15), they continued to sin and demanded more of God. Although He provided the manna and quail in response to their desire for bread and meat, their ungratefulness and continuing demands stirred God's anger and brought punishment.

> *God allows us to experience the consequences of our rebellion so He can restore us to His favor as people chosen to belong to Him.*

They responded much as we do today when we rededicate our lives, reaffirm that God is our Redeemer and our Security, and promise to live for Him. But because our heart is not steadfast and our confession is more for the sake of convenience, the results are not lasting. Many Christians demonstrate the same pattern as Israel—getting interested in church and serving the Lord for awhile and then falling away, only to return when life gets hard, the situation gets desperate, and they are forced to acknowledge their need for God. We don't deserve the patience and compassion God continues to exhibit toward us. Like Israel in captivity, God allows us to experience the consequences of our rebellion, to wander in the wilderness and once again be in bondage to sin. But it is only so that He can deliver us and restore us to His favor as people chosen to belong to Him.

God's faithfulness was reflected in raising up David as an unlikely leader but one with a servant heart and a shepherd's tender love and compassion. In contrast to those who only gave lip service to following God, David guided them with integrity. For God's people to persevere in faithfulness and obedience, we need to acknowledge the need for leadership and accountability. Whether a pastor or a personal friend and mentor to encourage and guide us, we need to be willing to follow someone whom God has equipped with leadership skills and wisdom and an authentic faith to lead us.

PRAYER: *Lord, I pray that You will never let me forget the wondrous things You have done in my life, Your faithfulness, compassion, and forgiveness. I don't want my confession and devotion to be insincere but a heartfelt commitment that lasts. Help me learn and grow from the consequences of failure. Give me a heart to follow and heed those You provide to guide, advise, and mentor me that I might walk in obedience to You.*

For the Glory of God's Name

*Key Verse: Help us, O God of our salvation, for the glory
of Thy name; and deliver us, and forgive our sins, for
Thy name's sake. (Psalm 79:9)*

In a time of punishment, Israel had been defeated and laid
waste. Obviously the consequences were pretty severe, and
the situation had been going on fairly long, maybe for generations. Initially their hearts were probably hardened and
bitter. They probably desired to be relieved of their servitude
in order to enjoy freedom and prosperity, but they finally
began to see their situation from a different perspective. They
were God's inheritance, and their subjection to suffering and
bondage was an insult to His sovereignty and glory. They
pleaded with God, *"How long, O LORD? Wilt Thou be angry
forever?"* (v. 5). They realized their suffering and defeat were
due to God's anger and punishment, but the situation continued until they finally realized that it wasn't about them. It was
all about God's glory and His reputation among the nations.

We, too, experience times of trouble and stress when we
are overwhelmed with problems that seem to have no solution. We plead with God to intervene and deliver us because
we want to be set free and relieved. Perhaps God's blessings
are withheld until we realize it is not for the sake of our comfort and convenience but for "His name's sake." He is the
One who should receive the glory when He forgives our sins
or brings relief from our trials. Too many testimonies are
focused on what happened to us and what we gained from
God doing something in our lives.

> *God's blessings are withheld until
> we realize deliverance is not for
> the sake of our comfort and convenience
> but for His name's sake.*

I have been convicted that a lot of my praying to be delivered from the barrage of critics and adversaries is simply because I don't like to be subjected to the pain and distractions they cause, to the threat to my reputation, or damage to my leadership. However, my attitude should be otherwise; unless God can be glorified through bringing judgment on my detractors, it is preferable that I continue to suffer. By allowing the pagan nations to prevail, Israel reminded God that He was being deprived of honor to which He was due, and His reputation was in jeopardy. The reproach they were experiencing as His people was also bringing reproach upon God since they belonged to Him, and He was not doing anything about their situation.

Our desire is for the nations to know God and become His people. Our passion should be to proclaim His glory among all peoples that they might find salvation and become the kingdom of our Lord. But for those who do not acknowledge His lordship, God will not forever tolerate their arrogance, independence, and skepticism. He will vindicate His people who have suffered among the nations that have persecuted believers and therefore brought reproach upon God. But when that has not yet happened—even in our personal life when we are oppressed and taken advantage of—we are to maintain our faith and confidence in God, giving thanks and praise to His name. It's all about Him!

PRAYER: *Lord, I confess that I usually pray for You to intervene in my problems and bless me because of my desire to be free from trials, criticism, and hardship. Help me realize it is only for Your sake and Your glory that You will show Yourself strong against my enemies.*

Yearning for God's Favor

Key Verse: O God, restore us, and cause Thy face to shine upon us, and we will be saved. (Psalm 80:3)

The heartfelt plea of Israel is apparent in this theme verse that is repeated three times. They were repentant, wanted to return to God and to be restored to His favor. They earnestly desired God to save them and deliver them from oppression. They longed once again for God's face to shine upon them. I love that expression. It makes me think of someone who beams with joy because of the pleasure of seeing me. It reminds me of the radiant faces and big smiles of my grandchildren when I arrive or how Bobbye, my wife, looks at the airport upon my return after an extended time of separation. It reflects the love and appreciation of an intimate relationship.

In contrast I can think of the visage of one who has been angry or displeased with me, especially a supervisor or one to whom I am accountable when I have let them down. I will always remember the scowl on my father's face when he confronted me for an act of disobedience. How miserable it was to encounter the disappointment of one you love. There was a longing to see on his face an expression of pride and pleasure that affirmed my behavior. This is what Israel was experiencing, and they chafed under the realization that they lacked God's favor. The tribes of Ephraim, Benjamin, and Manasseh especially were rebellious or indifferent toward God's authority and their allegiance to Him.

---

*Only when we call on His name and
promise not to turn back from Him
will His favor shine upon us.*

This Psalm is a picture of America to me. God had brought Israel out of Egypt, driven out the nations, and planted them as a vine in the Promised Land. He prospered them with blessings that were so abundant they overshadowed the mountains and extended to the sea! But the hedges were broken down. They no longer had the respect of other nations. Their produce was pilfered by others, and their power decimated. They did not have the joy and blessings that came only from honoring God and humbly acknowledging that He was the source of their success. Our forefathers came from other lands for the sake of religious freedom, and our nation was founded on principles that honored God. In planting a nation in the new world, God prospered us economically and materially to become the wealthiest and most powerful nation in the world. Yet we have become despised by the nations, our economy is in disarray, and the most basic moral values are being rejected.

Our plea needs to be for God to restore us and save us from our rejection of His lordship over our nation and society. We need to recognize His sovereignty and authority over us and in humility repent of the godless direction we are going. We should acknowledge that the crime, economic problems, immoral lifestyles, breakdown of marriage, and lack of respect for the sanctity of life are the consequences of our sin. But only when we *"call upon His name"* and promise not to *"turn back from Thee"* (v. 18) will His favor shine upon us.

PRAYER: *Lord, how desperately this prayer of Israel needs to be our plea as a nation. But also when my own sin destroys the fellowship with You that I long for, I pray that You would restore me to Your favor and allow Your face to shine upon me.*

Meekness and Submission

Key Verse: *"Oh that My people would listen to Me, that Israel would walk in My ways!" (Psalm 81:13)*

Meekness is a characteristic that is usually seen as negative and undesirable. Our connotation of a meek person is one who is shy, unassertive, and has low self-esteem. However, it actually means to be disciplined, not given to unrestrained behavior; it is one who is suscepti- ble to guidance and receptive to advice. The humility that accompanies meekness enables one to recognize authority, respond to admonishment, and give oneself to others with a servant heart. Jesus was described as meek and lowly because He was totally submissive to the Father's will. There was no resistance, stubbornness, or arrogance, but like a bridled horse He was yielded to the Father's control.

> *Our unwillingness to impose self- discipline, practice restraint, and walk in God's way deprives us of the fullness of His blessings.*

It is not human nature to be meek and submissive; in fact, it is the nature of sin to be self-centered. Pride leads us to assert ourselves, resist advice, and follow our own will, often resulting in conflict with others. God had richly blessed Israel. He had rescued them when they called to Him in times of trouble and provided for their every need in the wilderness. They should have been overwhelmed with rejoicing, celebrat- ing, and praising God. His goodness toward them should have resulted in their faithful submission to follow Him and trust Him. But instead, they refused to listen to God. In arro- gance they followed their own inclinations and self-will instead of walking in God's ways. This resulted in their being defeated by their enemies and deprived of God's provision for all their needs. Isaiah 65:2 says, *"I have spread out My hands all day long to a rebellious people, who walk in the way which is not good, following their own thoughts."*

God pleaded with them to listen to Him that He might admonish them. While "teaching" and "exhorting" are imparting and encouraging application of positive truth, "admonishing" relates to the things that are wrong, and it is for the sake of correction. How valuable it is to have a friend or colleague who cares enough to admonish us. But we don't always appreciate someone pointing out our faults. Sometimes the truth hurts. But when done in love, admonishment is for our own good and growth. It helps us see the blind spots. The issue is whether or not we hear and respond with meekness. Proverbs 12:15 tells us, *"The way of a fool is right in his own eyes, but a wise man is he who listens to counsel."*

Just as we often do, Israel in their stubbornness refused to listen to God and respond to His admonishment. In love He reminded them that He had brought them out of Egypt and blessed them. He would feed them with the finest provisions and subdue their enemies. Could our stressful lifestyle, financial burdens, and other troubles be due to following our own devices and opinion? Our allegiance to the gods of materialism and unwillingness to impose self-discipline, practice restraint, and walk in God's way deprive us of the fullness of His blessings.

PRAYER: *Lord, You have always proved Yourself faithful in times of trouble. Don't let my heart be stubborn, resorting to my own wisdom and devices, but in meekness let me hear Your voice and respond in submission to Your admonishment and guidance.*

Judgment on Behalf of the Weak

*Key Verse: Arise, O God, judge the earth! For it is Thou
who dost possess all the nations. (Psalm 82:8)*

We often have a problem accepting the fact that God
is sovereign over all the nations and rulers of the
world and then reconciling this fact with the preva-
lence of evil and injustice that is so common. Just as we
want to blame Him for our own suffering, we think that if
He is Lord, then He would do something about the afflicted
and destitute, especially when they are the victims of wicked
and despotic rulers.

Sometimes this incongruent reality is difficult to explain.
We succumb to the reasoning of media commentators after
the tragedy of September 11, 2001, when more than three
thousand people died as a result of terrorists hijacking and
flying planes into the World Trade Center and the Pentagon.
They said that God was either all-powerful or all-good but
not both. If He is all-powerful, then He is not good because
He would not have allowed this tragedy to occur. But if He is
all-good, then apparently He is not all-powerful, for He did
not and could not prevent this evil event. Of course such reasoning contradicts the truth of God's nature; He is all-powerful and completely good and holy. He does not use His power
to contradict the laws of nature or the consequences of evil
deeds of depraved humanity. But in His goodness and providence He does have a purpose through which He will ultimately be glorified.

By allowing evil rulers to prevail, God may seem to be
showing partiality to the wicked. We would presume that He
would *"rescue the weak and needy,"* and *"deliver them out
of the hand of the wicked"* (v. 4). We expect Him to cham-
pion the cause of the orphans and those who are destitute. As
I reflect on this Psalm, the words of a song I just heard come
to mind. It says, "God has no hands but our hands; He has
no feet but our feet." The church is called "the body of

Christ." We are His presence in the world today, and He has chosen to work in the world through us, His people. We are the ones who should be advocates for justice in the public place and reaching out to those who are unfortunate and victimized by the "system." But we should never lose sight of the fact that one day God will shake the foundations of the earth in judgment.

> ## We are God's presence in the world today, and He has chosen to work in the world through us, His people.

While traveling in West Africa years ago, I was unaware that our flight from Dakar to Abidjan would stop in Mauritania. We were not allowed off the plane, but as I looked out the window, all I could see was barren, desert wasteland and a few Arab-dressed nomads around the airfield. I had been told there were no known believers in this country. My heart was broken as I looked over the desolation. I turned back to my devotional reading in which I had been engaged and found myself reading Psalm 113. Verses 7 and 8 seemed to reveal a promise for the spiritually impoverished people I was seeing—"*He raises the poor from the dust, and lifts the needy from the ash heap, to make them sit with . . . the princes of His people.*" One day God will arise and judge the earth, for He, indeed, does possess the nations!

PRAYER: *Lord, I cannot understand why the wicked seem to prosper and people are subjected to injustice. Help me remain confident of Your sovereignty over the earth but also that You have chosen to work through me and Your church on earth. Make me sensitive to the plight of the afflicted and needy and be the one to minister to them.*

When God Is Silent

Key Verse: That they may know that Thou alone, whose name is the LORD, art the Most High over all the earth. (Psalm 83:18)

When we arrived as missionaries in Indonesia, I fully expected to see the power of God manifested in miraculous ways. My confidence in my calling and conviction in the power of the gospel led me to believe that God was just waiting for me to arrive, and the pages of Acts would unfold once again with multitudes being saved. It was discouraging to labor tirelessly and see no evidence of God's hand. I had sacrificed to be obedient to God's call and was serving Him faithfully but began to feel He was not doing His part.

Whether it is lack of fruit in our evangelistic efforts, a personal need that is not being met, or simply unanswered prayer, how do we respond when God is silent? Israel was going through a time when it seemed their enemies had conspired against them and were prevailing; they felt they would be destroyed if God did not intervene. They were crying out, *"Do not be silent and, O God, do not be still,"* (v. 1). In exasperation they were saying to God, "Do something!" Many times our problems are unresolved, the pressures of work and family continue to mount, financial stress or health needs get worse, and we wonder why God doesn't respond to our supplication. Doubts begin to arise, and God seems far removed and unconcerned.

> *God's ways are not our ways.*
> *His concern is more for our faith*
> *and growth and for His glory than*
> *dealing with our problems.*

We usually have a pretty good idea about what we think God should do. Israel reminded God how He had intervened and destroyed the troops of Sisera and Jabin at Kishon (Judg. 4) and how Gideon's three hundred had defeated the Midianites (Judg. 7). They told God He should *"make them like the whirling dust, like chaff before the wind . . . fire that burns the forest, and . . . sets the mountains on fire . . . pursue them with Thy tempest and terrify them with Thy storm"* (vv. 13–15). We could readily come up with some solutions for how we would like to see God deal with our enemies and our problems, but God's ways are not our ways. He has a higher purpose than simply blessing us with relief. He has a long-range perspective on the events swirling around us. His concern is more for our faith and growth and for His glory than dealing with our adversaries and problems.

Israel's appeal was right on target with the reason for asking God to act to humiliate and bring dishonor to those who threatened and oppressed them; it was so that they would *"seek Thy name, O LORD,"* (v. 16). When God is silent, and He doesn't seem to answer our prayers, maybe He wants us to realize that it is not about us and our needs. He could be using our situation to remind us and others that He alone is the Lord, that He is the Most High God with all power and authority. It is all about knowing Him.

PRAYER: *Lord, You are the Most High over all the earth. Forgive me for wanting You to judge those who oppress and conspire against me due to my own vindictive motives or just because I want to be free from conflict. My desire should only be for them to know You. Help me not to focus on myself and my needs but on what will glorify You. When You are silent, let me never doubt that You will act in Your timing and Your way, and it is in order for Your purpose to be fulfilled, not mine.*

Psalm 84

The Joy of God's Presence

Key Verse: For the LORD God is a sun and shield; the LORD gives grace and glory; no good thing does He withhold from those who walk uprightly. (Psalm 84:11)

Our greatest desire should be to dwell in God's presence each day. The yearning and fervent desire of our heart should be to have a conscious awareness that He is with us. He has promised to abide with us and never to leave or forsake us. The essence of our salvation experience is not just being saved from the penalty of sin or gaining assurance of eternal life in heaven, but it is the fact that Jesus Christ comes to dwell within us. How tragic to lose sight of the reality of abiding in Him. Life becomes pretty miserable when we struggle with temptations and attempt to bear our daily burdens in our own strength. Our failures come from resorting to our own wisdom and ingenuity rather than relying on God who is always with us.

We have had those times of blessing when we sensed God's presence and power and therefore long for that to be our consistent daily experience. In my prayer journal I have an item which reminds me, "Praise God for His presence in my life today." Sometime later I had added a parenthesis with the word *joy*. An awareness of abiding in God's presence is absolutely the source of joy that puts a song in our heart. When we have been there, we would never desire anything else. The ways of the world and the shallow, temporal pleasures that come from following self-serving and self-gratifying carnal values can never satisfy like being in God's presence. Enjoying one day with the Lord is better than a thousand apart from Him! Even if we don't enter into the fullness of God's blessing, just being at the threshold of that relationship is better than a lifestyle of sin.

> *When we are dwelling in the courts*
> *of the Lord, every aspect of our*
> *lives becomes an altar because life*
> *is an experience of worship.*

When we are dwelling in the courts of the Lord, every aspect of our lives—our home, our office, our cars—becomes an altar because life is an experience of worship. We find ourselves going from strength to strength as God empowers us and supplies all our needs. Our heart is simply the highway on which God is leading us on pilgrimage to Zion, the place of ultimate and perfect enjoyment of His presence and fullness. When we are dwelling in His presence, even "Baca," the valleys of weeping and sorrow, are turned into a spring of blessing.

The Lord becomes our dwelling place only by our trusting in Him. We enter into that secret place of the Most High by faith, believing and appropriating the reality of His presence. And notice what we have as a result. He is our sun and shield, enlightening us, shining His blessings upon us, and protecting us from all harm. He gives us a constant flow of grace, undeserved favor and mercy, and allows us to experience His glory. He will withhold nothing that is good when we walk "uprightly" or in the reality of these truths.

PRAYER: *Lord, You are my sun and shield, my protection and the source of all blessing. Give me a longing for Your presence in my life above all worldly attractions and desires. It is awesome to think that You will withhold no good thing if I will abide with You and walk in Your ways. Give me a desire for You and faith to trust You each day.*

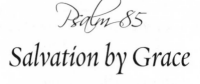

Salvation by Grace

Key Verse: Wilt Thou not Thyself revive us again, that
Thy people may rejoice in Thee? (Psalm 85:6)

I have a growing concern about the shallow approach we
take in evangelism and the assumption that we can personally choose to say the right words and change our eternal destiny. Historically there has been a tension between
Calvinism, a theological position that emphasizes the grace
and initiative of a sovereign God in one's salvation, and
Armenianism, which focuses on the free will of man to inde-
pendently decide whether or not to accept God's offer of
grace. Giving intellectual assent to a presentation of the gospel and praying a stereotype-worded prayer in order not to
be accountable for one's sins doesn't necessarily translate into
a God-glorifying, life-changing experience. Salvation is a
work of God's sovereign grace and is received genuinely only
when the convicting power of sin leads to heartfelt repentance. It is not so much for us as for God's glory. Failure to
recognize this truth results in a nominal Christian characterized by unfaithfulness and carnal living.

> **Salvation is a work of God's sovereign**
> **grace and is received only when the**
> **convicting power of sin leads to**
> **heartfelt repentance.**

Israel prayed that God would revive them, save them,
and restore them to a life in which they would rejoice and
bring glory to Him. This salvation was of God and was available only because of His loving-kindness. They reminded
Him how He had restored them in the past, delivered them
from captivity, forgiven their iniquity, and covered their sin.

He had every right to be angry with them; they had experienced His indignation for generations and wondered if it would be forever. Salvation was not something readily available that they could have by simply choosing to return to God whenever they were so inclined. They acknowledged it was *"Thy salvation;"* it belonged to God and was available only as He determined. God does not dispense cheap grace.

So what is the contingency for God to save and restore? *"His salvation is near to those who fear Him"* (v. 9). Godly conviction of sin grows out of a respect and reverence for God and recognition that we are separated from Him and need Him. The gospel came to Cornelius in Acts 10 because he "feared God." Jesus told the scribe who acknowledged that the foremost commandment was to love the Lord God completely: *"You are not far from the kingdom of God"* (Mark 12:34). True salvation isn't provided to one uttering a ritualistic prayer for the sake of eternal fire insurance! It comes from humble acceptance of God's grace and out of a desire and commitment to live for His glory. God saves and revives us that we might rejoice in Him.

In a beautiful word picture in verse 10, God's mercy and loving-kindness are merged with His truth and faithfulness when He pours out His grace to save us. Righteousness becomes a reality among His people and goes before them, bringing peace and prosperity to the land and in our lives.

PRAYER: *Lord, You have every right to be angry with me and to withhold Your blessings. I don't deserve Your salvation and loving-kindness. But I am grateful for Your grace, restoring me that Your righteousness might guide me, and I can rejoice in Your name.*

A Heart Focused on God

Key Verse: Teach me Thy way, O LORD; I will walk in
Thy truth; unite my heart to fear Thy name. I will give
thanks to Thee, O Lord my God, with all my heart,
and will glorify Thy name forever. (Psalm 86:11–12)

A personal relationship with God allows us to come to
Him for our every need. We have a right to bring our
supplications to Him and request His grace, His
strength, and His guidance. In the first five verses of this
Psalm, each appeal is on the basis of a related condition; the
request is justified by a need or contingency.

- *Incline Thine ear and answer me . . . for I am afflicted
  and needy. (v. 1)*
- *Preserve my soul . . . for I am a godly man. (v. 2)*
- *Save Thy servant . . . for I trust in Thee. (v. 2)*
- *Make glad the soul of Thy servant . . . for I lift up my
  soul to Thee. (v. 4)*

However, the answer to all of these appeals, which are
typical of our prayers, is not on the basis of our need or fulfilling the stated contingency as much as it is on one's confidence
in the nature of God. He is *"good, and ready to forgive,
and abundant in lovingkindness to all who call upon [Him]"*
(v. 5). We can come boldly to Him and call upon Him in our
troubles, confident He will answer because there is no one
like Him. He is not a distant, impersonal God. He is not judgmental and punitive, putting us on a guilt trip and delighting
in our groveling in the consequences of our own sin and failure. He delights in pouring out His loving-kindness, showing
mercy and delivering us.

> *All affections and desires should be brought into subjection and totally focused on one thing— reverence and awe of God.*

In response to this confidence in God as One who is *"merciful and gracious, slow to anger and abundant in lovingkindness and truth* (v. 15),*"* the psalmist makes five vows in verses 11 and 12 that should characterize our commitment and desire. These are: (1) an openness to be taught God's way, (2) a desire to walk in God's truth, (3) a heart that is focused on fearing the Lord, (4) a commitment to giving thanks to the Lord with his whole heart, and (5) a vision for glorifying God's name forever.

Central to these expressions is an appeal for God to *"unite my heart to fear Thy name"* (v. 11). It is an understanding that all the affections, desires, and distractions that are so prevalent and constantly demand our attention should be brought into subjection and totally focused on one thing— reverence and awe at the name of God. When everything is centered on God, He can teach and guide us in His truth, and His will is what will be done in our life. Our life will be a daily expression of giving thanks and glorifying Him.

That vision of God's greatness and awareness of the deeds that He has done will give us confidence beyond our personal concerns; it is a vision of all the nations one day coming before the Lord and worshipping Him.

PRAYER: *Lord, You are so good and readily pour out an abundance of loving-kindness when I come to You in times of need. May the focus of my heart and all the concerns of my life be united to fear Your name so that I will be giving thanks to You in all things, faithfully following Your will and always glorifying Your name.*

Reaching All Peoples

*Key Verse: The Lord shall count when He registers the peoples,
"This one was born there." (Psalm 87:6)*

Global missions has been revolutionized in recent years
by recognition that our task is not simply proclaiming
the gospel in as many countries as possible for whatever may result but is to make the gospel accessible to all
peoples. God's desire is that all the peoples of the world know
Him and become a part of His kingdom. He called Abraham
to leave his home and family so *"all the families of the earth
shall be blessed"* (Gen. 12:3). The psalmist tells us that *"All
the ends of the earth will remember and turn to the Lord,
and all the families of the nations will worship before Thee"*
(Ps. 22:27). When Jesus gave the Great Commission and told
us to disciple the nations, the expression He used was *panta
ta ethne*, which literally means all the ethnic-linguistic people
groups of the world. We no longer see the world as geopoliti-
cal nations but as more than eleven thousand distinct lan-
guages and cultures, all of whom God desires to be a part of
His kingdom. Psalm 67:3 says, *"Let the peoples praise Thee,
O God; let all the peoples praise Thee."*

God is tracking the progress of global evangelization and
noting which peoples have representatives in His kingdom.
Jesus said in Matthew 24:14, *"This gospel of the kingdom
shall be preached in the whole world for a witness to all the
nations (people), and then the end shall come."* Recently
researchers identified more than two thousand culturally distinct people groups that have not yet heard the gospel. But
that number is rapidly being diminished as mission strategies
systematically are penetrating this last frontier. Once the gospel has touched every people group, and a representative
remnant of believers has been gathered into God's kingdom,
Jesus indicated that will complete the Great Commission and
signal His return.

> *God is tracking the progress of global evangelization and noting which peoples have representatives in His kingdom.*

A strategy coordinator told about a volunteer team prayer walking in a remote area of China when they encountered a young man who spoke English. As they got acquainted and shared a witness of their faith and the claims of Christ over the next few days, the young man prayed to receive Christ. He was the first known believer among this people group. After praying in English, he asked if he could pray that sinner's prayer confessing Jesus as Savior and Lord in his own language. The strategy coordinator said, in relating this story, "Can you imagine the joy in heaven to hear Jesus confessed as Lord in that language for the first time?"

It was not just Israel, God's chosen people, who were enjoying the dwelling places of Zion, which represents the heavenly, eternal kingdom of God, but those from Babylon, Philistia, Tyre, and Ethiopia had come to know God. God is registering all born-again believers and their ancestry because one day there will be *"a great multitude, which no one could count, from every nation and all tribes and peoples and tongues, standing before the throne and before the Lamb"* (Rev. 7:9).

PRAYER: *Lord, Your desire is for all the peoples to know You. I am grateful that, because of Your grace, I heard the gospel and have the privilege of being a part of Your eternal kingdom. I pray that the concern and devotion of my life also would be to share the gospel with all peoples.*

Psalm 88

Dealing with Despair

Key Verse: O LORD, the God of my salvation, I have cried out by day and in the night before Thee. Let my prayer come before Thee; incline Thine ear to my cry! (Psalm 88:1–2)

This is a cry of desperation of one in total despair. It appears to be an appeal of one who is afflicted with a terminal illness or disfigured by an accident in which even his appearance is repulsive to others. Obviously there is a feeling of rejection and abandonment by family and friends. Life ceases to have meaning for individuals confined to a hospital bed or who have a disability which keeps them from engaging in meaningful and fulfilling work. The image is that of the aged and infirmed who seem to have lost their quality of life or multitudes of destitute people in Third-World countries simply struggling for survival. They are like those who are *"without strength, forsaken, [as if] among the dead"* (vv. 4–5). They feel that no one remembers them, and they have been cut off and separated even from God's hand of mercy and blessing.

But we are reminded that we are given life in order to live for the praise of God's glory. The purpose for which God extends life to us, regardless of the circumstances—the suffering and affliction we go through—is to serve Him and praise Him. Certainly we will spend eternity praising the Lord in heaven, but the psalmist makes a clever appeal for why God should extend his life: (1) God will not have an opportunity to perform wonders for those who have already died. (2) Departed spirits will not praise Him as those do in this life. (3) His loving-kindness cannot be experienced by those who have died but only in the circumstances and needs of those who live in the world. (4) The witness of God's righteousness and opportunities for Him to manifest His power exist in our lives now, not after we die.

> *God does deliver us from suffering,*
> *affliction, and despair. He grants*
> *us each day for a purpose, and we*
> *must trust in Him.*

Many times we cry out to God for help but sense no response. This Psalm is a reminder that we need to be perfectly honest and candid with God. We need to tell Him exactly how we feel. He is not interested in beautiful, syrupy platitudes when we are really feeling angry and rejected. We need to tell Him when we are feeling depressed and in despair. We should acknowledge when we feel that He has let us down and that we are hurting. Confess the hopelessness we feel when afflictions overwhelm us, or we go through the pain of a broken relationship or the despair of living with an incurable disease. Acknowledge the anger and grief we feel upon the loss of a loved one or bitterness when the infirmities of old age bring loneliness and make life meaningless. After all, God knows. Our relationship with Him is not enhanced by pretense and hypocritical expressions.

However, we must remember that the final verses and chapters of life have not been written. God does hear our cry. He is the God of our salvation, not only from sin, but He delivers us from suffering, affliction, and despair. We may feel as if we might as well be dead, but God grants us each day for a purpose, and we must trust in Him.

PRAYER: *Lord, I have not experienced the extent of suffering in which I despair of life, but help me trust You and always be honest in expressing my feelings and needs. Though I do sometimes feel abandoned and rejected, it is because I am focused on myself instead of realizing I live to bring praise to Your name.*

Psalm 89:1-18

God Is Over All of Heaven and Earth

*Key Verse: How blessed are the people who know
the joyful sound! O LORD, they walk in the light of
Thy countenance. (Psalm 89:15)*

I don't believe it was a mere coincidence in the inspiration of Scripture and formation of the Old Testament canon that Psalm 89 is positioned as it is. The pessimism of Psalm 88 is offset by an optimistic expression of confidence in the faithfulness and loving-kindness of our Lord. A fatalistic and hopeless diatribe of despondency moves into a song of victory and confession of God's providence over all the earth. Verse 11 declares that everything in heaven and on earth belongs to God and is subject to His control. *"The heavens are Thine, the earth also is Thine; the world and all it contains, Thou hast founded them"* (v. 11).

Rather than defeat and despair, a sense of God's presence elicits a song in our hearts. An awareness of His greatness erupts in worship and praise, diverting us from the misery of our own circumstances. God's loving-kindness and faithfulness are forever. The grandeur and spectacle of the heavens affirm His wonders and remind us that none is comparable to Him. He is awesome and is to be feared and reverenced above everyone and any earthly thing that would claim our attention and affections. He creates the mountains, rules the sea, scatters His enemies and is in total control over the universe. He is exalted because of His strong arm that symbolizes power and His mighty hand that represents authority. His throne is established on righteousness and justice, and every action is based on mercy and truth; these characteristics of His nature are unchanging and irrevocable. They are absolutely dependable.

> *God is awesome and is to be*
> *feared above everyone and any*
> *earthly thing that would claim*
> *our attention and affections.*

This passage must have been the inspiration for the familiar gospel hymn, "We have heard the joyful sound, Jesus saves, Jesus saves." For the psalmist declares that those who have heard the joyful sound, the good news of God's greatness, loving-kindness, and righteousness are truly blessed; for they walk in His presence—*"in the light of [His] countenance"* (v. 15). We live rejoicing throughout the day because we are lifted up and exalted by His righteousness; we are not left to the futility of our own efforts to live a righteous life. God is glorified when we allow His strength to be manifested in meeting our needs. He is our shield of protection, and by His grace we find favor. He is the One by whom *"our horn is exalted"* (v. 17); that is, our success and place of authority and leadership are established.

What is our responsibility as recipients of such favor and blessings and as those who have had the privilege of knowing the "joyful sound"? We are to declare God's loving-kindness, be witnesses to others of what we have discovered, and tell of His faithfulness to succeeding generations.

PRAYER: *Lord, I am so privileged to be among those who have heard the joyful good news of Your loving-kindness and experienced Your favor. Righteousness and justice are the foundation of all You do. Your mercy is forever. Help me live in Your presence that I might sing of Your glory and make known Your faithfulness to others.*

Psalm 89:19-52

God's Covenant Promise

*Key Verse: "But I will not break off My lovingkindness from him,
nor deal falsely in My faithfulness. My covenant I will not violate,
nor will I alter the utterance of My lips." (Psalm 89:33–34)*

Basic to our faith is our confidence in God and His Word.
He cannot lie and deceive, as that would be contrary to
His moral nature and holiness. What He says is true
and reliable. We base our hope on the fact of God's Word,
not what we feel, think, or rationalize about a situation or
issue. Why do we assume that we are saved from sin and
have the assurance of eternal life when we profess our belief
in Jesus Christ and His death and resurrection? It is because
that's what God's Word tells us. The eternal security of our
salvation is not due to our ability to live a holy and sinless
life but on God's faithfulness to keep His covenant and do
what He said He would do.

David had been anointed and chosen of God, but the
truth of what God had promised was not just for him and his
generation. This is a picture of how God would manifest
His covenant promise in the coming of Jesus Christ, the
descendant of David. The "throne of David" was established
as a prototype of the future reign of Christ. There had been
many times of trial that would lead God's people to doubt
His faithfulness, such as four hundred years of captivity in
Egypt, defeat by their enemies, and their eventual captivity in
Babylon. But God's ways are not our ways, and His time
frame is always a big picture perspective. Clearly the transgressions and sins of God's people, and of David himself,
would bring punishment and chastisement, but that would
not divert God's purpose from being carried out and His
promises fulfilled.

> *The eternal security of our salvation is not based on our ability to live a holy and sinless life but on God's faithfulness to keep His covenant.*

In a sense God also has chosen us who have trusted Him as Savior and Lord and given us an anointing of His Spirit. We, too, have a covenant relationship with Him. And notice what accompanies that relationship. It was not only applicable for David as king of Israel and as a prophecy regarding the coming Messiah and Redeemer but for us as His covenant people. As His chosen people, anointed by the indwelling of the Holy Spirit, we are established as His possession forever; this is not due to our efforts but by His mighty power. He provides us strength; as Paul recognized, *"I can do all things through Him who strengthens me"* (Phil. 4:13). He will go before us, crushing our adversaries, providing a spiritual armor so that the wicked one cannot deceive us. He gives us power and authority to fulfill His will whether over earthly dominions or in a spiritual task. It is this kind of relationship that results in a heart of worship and praise, constantly acknowledging and confessing God as *"[our] Father . . . and the rock of [our] salvation"* (v. 26). Also, our children and descendants will follow in that covenant blessing.

In spite of these awesome promises, apparently David had been defeated. He felt God had broken His covenant, and he asked, *"How long, O LORD?"* (v. 46). But his faith is not deterred as he closes by affirming, *"Blessed be the LORD forever!"* (v. 52).

PRAYER: *Lord, thank You for Your covenant promise. Often I feel rejected, especially when I experience the consequences of my own failure, but I rejoice in Your faithfulness. Give me faith to know with certainty that the promises and truths of Your Word are irrevocable and I can claim them as my own.*

Using Time Wisely

*Key Verse: So teach us to number our days, that we may
present to Thee a heart of wisdom. (Psalm 90:12)*

My self-image has never been consistent with my age.
My concept of "middle age" used to be an adult
thirty-five to fifty years old, and anyone beyond
fifty years of age was old. However, I now consider middle
age forty-five to sixty, and one cannot be considered old prior
to age seventy! The length of time between birthdays for a
child is long, but time seems to accelerate with the pace of
activities and studies once you are in school. That, however,
is only a precursor to the frequency at which the pages of the
calendar whiz by as an adult. The responsibilities of family
and career intermingled with all the pressures and demands
of life eliminate any semblance of margin. We find ourselves
looking back, wondering where the year has gone and,
indeed, wondering how our life has passed so quickly.

Time is an element of creation and belongs only in this
world. For a timeless and eternal God, there is little difference
between a thousand years and a day. But He who is everlasting created the world as our dwelling place, and we have a
stewardship to the One who gave us life to use the time we are
given appropriately. We no longer have the nine hundred plus
years of a Methuselah; typical longevity is only seventy to
eighty years. Though life may be extended for some, we need
to recognize that the years of productivity and influence are
limited. One with a heart of wisdom will understand this and
realize how important it is to use each day in serving the Lord
and living for Him.

> *We need to have the wisdom to use each day to the maximum, living in obedience to God's will, serving others and seizing every opportunity to make an impact on our world.*

In *The Screwtape Letters*, C. S. Lewis alerts us to the fact that one of Satan's most effective tactics is to get us to procrastinate. He lets us have plans for what we are going to do sometime in the future and good intentions for serving the Lord as long as we never get around to them. We are reminded that it is only in the present that time touches eternity, for the future is not yet reality and the past is simply a lost opportunity. God sweeps away each day like a flood in the night, but the marvelous thing is that He gives us a new one each morning! *"It flourishes and sprouts anew"* (v. 6) with fresh opportunities. We need to have the wisdom and foresight to use each day to the maximum, living in obedience to God's will, serving others and seizing every opportunity to make an impact on our world.

How sad if our days are the object of God's wrath and are consumed by His anger in His having to deal with our iniquities and secret sins. We need to pray that His favor would be upon us and that He would confirm our work. Paul reminds us in Ephesians 5:15–16 that we are to *"be careful how [we] walk, not as unwise men, but as wise, making the most of [our] time, because the days are evil."* Our desire should be that all our days would be filled with gladness and joy because we experience God's loving-kindness.

PRAYER: *Lord, the days You have given me are relatively few and pass by so quickly. Let me be a good steward of the life You have given and use each day as You desire. My life will be obedient to Your will only as each day is lived for Your glory. Give me wisdom that the work of my hands would find favor and be confirmed by Your blessing.*

Protected in God's Presence

*Key Verse: He who dwells in the shelter of the Most High will
abide in the shadow of the Almighty. (Psalm 91:1)*

We come to the verse and passage that I have chosen
to identify as the overarching theme of these devotional reflections. The primary issue throughout the
Psalms is a relationship with God in which we are constantly
abiding in His presence and acknowledging His providence.
The result is assurance of His provision. When we are constantly aware of being "in Him," we find ourselves overshadowed by His almighty power, controlling our destiny, avenging
our enemies, and making every provision for our protection
and blessing. That **assurance** comes from **affirming** our faith
and reliance on God, **abiding** in Him, and confessing, as in
verse 2, *"[He is] my refuge and my fortress, my God, in whom
I trust!"*

There is a popular cliché that says "The safest place is in
the center of God's will." However, we need to examine that
perception. Was Paul not in the center of God's will when he
was stoned, beaten, and imprisoned? Do missionaries suffer
and Christian martyrs around the world shed their blood
because they are out of God's will? Does God separate us
like the tares and wheat, putting a hedge of protection
around those who are obedient while leaving others to be
subjected to a fallen and sinful world? No one is exempt
from suffering; in fact, we are told that suffering is a part of
our calling. First Peter 2:21 says, *"For you have been called
for this purpose, since Christ also suffered for you, leaving
you an example for you to follow in His steps."* The problem is our thinking of safety in worldly terms of comfort and
the absence of suffering rather than in terms of our spiritual
security in Christ.

> *When we are "in Him," we are over-shadowed by His power; His presence makes every provision for our protection and blessing.*

God will protect us and deliver us, but it may not mean the absence of pain and affliction in this life. He is not only our shield but a bulwark that fortifies our security; however, that security may be spiritual. Recently four missionaries were killed in Iraq. Was this a contradiction to God's promise of protection from *"the arrow that flies by day,"* or *"the pestilence that stalks in darkness,"* or *"the destruction that lays waste at noon?"* (vv. 5–6). Not at all! Those who were slain were secure under the shadow of the Almighty. He was their refuge and dwelling place, and that was not taken from them. Though their life on earth was cut short from a human perspective, they lost nothing. The evil one could not touch them as God was faithful to *"bear [them] up"* (v. 12). God delivers us from fear! Abiding in Him liberates us from the fear and threats of what might happen to us.

God responds to this abiding relationship with a beautiful expression of assurance in the closing verses. He will deliver us because we love Him. He sets us securely on high because we know His name. He answers us because we call on Him. He is with us in trouble, will rescue us, honor us, satisfy us with a long life, and allow us to know and experience His salvation because of an abiding, intimate relationship with Him.

PRAYER: *Lord, may my only desire be to dwell in Your presence and abide under the shadow of Your protection. Help me not to look for security in worldly terms of personal comforts and safety, but recognize You are my security and my refuge; I shall not fear.*

Thanking God in All Things

Key Verse: It is good to give thanks to the LORD, *and to sing praises to Thy name, O Most High; to declare Thy lovingkindness in the morning, and Thy faithfulness by night. (Psalm 92:1–2)*

Praise is the key and the open door to an abundant life in Christ. We are told in 1 Thessalonians 5:18, *"In everything give thanks."* Paul said in Philippians 4:6 that we are not to *"be anxious . . . but in everything by prayer and supplication and with thanksgiving let your requests be made known to God."* Praise creates an awareness of God's presence that allows Him to take control of our feelings and emotions. Giving thanks, regardless of the circumstances, is an expression of faith in claiming the promises of God and the truth of His Word when all that we are experiencing seems to be to the contrary. An absolute guarantee of a victorious and blessed day is one that is begun on our knees affirming our confidence in God's loving-kindness being poured out upon us in all our needs throughout the day and then at night reflecting on His faithfulness.

> *A victorious day is one that is begun affirming confidence in God's loving-kindness and ends at night reflecting on His faithfulness.*

When the psalmist reflects on the greatness of God's works and all that He has done, it elicits unrestrained joy and a song in his heart. Unfortunately, our tendency is to be thankful only when God has done something to bless us or to intervene in our problems. If we don't see evidence of His hand at work, thankfulness is lacking in our heart. We need to realize that God's thoughts and purposes are very deep.

We cannot always understand them and why He does what He does, or why He fails to act in accord with our supplications and perceived needs. However, it is a "senseless" and "stupid" person who doesn't understand God's providence. God is worthy of praise for who He is; thanking Him in all things, whether aligned with our desires or not, is what allows Him to work because it is an affirmation of our faith in Him and His promises. Our praise and thankful hearts should never be contingent on God doing what we want Him to do.

One of the reasons it is hard to praise God in all things is because our perspective is distorted by the realities around us. It seems the wicked flourish, and we are subjected to worldly influences without realizing they will inevitably be destroyed. Even when our ears succumb to anxious thoughts and sinful influences, God renews our vision and gives us eyes to discern that which is opposed to His righteousness. He gives us a fresh anointing of the oil of His Spirit that we might *"flourish like the palm tree [and] . . . grow like a cedar in Lebanon"* (v. 12). God's desire is that we be like the stately cedars of Lebanon or the luxuriant palm trees of the tropics by being planted in Him and abiding in His courts. A wonderful concluding promise is that our lives will continue to bear fruit—even in old age—but that will be a testimony, not of our own strength and efforts, but that God is our rock. Appropriating His presence through praise assures us of no unrighteousness.

PRAYER: *Lord, as I begin each day, may my first thoughts be of You and my heart be lifted in praise and thanksgiving so that an attitude of joy will be sustained throughout the day. As I approach the latter years of life, I pray that I might abide in You and continue to be useful and fruitful in Your service. I long to see Your hand at work, but even when I don't, my confidence and faith will be in You, for You are my rock and my Savior.*

Power over the Natural World

*Key Verse: The LORD reigns, He is clothed with majesty;
the LORD has clothed and girded Himself with strength; indeed,
the world is firmly established, it will not be moved. (Psalm 93:1)*

We are hard pressed to find adequate analogies to portray the majesty and greatness of God. Seeing the grandeur of mountain peaks inevitably turns my thoughts to God and the majesty of His creation. I have felt the power of earthquake tremors and witnessed volcanic eruptions, both of which are expressions of power that defy man's control of the natural world. But nothing in nature consistently reflects the majesty and power of God as the constant swelling and crashing of waves on the seashore. Standing on an ocean beach produces an almost hypnotic fixation on the never-ending sequence of powerful waves splashing unceasingly on the sand and ocean currents erupting with an explosive roar.

I'll never forget seeing Victoria Falls for the first time. A mountain of mist on the horizon was visible from miles away. Long before the falls came into sight the roar and *"sounds of many waters"* (v. 4) was so loud, conversation was impossible. I stood entranced as an unbelievable volume of water plunged over the precipice into the Zambezi River without any let up. When I read, *"the floods lift up their pounding waves"* (v. 3), I recall arriving in Bangladesh after hundreds of thousands had perished in a tidal wave. A thirty-foot wall of water had been stirred up by a typhoon in the Bay of Bengal and pounded everything in its path as it moved inland for more than a hundred miles. The powerful current of the receding flood waters returning to the sea swept away people, livestock, houses, and everything else it encountered.

> *Natural disasters should alert us to the vulnerability of life and transitory nature of this world, but God is forever.*

How small and insignificant we must seem relative to these mighty forces of nature. But they are testimonies to the greatness and power of a God who *"is clothed with majesty . . . and girded . . . with strength"* (v. 1). Even natural disasters, rather than reflecting a world out of control, should be a reminder that God reigns, and His throne is firmly established over all the earth. When we witness the destructive power of storms, floods, and earthquakes, they should alert us to the vulnerability of life and the transitory nature of this world, but God is forever. The natural world of day and night, summer and winter, sun and rain, seedtime and harvest, and even floods and droughts confirm God's power on high; they are testimonies that He established the world, and our security is in Him.

Apart from our confidence in the truth of God's Word and faith in His grace and loving-kindness, the natural world around us of grass and trees, sunshine and rain, should remind us of His majesty and elicit an attitude of submission and praise as we stand in awe of His creation.

PRAYER: *Lord, I stand in awe of Your majesty when I behold the wonders of creation and realize You have established the world as a reflection of Your strength and might. You are everlasting, and I give to You my worship and praise, rejoicing that I can be in Your holy presence.*

Psalm 94
The Purpose of Godly Discipline

Key Verse: If I should say, "My foot has slipped,"
Thy lovingkindness, O LORD, will hold me up.
When my anxious thoughts multiply within me,
Thy consolations delight my soul. (Psalm 94:18–19)

Discipline is not something we usually relish. We commonly associate discipline with punishment for disobedience and wrongdoing, and it is usually painful. Whether it is a spanking as a child or being grounded as a teenager, discipline is not what we would define as a pleasurable or desirable experience. But those of us who are parents recognize that it is necessary to teach a child right from wrong, respect for others, and appropriate behavior. As children of God, we are blessed when God chastens or disciplines us; otherwise we would find ourselves no different from the wicked and godless people of the world who face His judgment and vengeance.

Proverbs 3:11–12 says, *"My son, do not reject the discipline of the LORD, or loathe His reproof, for whom the LORD loves He reproves, even as a father, the son in whom he delights."* This is quoted in Hebrews 12:5–6 to emphasize the fact that God loves us as His children and, therefore, He does not allow our selfish and sinful inclinations to go unchecked. An unloving father is indifferent to the behavior of his child. And, in fact, the chastening and reproof we experience is evidence we belong to God and He loves us. When I became president of the International Mission Board, a colleague congratulated me and said seriously, "I am going to pray that God keeps you broken every day." I did not appreciate the sentiment at the time but came to realize that if God did not constantly remind me of my failures and check my spirit with a painful word of criticism, admonishment, and something that made me aware of mistakes and wrong attitudes, I would easily become vulnerable to pride and insensitive to His guidance.

> *God loves us as His children and there-*
> *fore does not allow our selfish and sinful*
> *inclinations to go unchecked.*

God is not tolerant of sin, nor will He share His glory. The holiness of His nature demands that He be a God of vengeance, bringing recompense to the proud and the wicked. We must not miss the implication that sin and wickedness bring a blindness and insensitivity. Those who indulge in sin don't even recognize their wrongdoing or the fact that God sees and knows their actions and even their thoughts. Therefore we are blessed, indeed, by the assurance that God doesn't *"abandon His people, nor will He forsake His inheritance"* (v. 14); He teaches us through chastening. We reap the consequences of sin and the pain of disobedience so that we might avoid the judgment of the wicked. We learn from our adversity that we might gain relief. God's judgment is righteous, therefore those who belong to Him and are *"upright in heart will follow it"* (v. 15), and learn from it—growing in righteousness.

Even when we slip, God holds us up because of His loving-kindness. When anxiety overwhelms us, He comforts us and consoles us. He doesn't want us to be included in the destruction of the wicked, so He disciplines us; He is our security, our refuge.

PRAYER: *Lord, I usually don't welcome the painful experience of Your chastening, but help me to learn from it because it demonstrates Your love and that I belong to You. Enable me to respond appropriately to Your discipline that I might be upright in my heart and avoid a more severe judgment that comes from continuing in sin.*

Sensitive to Hear God's Voice

Key Verse: Today, if you would hear His voice,
do not harden your hearts. (Psalm 95:7–8)

We are continually reminded in the Psalms of what our relationship with God should be and how we should respond to His greatness. We worship a God who is not distant and impersonal, like the deities of other religions, but a God whom we know personally and intimately through Jesus Christ. That fact should cause us to sing for joy and to come into His presence each day, not with a melancholy attitude of beseeching Him with a litany of needs and requests, but with thanksgiving. Our joy should know no bounds when we realize that He is *"the rock of our salvation"* (v. 1). He is not only the source of our salvation but the One who makes it secure.

When we begin to comprehend God's sovereignty and greatness as the One who created the world and holds it in His hand, and that He is the One who made us and has given us life, we can only bow down before Him in humble adoration and worship. The fact that He is our God and we are His people is a relationship that is special and unique. Peter quoted several Old Testament passages in portraying us as *"a chosen race, a royal priesthood, a holy nation, a people for God's own possession"* (1 Pet. 2:9). John expressed the amazement we should all feel about this relationship when he wrote in 1 John 3:1, *"See how great a love the Father has bestowed upon us, that we should be called children of God; and such we are."*

> **We can be deprived of the blessings**
> **God has prepared for us if we become**
> **insensitive to His leadership and**
> **fail to walk in His way.**

Does this emotion of joy and sense of overwhelming adoration and thankfulness always characterize our attitude? Unfortunately, it is possible for even children of God to harden their hearts toward God, to be insensitive to His will and unresponsive to His guidance. This happened to the children of Israel in the wilderness. They rebelled against God. They lost their awe of Him and became disobedient. They had seen the mighty works of God and His miraculous power on their behalf but demanded their own way and refused to follow Him. God had prepared a "place of rest," the blessings and prosperity of the Promised Land, but they were not able to enter because their hearts were hardened.

In reflecting on this incident, 1 Corinthians 10:6 tells us that *"these things happened as examples for us, that we should not crave evil things."* We are the children of God; we belong to Him, and our salvation cannot be lost. But we can be deprived of the abundance of blessings God has prepared for us if we allow our hearts to be hardened, become insensitive to His voice and leadership and fail to walk in His way. How tragic if we should accept the salvation He provides and then continue to live for ourselves, neglecting to nurture a heart of worship and forfeiting the fullness of blessing and the abundant life God provides.

PRAYER: *Lord, I want to go all the way with You and enter into the fullness of blessing that is Your rest. Do not allow my heart to become hardened through unbelief and disobedience, but give me a heart that is sensitive to Your voice and submissive to Your will. May my worship be filled with joy and thanksgiving, for You are my God.*

All Nations Will Sing God's Praise

Key Verse: Tell of His glory among the nations,
His wonderful deeds among all the peoples. For great
is the LORD and greatly to be praised. (Psalm 96:3–4)

It is evident that the psalmist was a musician. He often appeals for us to sing a new song to the Lord; it is a prophetic reference to that new song of redemption when God's salvation will be revealed. And it is a song that is to be sung in all the earth by all peoples. This passage is an excerpt from the hymn of praise and worship recorded in 1 Chronicles 16 when the ark of the covenant was moved into the tabernacle. The ark symbolized the presence of God in the midst of His people. They were chosen of God and unique in their relationship to Him, but they were aware, even then, that they had been chosen for a purpose. Israel wasn't the only nation that was to praise the Lord; God was to be worshipped and praised by all nations. Therefore they were to *"proclaim good tidings of His salvation from day to day, tell of His glory among the nations, [declare] His wonderful deeds among all the peoples"* (vv. 2–3).

We are always looking for God to bless us, but it is awesome to realize that we can bless God. He who is exalted and on His throne is complete and has no needs, but we bless Him when we praise Him and ascribe to Him the glory and worship of which He is worthy. Imagine how it will bless God when all nations and peoples praise Him and give Him glory! Sadly, most of the peoples of the world are not worshipping and acknowledging God, nor do they know Him in all His splendor, majesty, strength, and beauty. They are still worshipping lifeless idols, living in fear and superstition of evil spirits, or ascribing strength and glory to themselves in humanistic pride. Not only is God great and sovereign over all the earth; He is to be feared and greatly praised. Therefore He has called us as His people to be witnesses to the ends of the earth. We are to proclaim His salvation, bear testimony to His power and wonderful deeds, and declare His glory.

> *God is to be worshipped and praised by all nations. Therefore we are to proclaim His salvation, testify of His power, and declare His glory.*

Our witness, and certainly the motivation to go as a missionary cross-culturally, is not driven by a sense of obligation or guilt. We will be faithful in our task of telling others of the Lord only when we are personally overwhelmed by God's love and greatness, and our hearts overflow spontaneously, giving Him praise and glory. This relationship with God is what causes us to tremble in His presence to the point that disobedience is unthinkable. It will compel us to live in holiness and bring our offering to Him, even the offering of our lives.

The closing verses remind me of Jesus' admonishment of the Pharisees on the occasion of His triumphal entry into Jerusalem. He declared that if the people did not praise Him, the very rocks would cry out. God is so great that not only should all peoples praise Him, but all creation is glad and rejoices: *"The sea roar[s] . . . the field exult[s] . . . the trees . . . sing for joy!"* (vv. 11–12). But it begins with us, His people, singing that new song of praise to His name.

PRAYER: *Lord, thank You for placing a song in my heart to bless and worship You. Help me declare Your glory and proclaim Your salvation until all the nations praise You, for You alone are worthy of all worship and honor and praise.*

Nature Testifies of God

*Key Verse: The heavens declare His righteousness, and all
the peoples have seen His glory. (Psalm 97:6)*

The first verse of this Psalm states emphatically and matter-of-factly the basic issues of life: (1) the Lord reigns; (2) let the earth rejoice. God reigns. He is God, and that takes care of everything. Our only response is to rejoice, for as long as God is on His throne—and He will reign forever—that covers all that we need. Could the following reference to letting the islands be glad be an oblique reference to unreached people groups who do not know God? If the whole earth is to rejoice, it is likely that those who do not know of Him are those who live on distant, isolated islands, cut off from commerce and interaction with the rest of the world. However, the rest of the Psalm indicates that God has been revealed to the whole earth through the world that He created.

All peoples have seen the lightning and heard the thunder. They have witnessed the majesty of a night sky full of stars and felt the mountains quake. The heavens declare the existence of a mighty and beneficent deity. Reverent response to the God of the universe invariably results in God making Himself known in further revelation. But sadly most of the world has rejected the testimony of nature and created their own gods. This is explained in Romans 1:19–20, *"That which is known about God is evident . . . for since the creation of the world His invisible attributes, His eternal power and divine nature, have been clearly seen, being understood through what has been made, so that they are without excuse."* Paul goes on to explain how they, rejecting God, became victims of futile speculations, their hearts were darkened, and they exchanged the glory of God for images they created themselves. They worshipped and served the created rather than the Creator, and the result was that God gave them over to their own lusts.

> *We need to be reminded that the natural*
> *world is a testimony of God's majesty*
> *and is designed to draw us to Him.*

That is certainly a picture of most of the world, even today. People in animistic cultures still worship and pray to idols; the perversion of other religions and the futile pursuit of false gods is a result of ignoring the Lord who is most High over all the earth. While we may not be so inclined, we need to be reminded that the natural world around us is a testimony of God's majesty and is designed to draw us to Him. The beauty of our world is God's way of blessing us that we may rejoice. However, the familiarity of our environment makes it so easy to take it for granted. My early morning quiet time is usually followed by a two-mile jog on the street where I live. Having just spent an intimate time with the Father, I feel that I have been ushered into the throne room as I revel in the colors of the eastern sky reflecting the rising sun. The splendor of dogwoods and azaleas in the spring and brilliant hues of the maple leaves in the fall declare that God reigns. Aren't we glad that the consistent cycle of day and night allows our bodies rest and renewal for the following day, and the stimulating diversity of changing seasons bears witness of God's glory? We should *"be glad . . . and give thanks to His holy name"* (v. 12).

PRAYER: *Lord, You are Most High over all the earth. Thank You for the beautiful world You created that testifies of Your glory. I pray that all peoples will eventually see Your glory and be made glad as they rejoice in Your righteousness and blessings.*

Psalm 98

Salvation Revealed to the Whole Earth

Key Verse: He has remembered His lovingkindness and His faithfulness to the house of Israel; all the ends of the earth have seen the salvation of our God. (Psalm 98:3)

The psalmist is obviously rejoicing in God's deliverance of Israel and how, by His mighty power and hand of authority, He had saved them from their enemies or some other catastrophe. Recognition that this salvation is of the Lord is significant; it wasn't the result of their own efforts and strength as a nation. Also, it was a testimony to all the nations that had witnessed what God had done. Surely in a time of defeat, or whatever they had been going through, they had begun to doubt God's faithfulness or His loving-kindness. They probably thought that He had forgotten His covenant with the house of Israel or questioned whether or not He really was a God of mercy. We sometimes go through these experiences as well. While waiting for God to intervene and bring relief from our problems, we allow doubts to emerge as to His goodness or wonder whether or not He really cares.

While this Psalm may have reference to an experience of Israel, it is a beautiful prophetic picture of the day when all the earth sees the salvation that God has provided in Jesus Christ. Jesus died for the whole world. That is not a testimony of universalism in which everyone will be saved regardless, but God's Word makes frequent reference to the day when all peoples will know His salvation. Jesus said in John 12:32, *"And I, if I be lifted up from the earth, will draw all men to Myself."* God says through the prophet Isaiah, *"Turn to Me, and be saved, all the ends of the earth; for I am God, and there is no other"* (45:22). And Habakkuk 2:14 tells us, *"The earth will be filled with the knowledge of the glory of the LORD, as the waters cover the sea."*

> *Our mission efforts are for the purpose*
> *of making His salvation known to all*
> *the earth so that God would not be*
> *deprived of praise and worship.*

All of our mission efforts are for the purpose of making His salvation known to all the earth so that no one might be deprived of the privilege of coming to God through Jesus Christ in repentance and faith. We envision that day when God's righteousness shall be revealed to all nations. God is being deprived of the praise and worship of most of the people throughout the world. His desire is that the whole earth would shout joyfully and break forth in songs of praise. The joy and assurance of salvation are something that elicits a spontaneous expression with song and instruments to the point that it seems all creation is joining us in praise. He wants every people group to know of the wonderful thing He has done in providing for their salvation that they might have that new song in their hearts as well.

It is important to get the gospel to all the world, for one day God is coming to judge the whole earth. It will be a judgment of righteousness and equity, and there are none who are righteous except those who are in Christ. And that will be the basis of judgment. Romans 2:16 says, *"On [that] day when, according to my gospel, God will judge the secrets of men through Christ Jesus."*

PRAYER: *Lord, I am filled with praise that You revealed Your salvation to me, and I was a recipient of Your grace. Use me that the whole earth may one day see Your salvation. Not all will believe, but no one should be deprived of the opportunity to know You and to receive Your salvation.*

Psalm 99

Standing in Awe of God's Holiness

Key Verse: Exalt the LORD our God, and worship at His footstool; Holy is He. (Psalm 99:5)

The Psalms frequently remind us of the appropriate response to the lordship and sovereignty of God. We are to sing songs of praise and exaltation; we are to rejoice and be glad. Here we are told that because the Lord reigns, the people are to tremble. We are grateful that we can have a relationship with a personal God through Jesus Christ; we can actually come into His presence and walk with Him, addressing Him as "Abba, Father." We are blessed to know Him as a loving and merciful God, full of compassion, who cares about our every need and desires to bless us. But our sensitivity to His greatness and moral nature is often neglected because of that intimate and personal relationship.

God is a holy God. That means there is absolutely no flaw or moral imperfection in His being and actions. His presence cannot be tainted by any implication of sin, iniquity, or injustice. That is why no one can be saved apart from the cleansing blood of Jesus Christ. No matter how much our goodness outweighs our sin, we cannot be accepted into heaven because all of our good deeds do not cancel out our sin nature. Justice demands the punishment of sin that all our defilement might be removed if we are to be received by a righteous and holy God. Even as we appropriate the atoning work of Christ on our behalf, we should tremble before His presence. He is so exalted that we are worthy only to bow at His feet and worship at His footstool.

> **When we comprehend His great and awesome name, our fear and reverence for Him should deter us from sinning.**

An awareness of His holiness and surety of His judgment in righteousness should compel us to live a holy life. When we begin to comprehend His great and awesome name, our fear and reverence for Him should deter us from any inclination to sin. First Peter 1:15–16 tells us, *"But like the Holy One who called you, be holy yourselves also in all your behavior; because it is written, 'You shall be holy, for I am holy.'"* Then Peter goes on to say that since God judges everyone's work impartially, *"conduct yourselves in fear during the time of your stay upon earth"* (1 Pet. 1:17). That impartial judgment will not be a measure of our rights and wrongs but will be based only on His absolute holiness. We love and praise the Lord because He is an approachable personal God who can be known, but He is worthy of our worship and should be exalted as we come into His presence with fear and trembling.

Moses, Aaron, and Samuel are given as examples of priestly leaders who called on the name of the Lord. They demonstrated their obeisance and need for God's leadership. In response, God answered them, guided them, forgave them when they failed and proved Himself faithful to His covenant promise. He will do the same for us when we hold Him in appropriate esteem with the honor and respect to which He is due. His holy and awesome name is worthy of exaltation and should make us tremble in His presence.

PRAYER: *Lord, I am unworthy of Your mercy and salvation and even to come into Your presence. I am far from holy and, therefore, tremble before You who are holy and exalted. I bow before You to receive grace as You judge in righteousness and equity. Never let the intimacy of knowing You personally allow me to belittle the awesome greatness of Your nature and authority.*

Access to God's Presence

Key Verse: Enter His gates with thanksgiving, and His courts with praise. Give thanks to Him; bless His name. (Psalm 100:4)

How does one comment on this beautiful and familiar hymn of praise? It is one of the first passages of Scripture I recall learning in Vacation Bible School and one I could quote if awakened in the middle of the night. My father would always read it at Thanksgiving dinner each year. God delights in our giving praise to Him. He is blessed by a thankful heart. It is sad that we are usually so preoccupied with our problems, disappointments and daily challenges that we engage in a personal pity party and come to God only to express our needs and requests. Even our service in time-consuming church activities or personal ministry is often out of a sense of obligation rather than with gladness of heart. This is a valuable reminder of how we are to approach God and come into His presence, not just in our quiet time of personal devotion but in a conscious awareness of a relationship with Him throughout the day.

> *The password that opens the gates of access to the Lord is thanksgiving, and praise transports us into His courts!*

One cannot avoid the image of God enthroned in a palace in splendor and majesty that is beyond our comprehension. How do we gain access to the Lord, surrounded by ministering angels and saints who have gone before? The password that opens the gates is thanksgiving, and praise transports us into His courts! As we are told in Psalm 22:3, God inhabits the praises of His people. We are to come before Him . . .

- with worship,
- with gladness,
- with joyful singing,
- with thanksgiving, and
- with praise.

He is worthy of our thanksgiving and praise simply because He is God. It is also in acknowledgement that He is the One who made us, and we owe total submission and gratitude to the One who has given us life and made us what we are. As His people we are as sheep, totally dependent on His provision, protection, and guidance. We are also drawn to Him in worship because . . .

- He is good,
- His love endures forever, and
- His faithfulness is unending, to all generations.

Finally, we are to realize that God desires for all the earth to come into His presence. He is worthy of worship and praise and has extended His loving-kindness that the peoples of every land would come before Him, knowing that He made them and that He is the Lord over all the earth.

PRAYER: *Lord, You made me and created me to serve You and to bless Your holy name. I pray that I might come into Your presence daily with thanksgiving and a heart of praise. You are worthy of all praise because You are good, and Your love is unending.*

Psalm 101
Living Blamelessly

Key Verse: I will set no worthless thing before my eyes . . .
it shall not fasten its grip on me. (Psalm 101:3)

A significant insight to understanding the implications of this Psalm is to note the number of times the psalmist says, "I will," or "I shall." Focusing our life on loving-kindness, justice, praising the Lord, and living blamelessly can happen only as the result of a deliberate decision. There are many references in the Bible to renewing our mind and setting our mind on things above. The function of our mind is to think and reason. It is used to form perceptions and then make choices based on those perceptions. I have often said in my teaching on spiritual warfare that Satan cannot make us do anything that we do not choose to do; we are responsible for the decisions we make. We choose our values and what will establish parameters for our behavior.

Among the decisions we should make is to hate and despise that which is evil. We should not tolerate it in any shape or form. Worldly, sensual behavior and images are all around us. A lot of the humor and entertainment we encounter are filled with lewd remarks and innuendoes that we may find funny. Then the line we draw regarding purity and principles for how we should live is fuzzy rather than representing clear, definitive convictions about what we allow ourselves to indulge in. Speaking ill of people, especially behind their back, or looking condescendingly on anyone is in conflict with the manner of life that reflects and honors God. If we find ourselves looking down on those who are unspiritual, the destitute, or immoral (especially those who have fallen), we need to realize that except for the grace of God, there go I! We should decide never to speak falsehood, practice deceit, or associate with those who would lead us away from the Lord. But note the two most prominent highlights relative to walking blamelessly.

> *The blameless way is a pretense unless it is reflected in our private lives because of our devotion to the Lord.*

One is to practice integrity in our heart, even at home where no one else sees us. It is not simply a matter of our reputation and how we act around others, but how do we behave in secret, when alone and in the privacy of our room? Traveling businessmen may be especially vulnerable to engaging in behavior on the road they would never indulge in at home. Do we watch movies that we would never view if our mother or pastor were with us or access Internet pornography when no one else is around? The blameless way is a pretense unless it is reflected in our private lives because of the genuineness and sincerity of our devotion to the Lord.

Second, we are *"[to] set no worthless thing before [our] eyes"* (v. 3). No habit that is unhealthy or ungodly should gain control of us. I continue to thank God that I had the kind of training and influence that led me to avoid smoking and drinking. We see addictive behavior all around us. It may not be gambling or drugs, but the prominence of obesity indicates that people have allowed unhealthy eating patterns to get control of them. We must not allow anything that is worthless to become an attraction and indulge in habits that are not profitable.

PRAYER: *Lord, it is amazing to think that I minister to You through a blameless life. Help that to be the desire of my heart and the basis for every decision. Give me a resolve not just to avoid sin but anything that is not profitable and do only that which glorifies You.*

Seeking the Lord in Times of Distress

Key Verse: "This will be written for the generation to come; that a people yet to be created may praise the LORD." (Psalm 102:18)

I t appears that one of the most prominent themes throughout the Psalms is distress, rejection, and seeking to cope in
the throes of depression. These lessons should shatter the
perception that "health and wealth" are the result of knowing and serving the Lord. The child of God is not exempt
from suffering and, in fact, will be reproached, ridiculed, and
ostracized by the world because our convictions and values
are so contrary to others. Also, God allows and uses our suffering to strengthen our faith and keep us dependent on Him
rather than allowing us to succumb to pride and any sense of
self-sufficiency.

This is an extremely dismal picture of one who feels God
has cast him away and forgotten him. The picture of emaci-
ated, starving refugees in Africa comes to mind. They are
nothing but skin and bones. Hollow, lifeless eyes send a
voiceless message that no one cares as they wither away. That
may be a reflection of one's spiritual condition, but many
have been to the place where they *"lie awake"* in misery, cannot eat, and worst of all, have no support, feeling alone *"like
a lonely bird on a housetop"* (v. 7). Whatever is our distress,
condition of suffering, rejection, and reproach by others, or
feeling of loneliness, the greatest need is not for deliverance
but to see the Lord. *"Do not hide Thy face from me in the
day of my distress"* (v. 2), is the expression of our real need.
We just need to know the Lord is there. However long we
have to suffer, we can survive, and even thrive, as long as
we are aware of the Lord's presence. That gives us confidence
that He knows our condition and needs, will hear our plea,
and answer our prayer. That confidence is expressed, beginning in verse 12, *"But Thou, O LORD, dost abide forever."*

> *God uses our suffering to strengthen our faith and keep us dependent on Him rather than allowing us to succumb to pride and any sense of self-sufficiency.*

There are possibly three interpretations of this Psalm, and all three may be valid. This seems to be a personal expression of need and a cry for help, but it could be a portrayal of the nation of Israel that was going through a time of reproach and famine. The request for the Lord to reveal Himself, to arise in compassion and be gracious, was not so that His people would be delivered from their suffering, but *"so the nations will fear the name of the LORD, and all the kings of the earth Thy glory"* (v. 15). If the other nations witnessed how God in His grace and power intervened and delivered them, it would be a testimony that would cause them to fear the Lord as well. Like Israel, we should realize that it is not just about us and our being blessed and having it good; if we are blessed, it is so we might be a blessing and God would be glorified.

A third perspective is that this passage could be symbolic of a world in sin, separated from God, but *"the appointed time"* (v. 13), when the Lord *"has appeared in His glory* (v. 16) . . . *looked down from His holy height* (v. 19) . . . *to set free those who were doomed to death"* (v. 20), is a prophetic picture of the redemption to be revealed in Christ. *"[The] people yet to be created"* (v. 18) who will praise the Lord are "Christians," so this is written for that generation to come.

PRAYER: *Lord, help me to realize that my greatest need is not to be blessed but to experience Your presence that I may be among those created to praise Your name. Use times of suffering and rejection to remind me of Your faithfulness and to draw me to You in faith.*

Psalm 103

Blessings in Superabundance

*Key Verse: Bless the LORD, O my soul; and all that is within
me, bless His holy name. Bless the LORD, O my soul,
and forget none of His benefits. (Psalm 103:1–2)*

This is my favorite Psalm. Although others deal with a
positive focus on God and acknowledgement of His
sovereignty, none is so upbeat in praising Him for a
litany of blessings and benefits. When we become mindful of
all that God has done and provided for us, we can only lift
up His name in praise with all of our being.

1. He has pardoned all our iniquities; there is no exception. *All* means "all"!
2. He heals all our diseases. Modern medicine may help,
   but God is the healer.
3. He redeems life from the pit, not only saving our life
   from hell but making this life profitable instead of a
   life of depression or failure.
4. He crowns us with loving-kindness and compassion.
5. He satisfies our years with good things—not just for a
   moment here and there.
6. He renews our youth, an encouraging promise for
   those advancing in age.
7. He performs righteous deeds; He intervenes with His
   righteousness and provides His strength.
8. He performs judgments on our behalf when we are
   oppressed and mistreated.
9. He makes known His ways and leads us as He did
   with Moses and others.

**When we become mindful of all that God
has done for us out of His limitless grace,
we can only praise Him with all our being.**

---

10. He is compassionate and gracious, blessing us even when we are undeserving.
11. He is slow to anger but abounding in loving-kindness.
12. He will not keep His anger forever; the Lord doesn't hold a grudge.
13. He does not deal with us according to our iniquities as we deserve, but according to His grace and mercy.
14. His mercy is higher than the heavens (and that is pretty high!) toward those who fear Him.
15. He has removed our transgressions from us; He not only forgives them but actually removes them and *"cleanses us from all unrighteousness"* (1 John 1:9). If you go north, you will eventually be going south as you reach the North Pole, but you can go east forever and never go west; our sins are gone!
16. He has compassion on us as a Father; we have the privilege of intimacy with Him.
17. He knows us in the depth of our being, our inclinations, our character, and our heart as well as our actions; therefore, He can provide whatever we need.
18. His loving-kindness is permanent and everlasting, not like the flowers and grass that wither and even our physical bodies that die.
19. He is faithful not only to us but to successive generations.
20. He has established His throne in the heavens, and His sovereignty is over all.

PRAYER: *Lord, I bless You and worship You, for You are so compassionate. You have not dealt with me as I deserve, but You have pardoned my iniquities and removed my sin from me. You heal me when I am sick, lift me from my depression, and continually provide grace and mercy.*

Psalm 104

The God of Creation

*Key Verse: O LORD, how many are Thy works!
In wisdom Thou hast made them all; the earth
is full of Thy possessions. (Psalm 104:24)*

E verything in the world was intentionally created by
God for a purpose. He makes all of creation fit together
in a way that only a sovereign and intelligent God could
do. The world and every detail of creation attest to His
splendor and majesty. Psalm 139 is a beautiful testimony of
God's providence. These two Psalms seem to go together as
Psalm 139 speaks of the creation of man and how God
designed every detail and knows beforehand the course of
our life. Here we read the psalmist's perspective on the creation account of Genesis, chapter 1. *"The earth was formless
and void, and darkness was over the surface of the deep; and
the Spirit of God was moving over the surface of the waters"*
(Gen. 1:2). Then God created light, separated the waters
between heaven and earth, and brought into being the dry
land.

> *Everything in the world was intentionally
> created by God for a purpose; every
> detail attests to His splendor and majesty.*

The creation account is described in an expanded, poetic
expression to show the majesty of God and His power over
the natural world. He laid the foundations of the world,
stretched out heaven like a tent curtain, covered the deep as
with a garment, raised up the mountains, pressed down the
valleys, and determined the boundaries of the waters that they
would not cover the earth. He formed springs to provide water
for the animals, trees for the birds, and grass and vegetation

for the cattle. The diverse natural environment was intentional as certain beasts were made for the tropical jungles and others for the rocky mountain slopes. He established the intricate food chain of interdependency among the various animals. The sun and moon that maintain the exact pattern of light and darkness needed to sustain life, and the seasons are the work of His hand. He fills the seas with life. All the animal kingdom depend on God and His created order to provide what they need to sustain life, and they are satisfied; the cycle of life and death and decay renews the face of the ground with organic matter.

What does this say to us? When we comprehend the creation of the natural world whether driving through a safari park, enjoying the splendor and beauty of a scenic forest setting, or sitting in the backyard as I do each morning, watching the squirrels, chipmunks, and robins scampering about, we should sense the awe of a Creator God and give Him glory. We should recognize that this did not happen by accident or by a meaningless process of evolution. We should acknowledge that this is the work of God, and *"in wisdom [He has] made them all"* (v. 24). This awareness should give us a sense of pride in our environment and a commitment to practice conservation and be stewards of the world in which God has placed us. But it is also a testimony to God's greatness and power. It should give us confidence in the security of the earth, in spite of threats of disasters and global warming; it should cause us to lift our praise to the Lord of all the earth.

PRAYER: *Lord, Your greatness is beyond comprehension. You created all things and are sovereign over the whole earth and everything in it. Your splendor and majesty is worthy of worship and praise. The purpose of my life, and the reason You have placed me in this awesome world is to sing praise to You as long as I live.*

Testimony of God's Providence

*Key Verse: Let the heart of those who seek the LORD
be glad. Seek the LORD and His strength; seek His
face continually. (Psalm 105:3–4)*

This passage begins a sequence of several lengthy "historical" Psalms which review, somewhat in detail, events in the history of Israel. I have often read through these narrative sections with less than full concentration due to my familiarity with the stories. They gain a significant relevance, however, when we approach them from the perspective of what God wants us to learn from reminding us of these experiences.

It seems we are given the conclusion at the beginning. God wants us **to seek, to sing,** and **to speak.** As we read of the events that follow, they are first of all a reminder that we are *"[to] seek the Lord and His strength"* (v. 4). We should be aware that we are not adequate within ourselves, and we must always rely on God's strength. However, we experience His strength for the challenges of life, not by looking for demonstrations of His power and expecting Him to work in our life but by seeking *"His face continually"* (v. 4). It is His presence that we should desire above all else.

> **We are not adequate within ourselves and
> must always rely upon God's strength
> by seeking His face continually.**

Second, this should cause us to *"give thanks to the Lord, call upon His name . . . and sing praises to Him"* (vv. 1–2). A heart of praise is what glorifies God. Experiencing His presence continually puts a song in our heart. And third, we are to testify of Him to others. *"Speak of all His wonders . . . make known His deeds among the peoples"* (vv. 2, 1).

As the psalmist reviews the sequence of history from God's covenant with Abraham until they finally gain possession of the Promised Land hundreds of years afterward, it is to remind us that God remembers and is faithful to His covenant promises. His timing is seldom in accord with our expectations, but that's our problem, not His. He usually has purposes beyond just the fulfillment of His covenant.

For example, He wants us, as He did Israel, to remember **His promise, His protection, His provision,** and **His providence.** Even though they disobeyed and suffered, He protected them, *"[permitting] no man to oppress them"* (v. 14). In His providence He had used foreordained circumstances to provide Joseph and raised Him up in Egypt to save them from famine. He called Moses to deliver them from four hundred years of slavery. He afflicted Egypt with the plagues and was able to bring them out with joy, even prospering them with the silver and gold of their oppressors. He provided bread and water for them in the wilderness and gave them the lands of other nations and tribes. This says nothing about the nation of Israel, but it says everything about the nature of God. As His people, we are assured of His promises, His protection, His provision, and His providence in our lives. But we must never forget that it is for the purpose of our keeping His statutes and observing His laws; we are to seek His face, sing His praise, and speak of His wonders.

PRAYER: *Lord, help me to learn from these lessons of history. It is wonderful to be reminded of Your faithfulness to Your covenant promises even though we may not see them fulfilled immediately. I want to seek Your face and sing Your praise continually that I might speak of Your wonders and testify of Your greatness to others.*

Psalm 106

Consequences of Sin and God's Mercy

Key Verse: Nevertheless He saved them for the sake of His name,
that He might make His power known. (Psalm 106:8)

The opening verses remind me of when I had been
caught disobeying my parents and been punished as a
small child. Feeling ashamed and full of remorse, there
was no limit to my expressions of wanting to do things that
would bring their pleasure and approval. So is the psalmist in
his effusive praise: *"[the Lord] is good; for His loving-
kindness is everlasting. Who can speak of [His] mighty deeds
. . . , or . . . show forth His praise?* (vv. 1–2) . . . *Remember
me, O LORD, in Thy favor* (v. 4); . . . *that I may rejoice in . . .
gladness . . . that I may glory with Thine inheritance"* (v. 5).
This is because of acknowledging that the people had sinned.
All of Israel's rebellion and sin are reviewed for the purpose
of showing God's faithfulness. He intervened in judgment
and righteousness. They suffered the consequences of their
sin, just as we do; but God, in His grace, saves us.

It is sad that we, like Israel, are guilty of a continual pattern of rebellion, in spite of being subjected to God's punishment. Our inclination is to sin, but we need to learn from our
mistakes and not to presume upon God's forgiveness and
mercy just because He has gotten us out of trouble before. In
spite of being delivered from Egypt by His mighty hand,
Israel rebelled and lost faith when they faced the obstacle of
the Red Sea. God brought them across with a miraculous
demonstration of His power, but they forgot His works and
complained against Him in the wilderness. God allowed disease to chastise them and an earthquake and fire to destroy
the ringleaders of rebellion, yet they made a golden calf, for-
getting God—their Savior—and abandoning His glory for a
graven image. Later they joined their pagan neighbors in
worshipping Baal; they provoked God with a rebellious spirit
at the waters of Meribah and made sacrifices to the demons
and idols of Canaan. Verse 40 says, *"The anger of the LORD*

was kindled against His people." God is a jealous God and will not share His glory. The holiness of His moral nature demands that sin be dealt with justly in consequences of punishment.

God does not show mercy because we deserve it; it is for the sake of His name and that He might demonstrate His power to save and forgive.

God's repetitive intervention and deliverance—His long-suffering and mercy—reflect how great His love is for His people. We should also recognize that usually God looks for someone to stand in the gap; He raises up a bold, moral leader like Moses or Phinehas, who will stand up against the crowd, take a stand for righteousness, and call the people to repentance. He also calls those who will intercede and will plead with God for the people. We need to understand why the people were inclined to disobedience and sin. (1) *"They . . . forgot [God's] works [and] . . . did not wait for His counsel"* (v. 13). (2) *"They did not believe in His word"* (v. 24). (3) And they did not obey the Lord and do what He commanded (v. 34). God does not show mercy for our sakes and because we deserve it; it is for the sake of His name and that He might demonstrate His power to save and forgive. It is so that we can give thanks and glorify Him among the nations.

PRAYER: *Lord, thank You for Your mercy and that You are willing to forgive and deliver me, no matter how often I sin. Help me not to be rebellious and forget Your works but to believe You, obey You, and praise You.*

Psalm 107

Testimony of Redemption

Key Verse: Let them give thanks to the LORD for His lovingkindness, and for His wonders to the sons of men! (Psalm 107:8)

This repeated theme is predicated on the introduction of verse 2, *"Let the redeemed of the LORD say so."* Those who have been redeemed should readily bear testimony and confess that they have been saved by the grace of God. Four times we are told to *"give thanks to the LORD for His lovingkindness, and for His wonders to the sons of men!"* (v. 15). Whereas in other passages we are reminded to remember His miraculous deeds and acts of power, this seems to be a specific reference to the wonder of His salvation and mercy that He has made available to men.

The context is obviously the redemption that God provided to Israel, but it is also a picture of the lostness of those without Christ. Verses 10–11 describe the lost as *"those who dwelt in darkness and in the shadow of death, prisoners in misery and chains."* Jesus spoke of Himself as the Light of the world and those who were separated from Him as living in darkness apart from the light. Those who have not been redeemed are literally walking dead men; though they have physical life, they abide under the penalty of death, in bondage to sin.

We were all at one time under bondage and in chains to the sin nature. The reason is because we *"had rebelled against the words of God, and spurned the counsel of the Most High"* (v. 11). Failure to live according to the Word of God is to transgress His law and His way; sin is the deliberate choice to follow our own way rather than the righteous guidance and counsel of the Lord. Isaiah 53:6 described it as, *"All of us like sheep have gone astray, each of us has turned to his own way; but the Lord has caused the iniquity of us all to fall on Him."* Romans 3:23 helps us to understand the reality of sin in explaining that *"all have sinned and fall short of the glory of God."* We should not think of sin simply as what we have done that is contrary to God's law, but it is the fact that we fall short of God's holiness and standard of righteousness that makes us sinners.

> ### *Sin is the deliberate choice to follow our own way rather than the righteous guidance and counsel of the Lord.*

Ephesians 2:1–3 paints a graphic picture of our lostness apart from Christ. We were *"dead in [our] trespasses and sins . . . walked according to the course of this world, according to . . . the spirit . . . of disobedience . . . liv[ing] in the lusts of our flesh."* The Scripture goes on to portray the lost as without hope and alienated from God. It is no wonder that the psalmist repeatedly exhorts us to *"give thanks to the LORD for His lovingkindness, and for His wonders to the sons of men"* (v. 15). How does one experience deliverance from sin and redemption from our lostness? There is another repetitive expression found in verses 6, 13, 19, and 28; *"They cried out to the LORD in their trouble; He delivered them out of their distresses."* Salvation comes only when one acknowledges his sin and cries out to the Lord. Until we confess our need and recognize our own inability to overcome sin, it is unlikely we will come to the Lord in repentance. But when we do, He delivers us from the adversary, satisfies our thirsty soul, calms the storm and turmoil in our life, and guides us as a ship into a haven of peace and rest according to His purpose.

PRAYER: *Lord, how thankful I am that You heard my cry of repentance and saved me from sin. I was separated from You and helpless, but Your mercy and grace delivered and saved me. Let me never be ashamed to testify of Your loving-kindness and redemption.*

Psalm 108

Courage through Praise

Key Verse: Through God we shall do valiantly; and it is He who will tread down our adversaries. (Psalm 108:13)

Praising the Lord at all times, even from early morning, is the key to a steadfast heart. When we *"awaken the dawn"* (v. 2) and begin the day with a song unto the Lord that flows from our innermost being, we are likely to walk confidently in His strength and blessings throughout the day. We will not be upset by disappointments and be batted back and forth emotionally by the circumstances and challenges we encounter. In fact, a positive attitude and optimism generated by faith and a heart of praise are a testimony to others. God is not only interested in blessing us and our experiencing His loving-kindness continually, but He wants it to be a testimony to others.

Israel was at the crossroads of the ancient world. The travel from Egypt in the south to Assyria in the north intersected the trade routes from the East converging on the shipping lanes of the Mediterranean. God's people were to be a testimony to the nations as they witnessed Israel giving thanks to the Lord and singing His praises. No other religion was characterized by a God of mercy and absolute truth. In a familiar and often-sung poetic passage—previously used in Psalm 60—God's exalted position as sovereign over the nations and peoples as well as the tribes of Israel is acknowledged. He not only set the boundaries of Shechem and Gilead and claimed the tribes of Manasseh, Ephraim, and Judah, but the pagan tribes of Moab, Edom, and Philistia were also subjected to His authority. Israel was to be the instrument of witness through which God would be exalted and His glory over all the earth would become evident.

> *Nothing draws the lost to the Lord as effectively as seeing someone walking in victory and living in the joy of the Lord.*

Habakkuk 2:14 says, *"The earth will be filled with the knowledge of the glory of the LORD, as the waters cover the sea."* As God's people, we are to be the ones who declare His praise among the nations. Nothing draws the lost to the Lord as effectively as seeing someone walking in victory and living in the joy of the Lord. However, there are many obstacles and adversaries in our task of witnessing daily where we live or in taking the knowledge of Christ to the nations. *"Deliverance by man is in vain"* (v. 12). It will not be successful by our own efforts or mission strategies; we need God's help if we are to claim the *"besieged cit[ies]"* (v. 10) and unreached people groups for Him. We must never forget that it is He who will overcome our adversaries. It is important to understand that He gives us courage and enables us to act valiantly. The emphasis must be on God's power and His strength; our dependence must be on Him. But that strength is often manifested in the courage that He gives us. We may tend to be shy and inhibited when it comes to witnessing to others. God gives us boldness and courage. In times of trial and hardship when an attitude of praise is elusive, He is the one who gives us the resources of faith to claim His promises, to recognize His sovereignty, to dig down deep and respond with the courage that is needed.

PRAYER: *Lord, go with me as with the armies of Israel. You are exalted above the heavens; Your loving-kindness is greater than I can comprehend. Since You are sovereign over the nations, You can surely take care of my needs. Give me confidence in Your deliverance and courage to declare Your praise among others.*

Psalm 109

Relinquishing Retribution

Key Verse: And let them know that this is Thy hand;
Thou, LORD, hast done it. (Psalm 109:27)

I t is not uncommon for us to reflect in our attitudes and prayers the egocentric feelings of the psalmist. "Lord, bless and be merciful to me, but judge my adversaries and enemies; give them the punishment they deserve." We don't have any trouble describing what we would like to see happen to those who make life miserable for us. *"Wipe them out, Lord; 'let his days be few* (v. 8) . . . *his children be fatherless, and his wife a widow'* (v. 9). Put a wicked person over them so they get a little of what they have done for others. *'Let [a] creditor seize all [they have]* (v. 11) . . . *[and] none . . . extend lovingkindness to him, nor . . . be gracious to his fatherless children* (v. 12) . . . *let their name be blotted out'"* (v. 13). Meanwhile, we pray that the Lord would *"deal kindly with me, . . . help me, . . . save me according to Thy lovingkindness"* (v. 21).

We all encounter people whom we feel have returned evil for good, or at least have been insensitive to what we have done for them. There are those who malign us and our reputation with lies and accuse us without cause. What should be our reaction? We naturally want them to get what they deserve, just as the psalmist appealed to God, but the main point is to leave it up to God. Only He discerns when justice instead of mercy is due and whether to dispense punishment or redemption. We are told in Romans 12:21, *"Do not be overcome by evil, but overcome evil with good."* It is hard to not respond in kind to those who are so vicious in their deceit and the hurt they have caused us, but the choice is either to become like them or demonstrate grace and forgiveness by continuing to do good. Jesus reminded us in His lessons on forgiveness in Matthew 18 that we are to continue to forgive no matter how often we are wronged, even up to seventy times seven, or without limit. Unforgiveness is one of Satan's favorite tactics, for he keeps us centered on ourselves—the fleshly nature of our needs, our rights, our space, our opinion—and how we have been wronged rather than on God and serving and blessing others.

It is hard not to respond in kind to those who hurt us, but the choice is to become like them or demonstrate grace by continuing to do good.

What we should desire above all else is for our adversaries to know the Lord and for them to experience His judgment in such a way so that they would know that He is the one who has done it. When God blesses them, in spite of their cursing, it should make them ashamed and aware of their sin. The first step toward repentance and a turn-around in behavior is to acknowledge one's selfish and evil deeds. God is always interested in redemption, and we should be also. We can be confident that He is faithful to assist the needy. When our heart is wounded and we are hurt by the betrayal of a friend or the intentional pain inflicted by an enemy, God will minister to us in loving-kindness when we turn to Him. But He is going to intervene in a way that will bring glory to Him. When our adversaries are put down, we will not be able to claim credit or gloat in their misfortune, for we will recognize that God is the One who has done it.

PRAYER: *Lord, there constantly seem to be those who slander, malign, and show disrespect toward me. Perhaps I deserve it but help me relinquish any retribution to You. Keep my heart from succumbing to a vengeful attitude. Show Yourself faithful and demonstrate Your loving-kindness in a way that makes clear to me and my adversaries that You are the One who has done it.*

Psalm 110

God's Lordship over All

Key Verse: The Lord is at Thy right hand; He will shatter
kings in the day of His wrath. He will judge among
the nations. (Psalm 110:5-6)

Jesus quotes the opening verse of this Psalm in His confrontation with the scribes and Pharisees in Luke 20:41–43. It is a prophetic reference to the Christ who would come and conquer sin and death, bringing them into subjection as a footstool under His feet. As a descendent of David, He should be under subjection to David's authority, yet David acknowledged Him as Lord. God is the Lord; He is all-powerful. David was His servant. But as His anointed, David was given a place of authority at His right hand until God, through Jesus Christ— the seed of David—established His rule over all.

As those who have come into His kingdom, we should recognize that Christ is at the right hand of the Father, interceding for us. There will come a day when He will judge the nations; kings and rulers who have ignored and rejected Him will be shattered. The prophet Haggai foresaw this as God said, *"I will overthrow the thrones of kingdoms and destroy the power of the kingdoms of the nations"* (Hag. 2:22). It seems that God is being rejected among most of the nations and peoples of the earth. In fact, many rulers and government authorities are responsible for actions that prohibit the gospel from being proclaimed and people coming to the knowledge of Christ. But one day Christ will be lifted up and others will be shattered. We often quote Philippians 2:10–11, *"That at the name of Jesus every knee should bow . . . and that every tongue should confess that Jesus Christ is Lord"* as a vision of universal salvation when everyone will accept the Lord. There will come that day of judgment when His lordship is undeniable; however, for many who never worshipped and confessed Him, that reality and acknowledgement will be one of judgment that seals their eternal destiny of lostness rather than a day of salvation. The nations will be filled with "corpses" of those who never knew God.

> *When God is ready to manifest His lordship and authority over the nations, He stirs the hearts of His people to offer themselves and join Him on mission.*

We have often used verse 3 to reflect on the growing number of mission volunteers and the increasing number of missionary candidates who are volunteering for overseas service. God is demonstrating His power in an accelerating harvest all over the world. Places are being engaged with the gospel that have been closed for hundreds of years. With this powerful manifestation of God's power, His people are volunteering freely. A generation of youth, especially, seems to be getting a passion for missions and is willing to go to the tough places and serve with abandonment. This is not a coincidence. When God is ready to manifest His lordship and authority over the nations, He stirs the hearts of His people to offer themselves and to join Him on mission.

Melchizedek was an ancient mystical priest who appeared to Abraham as a personification of God (Gen. 14:18) and is referred to in Zechariah and Hebrews as an illustration of the eternal existence of God. He represents God's unchanging purpose in establishing His covenant with His servants—redeeming His people and judging the nations.

PRAYER: *Lord, I am thankful that You are an unchanging Priest and King. I yield in subjection to You as One who will manifest Your power and authority over the nations. Thank You that I have been one of those who are blessed to know and confess You as Lord in this life. Use me to tell the nations of Your love and bring them under Your lordship as Your power moves among them.*

Source of Wisdom and Understanding

Key Verse: The fear of the LORD is the beginning of wisdom; a good understanding have all those who do His commandments; His praise endures forever. (Psalm 111:10)

Praise is the bookends of this Psalm that extols the glories, the character, and the works of God. We are to praise the Lord with all our heart and in sincerity, allowing no affection or interest to supersede our devotion to Him. But we are also to praise Him corporately with others in the assembly of believers because God is eternal, and His praise will last forever. As John Piper writes in *Let the Nations Be Glad! The Supremacy of God in Missions,* worship is the main thing because it is forever. We do missions because God is not yet being worshipped and praised among the nations. However, verse 6 is one that gives me encouragement in our missions task. It affirms the providence of God in fulfilling His purpose of global evangelism. Among His works that demonstrate His power is that of bringing the nations into His kingdom. All the nations will become His heritage just as Psalm 2:8 affirms, *"I will surely give the nations as Thine inheritance."*

God reveals His works to those who praise Him. Not everyone is aware of how God is at work in the world, but those who delight in the Lord see events and circumstances as the hand of God and a testimony of His splendor and majesty. He intends His works to be a testimony that will be remembered so we do not lose faith and our hearts will constantly be lifted in praise to Him.

Without the fear of God, we are left to our own discretion and lack of any absolute standard for judging right and wrong.

It is not only His works but His character and the nature of His very being that cause us to praise Him and fear Him. His righteousness is forever; it can never change. It is absolutely impossible for God to be tainted by sin or do anything that is not holy and good. He is gracious and compassionate and, in spite of our failures, will keep His covenant promises. All His actions are governed by truth and justice. His precepts—the guidelines and laws of moral behavior and relationships—are totally trustworthy.

This description is summed up by the fact that God is holy and awesome. While we respond to Him in love and praise for all He has done, our relationship to Him should be based on fear and reverence for the Lord. Verse 5 reminds us that this relationship is the basis of God's provision, *"He has given food to those who fear Him,"* and also is the foundation of wisdom and understanding. One who is wise will understand that obedience to God's commandments is not optional. Everyone needs discernment to comprehend situations, perceive the sometimes subtle distinctions between right and wrong, and make appropriate decisions. To perceive life accurately and have the ability to make proper judgments are contingent on wisdom, and wisdom begins with the fear of the Lord. Without the fear of God and understanding of His commandments and expectations, we are left to our own discretion with no absolute standard for judging right and wrong.

PRAYER: *Lord, I need Your wisdom and understanding. I stand in awe of You and worship You with fear, for You are holy and righteous and exalted above all. Lead me to understand and obey Your commandments that I might praise You with all my heart.*

Psalm 112

Results of Fearing God

Key Verse: Praise the LORD! *How blessed is the man who fears the* LORD, *who greatly delights in His commandments. (Psalm 112:1)*

Continuing the theme of the previous Psalm, we praise the Lord because of our fear and respect for Him and our delight in His commandments. This is an interesting and significant combination. Fear of the Lord doesn't mean walking a narrow line, constantly being afraid of what He might do to us if we fail, neither does it mean obedience that is driven by a guilt complex. Our awe and reverence for God actually bring us great delight in following His commandments and doing what brings praise to Him.

We are assured that the one who fears the Lord and delights in His commandments is blessed. Verse 10 explains that the wicked cannot understand this connection between reverence for the Lord and being blessed; they are vexed by the very concept. They, and all their desires, will melt away and perish, but the righteous will never be shaken. In fact, this Psalm is a litany of the blessings that are assured to those who fear the Lord.

Obedience is not driven by guilt. Our awe and reverence for God brings great delight in following His commandments.

- Their descendants will be mighty on the earth—respected people of influence.
- Their integrity (upright values) will influence and bless subsequent generations.
- Wealth and riches will be provided sufficiently for their household.
- Their righteousness endures forever; it will accrue to an eternal reward.

- They can see the light and hope, even in times of darkness and despair.
- Their righteousness is reflected in grace and compassion toward others.
- They are generous and gracious, lending to others in need.
- They conduct all their affairs with justice and fairness.
- They will never be shaken by setbacks and trials that upset others.
- They will not react in fear to bad news and with anxiety to foreboding rumors.
- Their heart is steadfast because their trust is in the Lord, not themselves.
- They do not fear and are confident their adversaries will eventually be overcome.
- They give freely to the poor because of their righteousness and sense of justice.
- Their strength and authority will be lifted up and exalted.

All of these blessings are what we should desire as a reflection of our character, values, and lifestyle. We don't become this kind of person by trying to follow a list of rules and a pattern of behavior. The Lord is the One who blesses us, pours His life into us, guides us, and gives us strength when we delight in Him and His commandments. We don't have what it takes to remain steadfast in the face of rumors and personal attacks. It is not our natural tendency to be gracious and give to others. We cannot guarantee that our influence will extend to future generations. These blessings are from God. Our responsibility is to fear the Lord, delight in His commandments, and praise Him.

PRAYER: *Lord, may I delight in Your commandments as a source of joy and blessing, not out of a sense of "oughtness." I am constantly beset with evil and threatening news; use this to strengthen my confidence and stand in fear of You, knowing the battle is Yours. I pray my life would reflect the character and behavior that comes from the fear of the Lord.*

Praising God All the Time

Key Verse: *From the rising of the sun to its setting the name of the* LORD *is to be praised. (Psalm 113:3)*

I t is really impossible to communicate adequately how exalted the Lord is and why He is worthy of praise. In an attempt to do so, the psalmist expresses the fact that the Lord is to be praised by everyone, everywhere, all the time! What does it mean to be a servant of the Lord? One who knows the Lord and has entered into a personal relationship with Him is one who blesses and serves Him. We serve Him by serving others and doing His will but also by coming into His presence, not seeking His help or presenting supplications relative to our needs but blessing Him by simply praising Him.

God is to be praised now and forever. There is not a time when He should not be praised. One day in heaven we will praise Him, and that will totally consume us for all eternity, but we should be praising Him all the time in this life as well. If there comes a moment when we are unaware of His presence, when we cease appropriating His presence through praise, we are left to our own devices and readily succumb to the carnal values and influences of the world.

> **We readily succumb to the carnal values and influences of the world whenever we cease appropriating God's presence through praise.**

I love the picturesque expression used in verse 3 to emphasize that the Lord is to be praised everywhere. Our initial impression may be correctly linked with the previous verse that God is to be praised from the time we get up in the morning until we retire at night—all day long. But I like to think of the rising sun in the east sweeping across the world in a continuous pattern that envelopes all the nations, lands, and peoples. Even as it sets in our hemisphere, it is rising on other parts of the world on its westward journey. In my office is a chronograph, which is a map of the world that moves from left to right, indicating the time in every part of the globe. Following the rotation of the map, in the opposite direction is a moving pattern of light and darkness consistent with day and night around the world. Everywhere the sunlight travels, the name of the Lord is to be praised. It is an encouragement in our mission task that one day, everywhere, all the peoples will know and praise the name of the Lord.

Why is the Lord so worthy of praise? Because His glory is higher than the heavens and His sovereignty is over all nations. No one is like the Lord, yet He humbled Himself and became a man so that we could know Him. This is expressed in Philippians 2:5–7, *"Christ Jesus, who, although He existed in the form of God, . . . emptied Himself, taking the form of a bond-servant, and being made in the likeness of men."* This enabled Him to identify with the poor and needy and those who are on the ash heap of sin. He lifts up the most despised and destitute and enables them to become children of God. We can become fruitful, significant, and profitable, as a once barren mother has the joy of having children, and everyone can have the privilege of becoming a part of God's household.

PRAYER: *Lord, the most significant thing that really matters in life is praising Your name. May my lips, my heart, my attitude, and my behavior bless and glorify Your name today from the moment I awaken until I fall asleep at night. Thank You for lifting me out of sin that I might be Your child. I rejoice that You will one day be praised everywhere, all the time, for You are truly exalted above all.*

Psalm 114

God's Dominion over All Nature

Key Verse: Tremble, O earth, before the Lord,
before the God of Jacob. (Psalm 114:7)

God manifested His power and sovereignty in delivering His people from Egypt and providing a sanctuary in His presence. His dominion was demonstrated over the sea, the rivers, and the mountains. In turning back the waters of the Red Sea for the sake of liberating and blessing His people and holding back the waters of the Jordan that they might enter the Promised Land, God showed His power over creation. The majestic mountains and the sea were created for His glory. If He can turn a rock into a pool of water and a mountain of flint into water to satisfy the needs of His people, what can He not do for us?

Families that are victims of hurricanes, floods, and tornadoes and have had their homes destroyed may feel that they have lost everything. When a business investment turns sour and one's life savings vanish, there may be a sense of hopelessness. Yet God is a God of beginning again. He is a God of redemption and has the power to restore the fortunes of those who will trust in Him. He is the one who plants courage in our hearts and a steadfast resolve not to succumb to adversity but to grasp firmly the vision of restoration and hope. God is able to take the drought of a farmland, the loss of a job, a handicap or disability, and turn it into a victory, a new direction, and hope.

> *If God can turn a rock into a pool of*
> *water to satisfy the need of His people,*
> *what can He not do for us?*

The whole earth trembles before Him. All of nature is subject to His will. Therefore we should stand in awe before Him, acknowledging His power and realizing there is no challenge or problem beyond His ability to intervene and bring blessing. Israel was subjected to slavery in Egypt for four hundred years; they wandered in the wilderness for forty years. Surely they had doubts about whether or not God cared. They probably felt forsaken and often wondered if He had the ability to deliver them.

Someone may find himself in the same situation, having gone through a failed marriage, the loss of a loved one, or declining health. The loss of a job may leave one wondering how his family will be supported. We may not have a clue how God can work things out, but He has prepared a sanctuary for His people. There is no element of nature and society that is apart from His dominion and ability to use for His purpose. Others may be in bondage to sin, much as Israel was in Egypt, living among people of a strange language. The church and God's chosen way of life have been rejected in choosing to speak the language and ways of the world, feeling self-sufficient, and opting for a lifestyle of personal gratification. Yet the emptiness has become apparent, and life is headed for a dead end. We are urged to return to the fear of the Lord and allow Him to intervene in His wisdom and power to fulfill His purpose for us.

PRAYER: *Lord, I am often subjected to situations and trials I cannot understand and cannot see the light at the end of the tunnel. Help me realize that there is nothing that is not under Your dominion, and You will accomplish Your purpose in my life if I will allow You to intervene by bringing my life into subjection to You and standing in awe before You.*

Psalm 115

Worthy of Worship and Praise

*Key Verse: Not to us, O LORD, not to us, but to
Thy name give glory because of Thy lovingkindness,
because of Thy truth. (Psalm 115:1)*

We can identify many challenges and issues in our life that seem so complex, creating problems and stress and robbing us of peace and a sense of well-being. We may find our efforts to know God are a struggle, and a consistent, victorious relationship is elusive. It comes down to a simple matter of whether we live for ourselves and strive in our own strength or relinquish all that we need to God. God is truth; His way is one of grace and loving-kindness. He meets our needs not for our sake but that He might receive the glory of our faith and worship. Otherwise, we would take credit for success and working out our problems, which in essence is idolatry, instead of giving glory to God. Putting anything above God, even exalting oneself in a futile self-confidence, is no different from the stone and wooden idols worshipped by Israel's pagan neighbors.

The tribes and nations surrounding Israel had their gods enshrined in temples. They were carved images that could be seen, but the people were asking, "Where is Israel's God?" They could not comprehend a God that was spirit and resided in the heavens. They did not have the capability of believing in One they could not see and touch; they did not have the faith to believe in One they did not create themselves. Although many cultures around the world still worship idols made of wood and stone—it is not just a feature of ancient animistic beliefs from the Old Testament—a lot of modern, educated people give preeminence and devotion to that which is their own creation.

God's way is one of grace. He meets our needs not for our sake but that He might receive the glory of our faith and worship.

Humanism is the dominant religion of our contemporary culture. It is the philosophy that I am supreme and capable of handling life in my own power and abilities. There is no absolute truth, but truth is what in my own wisdom and understanding I choose to believe. I determine my own values, and just as idols are the work of man's hands, the focus of one's life and that to which one is devoted is the work of his own mind and desires. Just as carved images have eyes but cannot see, ears but cannot hear, hands but cannot feel, and feet but cannot walk, so are those who create their own gods of materialism, hedonism, and pleasure. They exalt themselves over God. There is no future and hope; there is no power over sin and no resources in times of need.

We should remember that God is a living and personal God. He sees and knows our every need. He walks with us, speaks to us; and with His hands He becomes our help and shield. He is mindful of us and chooses to bless us—those who fear the Lord. God is sovereign and does whatever He pleases and chooses to do. It doesn't matter whether one chooses to accept Him and acknowledge Him as Lord or not; He is Lord! Therefore, we should bless Him by yielding our lives in submission to His lordship and praising Him now and forever!

PRAYER: *Lord, I have a tendency to want recognition, affirmation, and praise, but help me focus only on Your glory, for You are truth and filled with loving-kindness. Don't let me create an idol of anything that is exalted and esteemed above You, for You are Lord. You do whatever You please and are worthy of all praise and glory.*

Psalm 116

Responding to God's Grace

Key Verse: I love the LORD, because He hears my voice and my supplications. Because He has inclined His ear to me, therefore I shall call upon Him as long as I live. (Psalm 116:1–2)

This has always been one of my favorite Psalms, perhaps because of the way it begins: *"I love the Lord because. . . ."* It is always a blessing just to pause and think of all the Lord has done for us, to meditate on His marvelous, matchless character and to be reminded of why we love Him. The list would be endless, but the psalmist compiles them into three distinct categories.

1. I love the Lord, because *"He hears my supplications [and] . . . inclines His ear to me"* (v. 1). We all go through times of distress and sorrow. There are times we feel that things are hopeless, and it is as if *"the cords of death encompass me"* (v. 3). But we call upon the Lord and find that He hears us and delivers us. His love is so great that He is sensitive to our needs; His ear is inclined to hear us, waiting for us to call upon Him and beseech Him in our time of need.

2. I love the Lord, because *"He is gracious . . . righteous . . . and compassionate"* (v. 5). When we are *"brought low"* (v. 6), humbled and humiliated, usually due to our own sin and failure, God does not gloat over our suffering, reminding us of our wrong choices. He saves us and lifts us up, returning us to a restored relationship and rest.

3. I love the Lord, because *"He has rescued my soul from death, my eyes from tears, my feet from stumbling"* (v. 8). Wow! Not only does He save us from the condemnation of sin and the penalty of death; He heals our pain and comforts us in our sorrows and then keeps us from stumbling and falling into sin again.

> *It is a blessing to meditate on the Lord's character and all He has done for us and be reminded why we love Him.*

So what is our response to all that the Lord has done for us? *"What shall [we] render to the* LORD *for all His benefits?"* (v. 12). We love Him; therefore our response will be to:

- Call upon Him as long as we live.
- Walk before the Lord faithfully in fellowship with Him throughout this life.
- Accept His salvation and lift it up in praise to Him.
- Commit our life to the Lord and live as a testimony to Him before others.
- Recognize how precious His provision is for us, even in death.
- Offer a sacrifice of thanksgiving, always calling on the name of the Lord.

If we love the Lord, it will be evident to others. It is not just a matter of our thanking Him and acknowledging His grace, but it should be reflected in a covenant relationship through which we serve Him faithfully in worship *"in the courts of the* LORD*'s house"* (v. 19) and in our daily life.

PRAYER: *Lord, I love You. Thank You for hearing my prayer, responding to my need, and delivering my soul. I will live for You and call upon Your name as a testimony to others. Help my life to be a reflection of my love for You.*

Praise of All Nations

Key Verse: Praise the Lord, *all nations; laud Him, all peoples!" (Psalm 117:1)*

It is well-known that Psalm 117 is the shortest Psalm and chapter in the Bible. A fact that may not be as well-known is that it is also the middle chapter of the entire Bible. Actually, the middle of the Bible is between Psalm 117 and 118 since there are an even number of chapters. There are the same number of chapters from Genesis 1 to Psalm 117 as there are from Psalm 118 to Revelation 22. Not only is Psalm 117 in the middle of the Bible; these two short little verses represent the central theme of the entire biblical narrative. What the Bible is all about is God's desire and plan for all the nations and peoples of the world to know His truth, experience His loving-kindness, and praise Him!

This is why God called Abraham, in Genesis, to leave his home and family; it was so that through His seed (descendant—Jesus Christ) *"all the families of the earth shall be blessed"* (Gen. 12:3). Most of the Old Testament narrative tells about God's intervention in the lives of His chosen people, Israel; it was about their being a missions people to *"proclaim good tidings of His salvation . . . tell of His glory among the nations, His wonderful deeds among all the peoples"* (1 Chron. 16:23–24). In Psalm 67:1 they prayed, *"God be gracious to us and bless us, and cause His face to shine upon us."* But God would bless them, as expressed in the next verse, only for the sake of His way being made known on the earth and His salvation known among all nations.

> **The Bible is all about God's desire and plan for all nations to know His loving-kindness and praise Him!**

When we get to the Gospels in the New Testament and the story of Jesus coming to die on the cross, we usually have an egocentric perspective as if it were all about us and our salvation. But Jesus explained why this was necessary in Luke 24:46–47 from a different perspective, *"Thus it is written, that the Christ should suffer and rise again from the dead the third day; and that repentance for forgiveness of sins should be proclaimed in His name to all the nations."* His death and resurrection were fulfillments of God's purpose of providing a message and way of redemption for all nations. Then we get to the end of the Bible. In Revelation 7:9 the apostle John had a vision of *"a great multitude, which no one could count, from every nation and all tribes and peoples and tongues, standing before the throne and before the Lamb."*

One day every nation, people group, and language will be represented among the redeemed around the throne of God, praising Him and the Lamb that was slain for the sins of the world. The familiar verse we all know, John 3:16, tells us that *"God so loved the world."* His desire, His purpose, and the entire biblical narrative are about His being praised and worshipped by all nations and all the peoples of the world. Therefore, we should be faithful and diligent to proclaim His glory and tell of His salvation that all the peoples of the world would know that He is the true, living, and everlasting Lord.

PRAYER: *Lord, Your loving-kindness toward me, and others, has been great. Give me a heart for all peoples. Just as You desire the praise of the nations, may the driving passion of my life be to proclaim Your truth and glory until all peoples praise You.*

Psalm 118:1-9

Avoiding the Fear of Men

*Key Verse: The LORD is for me; I will not fear;
what can man do to me? (Psalm 118:6)*

The fear of men is one of Satan's most subtle schemes to get us to compromise our convictions and conform to the ways of the world. Every teenager knows the power of peer pressure. Acceptance by others is a powerful force that often determines our behavior. Much of the stress we experience comes from our attempt to guard our reputation and our concern for what people think of us. Because our lives are lived out within a social context, loneliness and rejection are among the worst consequences we can imagine. No one wants to be an outcast and looked down on by others; it is natural to want to be popular and to do whatever it takes to be accepted.

The clumsy child who is not chosen to be on anyone's team knows the cruelty of rejection. Many Christian students allow themselves to get pulled into drinking, partying, and promiscuous behavior because they fear what their friends may think of them. We have to have the latest toys and gimmicks and wear the latest fashions so that we can be acceptable. In fact, striving to attain status in the eyes of others drives many families to overindulgence and incurring debilitating indebtedness. Even in serving the Lord and speaking, we sometimes succumb to concern about what people are going to think rather than focusing only on pleasing God and being obedient to Him.

> *The fear of men is one of Satan's
> most subtle schemes to get us to
> compromise our convictions and con-
> form to the ways of the world.*

IN THE SECRET PLACE

What can offset this devious and natural desire to please men? What can deliver us from the fear of what people may think or what they might do to our reputation? It is very simple: We should remember that the Lord is for us! He responds when we call upon Him, and He answers us. He sets us *"in a large place"* (v. 5), a place of sufficiency and blessing and prosperity. He brings others alongside to help us and support us. One of the greatest strengths we have is a support group of friends. It may be at church or through other believers and friends who are always available to encourage and support us. I have observed that the missionaries who endure trials, family issues, and adversity that cause others to leave the field are those who experience the body life of a team that provides the love and support they need. That is a blessing from the Lord!

There will always be those who attack us, malign us, and reject us. We will encounter those who may take advantage of us and hurt us financially or maliciously smear our reputation. If our trust is in men and our confidence in princes—catering to people of influence—then the fear of men, concern for reputation, and peer pressure will always bring us down. The Lord is our refuge, and we can trust in Him. The favor of man comes and goes, but God's loving-kindness is everlasting. Even when we fail, He keeps coming back with more mercy toward those who fear Him because He is good. *"Give thanks to the* LORD*"* (v. 1) and be constantly reminded, *"His lovingkindness is everlasting"* (v. 1). And that is worth trusting!

PRAYER: *Lord, I am criticized and judged and my reputation threatened, but I will not fear what man can do to me. You are my refuge, Your loving-kindness is everlasting, and I will trust in You rather than being intimidated by others.*

Psalm 118:10-29

Rejoicing in Each Day

*Key Verse: This is the day which the LORD has made;
let us rejoice and be glad in it. (Psalm 118:24)*

Igrew up hearing verse 24 quoted almost every Sunday whether in a prayer or call to worship by the pastor. It left an impression that Sunday was made by the Lord as the day of worship; I failed to appreciate the fact that He had made every day, and we are to rejoice and be glad in each day that He gives us. I have heard so many people who have been through a critical illness in the later years of life, or someone who is living with a terminal disease, testify to the joy of living each day as a gift from God. It is unfortunate that we don't realize that reality earlier in life. Days flow into days, overscheduled and filled with demands. We tend to hit the ground running each morning, sometimes with a brief prayer to give token acknowledgement of God in our life and then fall in bed exhausted at night without an attitude of praise ever crossing our mind. We miss the joy of the journey in failing to realize that every day God has prepared bountiful blessings for us. He has created unlimited potential for us, and we should rejoice in the opportunities He provides.

> **We miss the joy of the journey in
> failing to recognize and rejoice
> in the blessing and opportunities
> God provides every day.**

While the above perspective on our daily lives is valid and true to Scripture, this prophetic Psalm is actually speaking of the day of the Lord when God will do a marvelous thing in providing redemption and salvation. God will take Christ, rejected by Israel—those called to prepare for and build the kingdom of God—and He will become the *"chief corner stone"* (v. 22), the foundation on which God's kingdom will be built. Verse 26 was echoed in the praise of the people who welcomed Jesus as the Messiah on the occasion of His triumphal entry into Jerusalem. They proclaimed, as recorded in all four Gospel accounts, *"Blessed is the one who comes in the name of the* LORD*"* (v. 26), but they did not realize that He would build His kingdom by dying, and before the week had passed He would be crucified.

We need to look beyond the messianic prophecy, however, to realize that we are blessed whenever we come into any situation "in the name of the Lord." The psalmist spoke of being surrounded by the nations in verse 10, but "in the name of the Lord," they were overcome and extinguished. Even when there are those who would push us down and cause us to fall, they will be *"cut off"* (v. 10), and the Lord will help us when we approach these challenges "in the name of the Lord." He becomes our *"strength . . . [our] song . . . and [our] salvation"* (v. 14).

The Lord does discipline us, sometimes severely, but we have assurance we will live because we belong to Him. We will enter into His kingdom through gates of righteousness because He is our salvation, and His right hand of authority has been valiant on our behalf. He is a personal God—*"my God"* (v. 28)—and we are to give thanks to Him and extol Him, *"for He is good"* and *"His lovingkindness is everlasting"* (v. 29).

PRAYER: *Lord, help me to greet each new day with rejoicing and confront every challenge in the name of the Lord. You are my God, personally, because of the salvation You have provided through Jesus Christ. I will give thanks and praise You always.*

Psalm 119:1-16

The Basis for Life's Values

Key Verse: How blessed are those whose way is blameless, who walk in the law of the LORD. (Psalm 119:1)

This longest Psalm of 176 verses, and the longest chapter in the Bible, is an amazing literary expression. It is written as an acrostic with twenty-two stanzas that alphabetically follow the twenty-two letters of the Hebrew alphabet. While it is the inspired Word of God, the text is about the Word of God with almost every verse making reference to it.

What is it that determines our life values and priorities? Are there foundational convictions that guide all our decisions and determine our behavior so that our direction and purpose in life is established? God has given us His precepts and laws. He has borne witness to His testimonies of the way that is right that we are to follow. We have assurance that we can walk according to His will and avoid unrighteousness if we intentionally decide to accept His precepts and diligently follow them. Once that decision is made, it takes care of a lot of future options as we encounter temptations or consider equivocating in our commitment. The result is a life that is blessed, happy, and content. This is because we have chosen four strategic guidelines:

1. To follow the way of integrity that is blameless.
2. To walk or live according to the law of the Lord.
3. To observe God's testimonies and promises—the record of His faithfulness.
4. To seek Him with all our heart.

It is wonderful to be able to read God's commandments and expectations and not be ashamed. We can only worship and praise the Lord if our heart is upright, obedient, and faithful, for He has blessed us in revealing His way to guide us. He will not forsake those who are conscientious about following His statutes.

It is wonderful to be able to read God's commandments and expectations and not be ashamed.

Perhaps David was a young man as he wrote this and understood all the temptations of passion and ambition. Like many today, he wanted to live a pure life for the Lord, but he lacked the ability to resist temptation. He once again found four keys.

1. Live according to God's Word—always let that be the standard and guide.
2. Seek God with the whole heart—that is to be one's desire above all else.
3. Treasure God's Word in your heart—learn it and make it a part of your life.
4. Consider God's ordinances and precepts in making every decision, for they are more valuable than riches; we are to find delight in them and meditate on them.

PRAYER: *Lord, I earnestly desire the fullness of Your blessings and want to keep my life pure and blameless. Give me a heart to seek You above all else so that sin, worldly ambition, and self-gain have no attraction for me. Help me treasure Your Word in my heart, make Your law and Your statutes the foundation of my convictions and life values, give heed to Your testimonies, and find joy and delight in following them.*

The Counsel of God's Word

Key Verse: Thy testimonies also are my delight;
they are my counselors. (Psalm 119:24)

We usually have the idea that we need to keep God's law and adhere to His commandments in order to be blessed. However, in a reversal of that concept the psalmist asked God to bless him and deal with him graciously in order that he might keep God's Word. We should pray that God would open our eyes of understanding and give us insight to discern the wonderful truths in His Word. Too often we just read the Bible as an obligation and perfunctory practice, or for inspiration, and fail to comprehend the richness of the truth it reveals.

We should not think of the precepts, commandments, ordinances, etc., in legalistic terms of the Old Testament laws. They are rather a way of life God is teaching us that will bless us and glorify Him. How wonderful if we could have such a longing for God's way to characterize our life that our soul would be crushed and our heart broken by any failure or wandering from His commandments. The appeal that God would deal bountifully with us, open our eyes, rebuke the arrogant, and take away our reproach and contempt is based on the rationale that we would keep His Word, observe His testimonies, meditate on His statutes, and that they would be our delight and counselor. There would be little need for counseling to straighten out emotionally disturbed lives if God's Word were allowed to be our counselor and we would follow its teaching and admonition faithfully.

There would be little need for counseling to
straighten out emotionally disturbed lives
if God's Word was our counselor.

In the following section, the psalmist is really down—
"my soul cleaves to the dust (v. 25) . . . *my soul weeps because
of grief"* (v. 28). We should always feel remorse when we
become aware of sin and our failure to keep God's laws. Sin
is a matter of independence and pride, choosing to follow
our own will and indulging in selfish gratification. But
because we belong to God, His Spirit will rebuke us when we
become arrogant. In response to our repentance, He revives,
restores, and strengthens us so that we might understand His
precepts, meditate on His wonders, choose the faithful way,
cleave to His testimonies, and run the way of His commandments. The result of this renewal will be the enlarging of our
heart for God and avoiding being put to shame for our failures and shortcomings.

Finally, in a passage that reflects a summary of the entire
Psalm, our prayer should be:

1. Teach me the way of Thy **statutes**—authoritative
   decrees.
2. Give me understanding to observe Thy **law**—binding
   rules of conduct.
3. Make me walk in the path of Thy **commandments**—
   mandates or edicts.
4. Incline my heart to Thy **testimonies**—affirmation and
   proof.
5. Revive me in Thy **ways**—a direction or manner of
   living.
6. Establish me in Thy **Word**—God's verbal and written
   instructions.
7. Turn me to your **ordinances**—proscribed parameters
   of behavior.
8. Make me long for Thy **precepts**—a standard or moral
   rule.

PRAYER: *Lord, You have given me all I need to guide
and direct my life, my conduct, and my behavior.
Give me discernment and understanding and a heart
that loves Your Word so I might live according to
Your precepts and standards.*

Psalm 119:41-72

The Reliability of God's Word

*Key Verse: Teach me good discernment and knowledge, for
I believe in Thy commandments. (Psalm 119:66)*

W e get assurance of God's loving-kindness and salvation from His Word. Once we have received God's
salvation through trusting in Christ, there should
be an obvious change of lifestyle, values, and perspectives
because the Holy Spirit abides within us, guiding us and pro-
ducing Christian character. We experience the evidence of
God's loving-kindness each time we confess our sins and find
release from guilt because of His forgiveness and cleansing.
But we know that we can be saved by trusting in Christ
because that's what God's Word tells us. We are told of God's
loving-kindness and believe it by faith before there is any
empirical evidence or emotional experience of its reality. Our
answer for a skeptical world is simply that God said it! That
makes it true, and we believe it.

While many people would consider it confining to be
bound by God's law, it is actually liberating. *"So I will keep
Thy law continually, forever and ever. And I will walk at lib-
erty"* (vv. 44–45). The decision to follow the precepts of God
takes care of a lot of dilemmas and decisions. It sets us free
from the power of sin and selfishly motivated behavior. If we
do not live in submission to the lordship of Christ and His
way, we remain under bondage to our old sin nature. If we
love and delight in God's commandments, figuratively lifting
up our hands in surrender to His statutes, we are not ashamed
to say, "This I believe."

> *Our answer for a skeptical world is
> simply that God said it! That makes
> it true, and we believe it.*

God's Word is our comfort in times of affliction. It is our hope in times of doubt and despair. When we go through difficult trials, the promises of the Bible and messages of God's love and providence bring comfort and peace. Jesus said in John 14:27, *"Peace I leave with you; My peace I give to you; not as the world gives, do I give to you. Let not your heart be troubled, nor let it be fearful."* This is God's Word and assurance of His grace, for all He has promised is based not on our circumstances but on His character. Abiding in His Word also makes us indignant toward that which is wicked and those who ignore and forsake God's law.

Observing God's precepts, remembering His ordinances, and loving His law makes it natural for us to think of them and meditate on them, even in the night. They become a song in our hearts. Although we may be surrounded by a wicked world, we seek our companions among those who fear the Lord and keep His precepts, for they are an encouragement in our faithfulness and obedience. We are told in verses 66–67 and 71 that affliction is God's way of teaching us when we go astray; it brings us back to His Word, and teaches us the validity of His statutes. We discover our own inadequacy and that opens our heart to be taught discernment and knowledge. Our prayer should always be that God would give us sound judgment to make decisions and choices based on the truth of His law and commandments. It is worth more than great wealth.

PRAYER: *Lord, give me discernment and knowledge that I might walk in Your truth, following Your laws. Set me free from sin through obedience to Your Word. Use the trials and afflictions that inevitably come to draw me back to the precepts and principles that should guide my life, correcting behavior and attitudes that are contrary to Your way.*

Psalm 119:73-96

God's Truth Is Always Relevant

Key Verse: Forever, O LORD, Thy word is settled
in heaven. Thy faithfulness continues throughout
all generations. (Psalm 119:89–90)

A real testimony of faith is to believe God even when His promises don't seem to be fulfilled. Hebrews 11:1 says, *"Faith is the assurance of things hoped for, the conviction of things not seen."* The psalmist was going through times of affliction but did not waver in his confidence in God's faithfulness and loving-kindness. Although the wicked and the arrogant, who were the cause of his troubles, had not yet been judged, he continued to delight in God's law and wait for His Word to be fulfilled. That steadfastness was an encouragement to others who feared the Lord and knew God's testimonies. We should remember that our remaining faithful in response to trials is a testimony to others.

Our prayer should not be just to walk in righteousness and obedience but that God would help us have a heart that is blameless. If our motives and attitudes are not pure, it is unlikely that our conduct will be.

The theme of suffering and adversity continues. Many saints around the world experience years of persecution without deliverance. Those who seek to live with integrity are maligned by lies until their soul literally languishes in suffering and grief. But we are not to forsake God's precepts or lose confidence in His faithfulness. When Shadrach, Meshach, and Abednego were thrown into the fiery furnace by Nebuchadnezzar, they affirmed their belief that God was able to deliver them, but even if He didn't, they were not going to serve other gods. This portion of Psalm 119 expresses the confidence and commitment of Habakkuk 3:17–18, *"Though the fig tree should not blossom, and there be no fruit on the vines, though the yield of the olive should fail, and the fields produce no food, though the flock should be cut off from the fold, and there be no cattle in the stalls, yet I will exult in the* LORD, *I will rejoice in the God of my salvation."*

> ### God's Spirit illuminates the meaning (of Scripture) and enlightens our understanding that we may apply it to our life situation.

Just as God established the earth, so has His Word been established. He is unchanging and cannot lie; therefore His ordinances and what He has spoken stand true forever; they are relevant for all generations. I have little respect for dispensational theories of biblical interpretation in which certain truths were only applicable to a specific era. Some interpret portions of the Scripture as if they were outdated and apply only to the biblical context. But God established His truths and precepts to govern and guide life; they always have a contemporary application because they are based on His nature and wisdom for all time. Just as all Scripture is inspired by God, it has also been preserved by Him, and His Spirit illuminates its meaning and enlightens our understanding that we may apply it to our life situation. Our confidence in God's Word enables us to survive and endure trials. We often would be overwhelmed and succumb to despondency and hopelessness if we failed to remember His precepts and delight in His law.

PRAYER: *Lord, give me a faith to accept Your Word as true, whether I see any evidence of it being fulfilled or not. You have promised loving-kindness and deliverance in times of trouble, but may I delight in Your law and remain faithful even in the midst of suffering. Give me wisdom to apply the truth of Your Word in the practical situations of life each day.*

A Guide for Life's Decisions

Key Verse: Thy word is a lamp to my feet,
and a light to my path. (Psalm 119:105)

Decision making is a constant challenge throughout life. It should not be a problem choosing between right and wrong, but the morally neutral decisions regarding the course of life often put us in a quandary of indecision. God's Word is like a lamp illuminating our pathway. If you have ever walked anywhere on a dark night, especially on a rocky precipice, you don't shine the flashlight on your companions or the surrounding scenery to see what may be lurking in the shadows. You keep the beam of light focused on the path in order to see where to step. No matter how strong the light, it doesn't shine all the way to your destination but only far enough to take the next few steps safely and securely.

God's Word is not a road map that will outline the course of your life into the distant future, providing a specific answer to all of life's questions, but it is like a guide that shows the way. When you are obedient and faithful to live according to its truth, you will find life unfolding as God intended because His hand is upon you. Usually we see God's Word as telling us how to live in terms of behavior and conduct but not necessarily relevant to practical decisions regarding school and careers, purchases and investments, and the multitude of issues we face each day. That misses the point entirely. When we live according to God's Word, it puts Him in control. We will not be diverted by selfish motives and an independent spirit that leads us contrary to God's will. We do what we know to do, and God will take care of the uncertainties. We can make decisions in confidence, unconcerned about making a wrong choice, because God is leading us. Our impressions and inclinations are shaped by a heart of obedience and desire to do His will.

> *God's Word is not a road map that will outline the course of your life, but it is like a guide that shows the way.*

Therefore, we are to meditate on His Word constantly because it gives us wisdom and insight. We are constantly making choices based on perceptions and responsibilities, and they affect our relationships and our attitudes. We may not connect God's specific laws and ordinances to what we are doing, but delighting in them, feeding on His Word, and meditating on them will keep us aligned with His wisdom and from wandering into sin. This will make one wiser than one's enemies, teachers, and the elderly sage. Their wisdom is based only on experience while the testimonies and precepts that guide us are from God.

When we do not turn aside from God's ordinances and His guidance, it gives us a teachable spirit (v. 102) and understanding that is sweet and satisfying. That teachable spirit is what allows God to guide our pathway and decision making. Finally, we should pray that our heart would be inclined to perform God's statutes. That means that they would become the default way of life. We would hate every false way, His truth would be the joy of our heart and decisions would be consistent with God's will.

PRAYER: *Lord, though I sincerely desire to live for You and am committed to be obedient to Your commandments, I often find myself in a dilemma in making decisions. Don't let me resort to my own wisdom and insight, but let me always be guided by Your Word.*

Psalm 119:113-136

A Deterrent to Sinful Influences

Key Verse: Thou art my hiding place and my shield;
I wait for Thy word. (Psalm 119:114)

The real reason the church is having a diminishing influence on our society is not because of the prominence of atheists, humanists, and those who disregard God, but double-minded Christians. They claim to be believers and go to church, but their lives are guided by worldly values and ambition. They give general assent to what they hear preached on Sunday and token respect for the Word of God but don't apply its laws and precepts in decisions and moral choices. Divorce is as common among churchgoers as the general public, and just as many teenagers in church get pregnant out of wedlock as those who never attend. There is no reticence to compromise what the Bible teaches for the sake of convenience or personal gain. The greatest good for many is not holiness and obedience but whatever brings pleasure, comfort, and personal success.

Peer pressure is a powerful force to turn aside from the narrow way defined by God's precepts and commands. It may not take the form of actual taunting and ridicule but appears as a subtle pressure to conform to how others live. We are made to feel like misfits when we opt for integrity, purity, and living for the Lord instead of for ourselves. *"Depart from me, evildoers"* (v. 115), *"Do not let the arrogant oppress me"* (v. 122), and *"Redeem me from the oppression of man"* (v. 134), should be our prayer. We need the discernment to recognize values and influences that may not appear to be evil or deceitful but cause us to wander from God's statutes.

We need discernment to recognize influences that may not appear to be evil but cause us to wander from God's precepts.

IN THE SECRET PLACE

How do we avoid these influences and actions that would cause us to be ashamed? We sustain a love for God's laws and faithfully observe them. We remain safe from temptation by hiding in that secret place of His presence. Dwelling under the shadow of His wings is like a shield repelling all that is contrary to His way of life. Jesus speaks of it as the "abiding" life. In John 15:7 He says, *"If you abide in Me, and My words abide in you, ask whatever you wish, and it shall be done for you."* We maintain that sense of fellowship with the Father; He becomes our hiding place from the pressures and temptations of worldly influences, only as His words abide in us. That is what this entire Psalm 119 is about—our adhering to the Word of God, learning it, meditating on it, and delighting in it. It is about loving it more than gold and finding it sweeter than honey and anything else we might experience. Of course our fear of the Lord and respect for His moral nature are also deterrents to sin. Assurance of His judgment on those who ignore His way motivates us to be grounded in His law.

We should not always be looking for immediate rewards and blessing. We will go through times of discouragement, oppression, and suffering, waiting for God's judgment on the wicked and His compassion toward us. These are times of testing that enable us to grow in our faith and for God to teach us His testimonies and give understanding.

PRAYER: *Lord, the pressures of worldly values are so prominent and subtle. I'm grateful that You have provided a shield and hiding place in Your Word. Help me to abide in You, and Your Word to abide in me, that I would not be diverted from Your way.*

Psalm 119:137-160

Realizing our Need for God

Key Verse: Trouble and anguish have come upon me; yet Thy commandments are my delight. (Psalm 119:143)

It is unfortunate that we have been conditioned to see laws, and especially the biblical commandments of God, as restrictive, legalistic, and confining rather than something to liberate us to a more blessed and prosperous life. The emphasis shifts with this passage to focus on God. His words and precepts reveal His character of purity, righteousness, and faithfulness. His commandments and testimonies represent everlasting truth. They reflect a character that cannot be defiled. There is no spot or deficiency in Him; therefore, His words are a blessing and delight. They have a cleansing effect on those who obey them and make one even more zealous to follow them. They give understanding and are the source of the abundant life that He has promised to those who walk according to His way.

But like the psalmist, we should always be aware that we are unable to follow God's way, obey His commandments, and abide in His Word in our own strength. In fact, the Scripture tells us that the purpose of the law is to reveal our sinfulness that we might in conviction come to God for help and in faith receive His salvation. Romans 7:7 says, *"I would not have come to know sin except through the Law."* The apostle Paul goes on to say in Galatians 3:19 and 24, *"Why the Law then? . . . [It] has become our tutor to lead us to Christ, that we may be justified by faith."* We don't keep the law in order to be saved and to be judged as righteous. It reveals our sin and helplessness. It causes us, like the psalmist, to cry out in trouble and anguish, to cry for God to answer us in our need and save us, for no one is capable of meeting God's expectations through his own efforts.

> *We should always be aware that we are unable to follow God's way, obey His commandments, and abide in His Word in our own strength.*

We should wake every morning, acknowledging our need for God's help and strength—*"I rise before dawn and cry for help"* (v. 147). Even though we have a heart for God and desire to walk according to His Word, we should never be presumptuous about our ability to be faithful and obedient. We need to abide in Christ as we let His words abide in us. We are dependent on His help and His strength to *"plead [our] cause and redeem [us]"* (v. 154). We must wait (hope) in Him as the One who enables us to live according to His truth. Then we look forward to quieting our hearts after a busy day to meditate on His Word and reflect on His faithfulness!

If we feel a lack of intimacy with God and sense that He is far away, then we should meditate on His Word and His promises. They give assurance of His loving-kindness. He will revive us according to His truth that is everlasting. He will rescue us from affliction and from our adversaries— those who would influence us to turn aside from God's testimonies. Never allow doubt to erode the conviction that *"the sum of [His] word is truth"* (v. 160). His Word is absolutely trustworthy.

PRAYER: *Lord, I do sincerely love You and desire to follow Your Word and live according to Your law, but I am constantly failing. Help me realize that You are my hope and depend on Your strength as the One who enables me to walk in Your truth.*

Psalm 119:161-176

A Matter of the Heart

Key Verse: Those who love Thy law have great peace, and nothing causes them to stumble. (Psalm 119:165)

We are reminded that God knows what we do. There is no pretense or hidden sin, *"for all my ways are before Thee"* (v. 168). Hypocrisy, in supposing to be righteous and to abide by God's laws while doing otherwise, is mere self-deceit. Obedience and living according to God's Word are matters of the heart, which determines our motives and is the place of our affections. Genuine and authentic commitment begins with a *"heart [that] stands in awe of Thy words"* (v. 161). It is followed by loving and delighting in God's Word, as so often expressed by the psalmist. Verse 111 indicates, *"[God's precepts and testimonies] are the joy of my heart."*

Remember other references where the psalmist prays for understanding, *"that I may observe Thy law, and keep it with all my heart"* (v. 34). In verse 36 he prays, *"Incline my heart to Thy testimonies,"* and in verse 80, *"May my heart be blameless in Thy statutes."* A blessed and victorious life is not just a matter of legalistic obedience, avoiding wrong deeds and doing what is right in our conduct; it comes only from a pure heart that seeks God and desires Him above all else. The key to walking according to the law of the Lord and living in sync with His Word is expressed at the very beginning of this lengthy Psalm. The conclusion of all we have been reading and reflecting upon is indicated in the second verse. *"How blessed are those who observe His testimonies, who seek Him with all their heart."* And perhaps the key verse for practical application of all that is said in these 176 verses is verse 11, *"Thy word I have treasured in my heart, that I may not sin against Thee."*

> *A blessed and victorious life comes
> from a pure heart that seeks God
> and desires Him above all else.*

As the psalmist reaches a conclusion, he reflects that to know and follow God's Word is like discovering a great treasure. It causes him to hate and resist falsehood. It gives him great peace because with a pure heart he can live before God with openness, honesty, and transparency. Finally, the closing stanza is an antiphonal expression of supplication and response based on the fact that God teaches us His statutes, His commandments are righteous, we have chosen His precepts, and His law is our delight. Our desire should be expressed by the seven components of the psalmist's concluding prayer:

1. Hear my cry.
2. Give me understanding.
3. Receive my supplications.
4. Deliver me.
5. Let my lips utter praise and sing Thy Word.
6. Let your hand be ready to help.
7. Let my soul live that it may praise Thee!

PRAYER: *Lord, give me a heart that desires You and loves Your Word. I have been so blessed to have knowledge of Your law, understand Your commandments, receive Your testimonies and discern Your precepts. Give me strength to live accordingly as I abide in You and allow Your words to abide in me.*

Psalm 120

Avoiding Trouble

*Key Verse: In my trouble I cried to the LORD,
and He answered me. (Psalm 120:1)*

There are two reasons implied as the cause of trouble we may be experiencing. One is a habitual misuse of the tongue in lying and propagating deceit, and the other is not being careful and circumspect about those with whom we associate. Both will bring misery and defeat to our lives. But we have the beautiful promise of assurance that the Lord hears us and answers us when we confess our need and turn to Him for help and strength.

The earlier verses could be interpreted as a cry for deliverance because one has been the victim of deceit and the lies of others. It is not uncommon to be the subject of gossip. The office grapevine and rumor mill can be vicious. The "talk" is usually generated by a perception that is communicated as fact but sometimes is the deliberate and malicious intent of someone to hurt us or our reputation. When we react defensively, it often serves only to give credibility to the lies. We have all been hurt and disappointed by those who have deceived us, making promises that weren't fulfilled. I have found that wounds from the lies and deceit of others penetrate like *"sharp arrows of the warrior"* (v. 4) deep within my heart and are among the hardest to get over; it is necessary to turn to the Lord to heal and cleanse our soul from bitterness.

However, I feel this reference is more likely about one who has succumbed to lying and deceit, perhaps to protect his reputation or to gain some personal advantage over others. We all know the terrible tangled web of deceit and how one lie leads to another. Subtly we can come to believe our own lies and become victims of self-deceit. Many references throughout Scripture tell us that the heart is deceitful above all things and the tongue is the most difficult member of our body to control. We need the Lord to deliver us from deceit and guide us that we might walk in truth and speak with integrity.

We need the Lord to deliver us from deceit and guide us that we might walk in truth and speak with integrity.

Another area in which we need the wisdom and help of the Lord is in our association with others and the company we keep. I can remember being cautioned by my parents to be discerning in the friends I hung out with. It is so easy to follow the crowd and get in with those whose attitudes are rebellious and activities are morally questionable. Meshech was one of the grandsons of Noah; his tribe was the focus of prophecy in Ezekiel and is referred to in Revelation as "Gog and Magog," the peoples that would be deceived and follow Satan in the end-times. Kedar was one of the sons of Ishmael, from whom the Arabs have descended; their inclination to war and violence instead of peace is apparent throughout history. Israel had *"sojourn[ed] in Meshech . . . [and] dwel[t] among the tents of Kedar"* (v. 5). They had succumbed to their influence, contrary to their own convictions and desires, because they were associating with the wrong crowd. If we are to live for the Lord, we need to choose our friends carefully. Certainly we need to relate to those who are lost in the world but should not identify with them to the extent that we become victims of their influence.

PRAYER: *Lord, help me respond with grace to the sharp arrows of criticism and verbal attacks of others and always to speak with integrity, choosing my friends appropriately. Help me guard my words and never lie or practice deceit in order to enhance my self-image but be committed to truth whatever the consequences.*

Psalm 121

God—Our Protector and Guide

Key Verse: I will lift up my eyes to the mountains; from whence shall my help come? My help comes from the LORD, who made heaven and earth. (Psalm 121:1–2)

This is often referred to as "the traveler's Psalm." It is one of the most beautiful expressions of God's constant presence and watch care as we go and come. The visual image that triggers confidence in the Lord's protection is the majesty of the mountains. They remind us that God created the heavens and earth. If His power and sovereignty over the whole earth can bring the mountains into existence, it's a small thing for Him to care for us. There is also the connotation of acknowledging that our help comes from one who is exalted and over all; the mountains seem to remind us of how high and lifted up the Lord of heaven and earth is, yet He is available and cares for us.

We can look to the Lord for help because He is our security, our protection, and our guide. Israel's confidence was in a God who neither slumbered or slept; after all, sleep is only a need of our created bodies. God is alert at all times, watching over us, knowing our needs. We probably could not comprehend the things that have not happened to us because of God's providence and protection. We are aware of when we are threatened, delivered from danger, survive an accident, and we thank God for delivering us, but we do not know all the things that did not happen because He was caring for us. God keeps us from stumbling. We usually think of that in the physical realm in terms of not being hurt as a result of our own fallibility, weakness, clumsiness, or neglect, but God keeps us from stumbling by falling into sin and going astray.

> *If God's power and sovereignty over the earth can bring the mountains into existence, it's a small thing for Him to care for us.*

Too many Christians fail to understand the eternal security of the believer in Jesus Christ. We accept Jesus by faith as the source and provider of our salvation from sin but tend to think we have to hold on to salvation through our own efforts of sinlessness. But the security of "once saved, always saved" is due to God's grace and the fact that our salvation is all Him. We were initially saved from the penalty of sin when we trusted in Christ, but because we are in Him, God holds us in His hands. He saves us from the power of sin. He guards our way, our actions, and our hearts; *"He will keep [our] soul"* (v. 7).

God is always with us, at our right hand, deflecting the temptation and allure of the world that are constant, like the penetrating heat and rays of the sun. God is like a shade on a hot summer day when we would be overcome by the heat. He protects us from the more devious and subtle temptations and dangers of sin that come in the night, due to the darkness of our heart and baser instincts. He not only protects us from danger and sin, but He guards our way, directing our path, where we go, and what we do that we might remain securely in His will. Some say this Psalm describes the concept of a guardian angel. Whether that is the case or not, we should always look to God, knowing that He is ever present; He cares about us and will never leave us or forsake us.

PRAYER: *Lord, I lift my eyes to You as the One who made heaven and earth. Guard my ways that I might not slip and stumble into sin. Watch over me and protect me when I travel and at all times, for You are my security now and forever. Thank You for being my shade of protection against harm and evil and for the assurance You keep my soul secure.*

Psalm 122

Belonging to the Body of Christ

Key Verse: I was glad when they said to me, "Let us go to the house of the LORD." (Psalm 122:1)

Corporate worship is something that can easily be neglected, especially in a mobile society where one has no identity with a local congregation. Even when we live in a community for years, the worship and preaching may become routine and be taken for granted. We tend to rationalize that our relationship with God is a personal thing, and we don't have to participate in a church to be nurtured in our faith. However, when one is born again, the Scripture teaches us that the Holy Spirit within us draws us together into a fellowship with other believers. We are the "body of Christ" in the world today. As a collective group of believers, we are to worship, to witness, and to carry on the ministry of Christ. Also God has created the church for the purpose of our growth in discipleship and the Word, that we might be encouraged and strengthened in our walk with the Lord.

Too many people look on church attendance and participation from the perspective of whether or not they get anything from it. The worship service may not be stimulating, and the sermon may be boring, so we rationalize that it doesn't do us any good. We may consider the people who attend to be hypocrites whose lives do not reflect what they profess on Sundays. But we must remember that it is not about the style of worship, the sermon, or other people but our relationship with God and worshipping of Him. Our focus should be on Him, and regular participation in corporate worship is essential to maintaining the focus of our daily lives. Hebrews 10:24–25 says, *"Let us consider how to stimulate one another to love and good deeds, not forsaking our own assembling together, as is the habit of some, but encouraging one another."* We must not succumb to a self-centered perspective on church membership and attendance as if it is about us and what we get out of it; we have an obligation to others. The church is a context for us to encourage and minister to others that we all might live out our faith in the world more effectively.

> *The church is a context for us to encourage and minister to others that we all might live out our faith in the world more effectively.*

The tribes of Israel looked forward with rejoicing to occasions for going up to Jerusalem to worship at the temple, the house of the Lord. It was a testimony for them that they belonged to God and reflected a thankful heart; it was an acknowledgement of what God had done for them. We are encouraged to *"pray for the peace of Jerusalem"* (v. 6) with the promise that those who love and seek the good of the city will prosper and be blessed. The context of blessing the place where God was worshipped in biblical times has been distorted by many evangelicals to support the current political regime of Israel. While Israel is God's chosen people, and He has promised to deal with them uniquely in a special dispensation (Rom. 9–11), that does not justify allegiance to a godless, secular government that restricts the proclamation of the gospel. The only way for Israel to know peace is to know the Prince of Peace, Jesus Christ, and our prayer for Jerusalem should be that Israelis, and Jews everywhere, would come to know Him as Savior and their Messiah, not that God would bless and protect them politically.

PRAYER: *Lord, thank You for the privilege of corporate worship. I pray that I would have a proper attitude about participation in church, that it would be an experience of meeting You, a time of personal renewal, and expression of ministry to others.*

Psalm 123

Keeping Our Eyes on Jesus

Key Verse: To Thee I lift up my eyes, O Thou who
art enthroned in the heavens! (Psalm 123:1)

Igrew up with a song that is still sung occasionally; it was always a meaningful and inspirational reminder that put everything into perspective.

> *"Turn your eyes upon Jesus; look full in His*
> *wonderful face, and the things of earth will*
> *grow strangely dim in the light of His glory*
> *and grace." (Helen H. Lemmel, 1922)*

It is easy for things to get distorted as we seek to cope with all the pressures and demands of life. We feel victimized by circumstances, the actions and attitudes of others, and events over which we have no control. Relationships with family members are often strained, and the atmosphere at school or in the workplace is far from ideal and tends to get us down. Escalating war and global news make the future appear dismal, and news of rising crime rates, a floundering economy, and environmental pollution create discouragement. But our attitude and perspective tend to change when we turn our thoughts and attention to Jesus instead of the things of earth. We can choose to view reality according to the temporal, material, human world around us or from the perspective of the One who is enthroned in the heavens and sovereign over the universe.

We can choose to view reality according
to the world around us or from the
perspective of the One who is
sovereign over the universe.

Several admonitions throughout Scripture remind us, as Colossians 3:2, to *"set your mind on the things above, not on the things that are on earth."* How we view things is a matter of choice. When we turn our eyes on Jesus, we not only are reminded of a God who reigns with all power and authority, but we see a personal God who cares about us and is gracious toward us. He is sensitive to our needs. He knows our heart and our feelings and understands that in this world we will encounter scoffing and contempt for our faith. There is a growing tension between humanists who advocate godless secularism, wanting to limit religion to only private expression, and those who seek to live out their faith openly in society. Those who are arrogant and proud ridicule those who would value the sanctity of life and want to honor God in the public place.

We can feel hopeless and despondent when we look only on the trends within society, so it is important that *"our eyes look to the LORD our God"* (v. 2). We may be struggling financially, dealing with a health problem, or burdened by a friend or loved one who is not walking with the Lord. Our only option is to lift up our eyes to the Lord, recognize He has the power to deal with our personal issues as well as the problems in our world, knowing that He will be gracious to us. Just as the servant has no authority but must rely on his master to provide for his needs, so must we turn to the Lord and trust Him. Our problems and the things of earth will diminish in significance when we behold His glory and grace!

PRAYER: *Lord, I am so often discouraged and depressed due to the circumstances around me. Don't allow me to be distracted by the things of the world but always to lift my eyes to focus on You and Your glory, confident of Your power and grace.*

Psalm 124

Our Defender and Deliverer

Key Verse: Our help is in the name of the LORD,
who made heaven and earth. (Psalm 124:8)

Lessons throughout Scripture constantly teach us and remind us of our need to trust the Lord and rely upon Him. A sense of self-sufficiency and reliance on one's own abilities brings a certainty of defeat by one's enemies or being overcome by the problems that are common to life. We are so weak and vulnerable, but the Lord is the one who made the heavens and earth and is sovereign not only over the nations but over the affairs of men. We are "in Christ," and He has said in Matthew 28:18, *"All authority has been given to Me in heaven and on earth."* No power in all the universe exceeds the power and authority of our Lord Jesus Christ. One of the reasons the Lord allows us to be subjected to temptation and trials is to bring us to the end of ourselves and recognize that He is our source of power. He is our hope in times of despair, and His help is always available when we trust in Him rather than trying to do it ourselves.

> *A sense of self-sufficiency and reliance*
> *on one's own abilities bring a*
> *certainty of being overcome by*
> *problems common to life.*

Israel had experienced defeat in battles when they were overpowered by the enemy. It brought them to the realization that they would have literally been destroyed had God not intervened on their behalf. I recently watched a newscast that showed raging floodwaters racing through a town, washing away houses, cars, trees, and everything in its path. Sometimes we feel that is what is happening to us as adversity accumulates. Life is a swirl of escalating problems, and it seems everyone is against us. Sometimes the attacks are personal *"when men rose up against us . . . their anger was kindled against us* (vv. 2–3), and it seemed we would be *"torn by their teeth"* (v. 6). This is how I felt during my election as president of the IMB as I came under attack by those in opposition; rumors and publicity maligned my reputation, but it seemed an impermeable shield did not allow me to be touched. There was nothing that I could do; to be defensive would simply feed the controversy and the opposition. I felt that I would be destroyed. My inclination was to run from this responsibility and seek the security of anonymity away from the crowd and public attacks—*"Had it not been the* LORD *who was on our side"* (v. 1). Obedience to Him does not exempt us from attack, but when we rely on Him, He will deliver us.

In a more common and personal way, we need to realize that it is the Lord who stands beside us, gives us strength, and enables us to escape being entrapped by sin and temptation. Those who take pride in thinking they are strong and capable of withstanding temptation are those who are most vulnerable and likely to fall. Sin is like a snare that can allure us and entrap us before we know it unless we are relying on the Lord and recognize that He is our help and our strength. When we call upon His name, we are expressing all that represents as our Redeemer, our Protector, our Healer, our Stronghold, and our Shield. Because we belong to Him we can be confident He is on our side; He is for us, and He is our Defense and our Deliverer.

PRAYER: *Lord, thank You for standing by me in times of need. Thank You for the confidence that You are for me and are my help and defender, even when I don't deserve it. Don't allow me to succumb to pride and self-reliance but look to You in times of need.*

Psalm 125

A Hedge of Protection

*Key Verse: As the mountains surround Jerusalem,
so the LORD surrounds His people. (Psalm 125:2)*

The theme of the previous Psalm that God is our help is reinforced by the assurance of the security He provides. Those who trust in the Lord in times of need or personal attacks and temptation, rather than depending on self-reliance, are *"as Mount Zion, which cannot be moved"* (v. 1). The psalmist continually returns to the image of the mountains; there is nothing so massive, so strong, and secure. But of special significance was Mount Zion. This was where Jerusalem was located. The temple and place of worship were there, and it came to be understood as the place of God's presence. Zion often refers to heaven and that future kingdom of God that is eternal. So it is a beautiful promise that *"those who trust in the LORD are as Mount Zion"* (v. 1). They are secure forever.

During the years we lived in Indonesia and Thailand, my assignment entailed a good bit of travel. Sometimes I would be gone to India for as long as a month at a time; administrative responsibilities would require constant travel, sometimes to remote and dangerous places. Before leaving for the airport, or sometimes the night before, we would always gather as a family to review my itinerary and where I would be, to discuss schedules and activities at home while I was gone and pray for God to be with us. My wife, who has a beautiful gift of memorizing and praying Scripture, would often pray, *"As the mountains surround Jerusalem, so may the Lord surround you"* (v. 2). It was a prayer of protection that God's presence would be a hedge of protection around me just as the mountains encircled the city of Jerusalem.

IN THE SECRET PLACE

> *It is not so much protection from danger and harm that we need as it is protection from wrongdoing and evil.*

This was the sense of security expressed by the psalmist and the confidence he felt in the Lord's protection. But the primary protection was not from external attack or those who would threaten to harm him; it was protection from wickedness. As God's people who dwelt in His presence and were surrounded by His hedge of protection, they were to do good and reflect the righteousness of God that brings honor to Him. They had confidence in God's goodness because they were upright in their hearts. They knew that the holy and moral nature of God required that they be punished *"with the doers of iniquity"* (v. 5) if they turned aside to do wrong. God's protection assured them of peace only as they did not allow the *"scepter of wickedness [to] rest upon the land"* (v. 3).

We, too, can have peace and assurance of God's hedge of protection, but it is not so much protection from danger and harm that we need as it is protection from wrongdoing and evil. We can be confident of our security that is as unmovable and strong as the mountains around Jerusalem when we trust in the Lord, do good, and maintain a heart that is upright.

PRAYER: *Lord, I know that my salvation is secure and I will abide forever, but help me to trust You to be a hedge of protection that is immovable each day. As the mountains surround Jerusalem, surround me with Your presence that my heart would never fail to be upright and my hands would not do wrong today and always.*

Psalm 126

Brokenness Leads to Joy

*Key Verse: Those who sow in tears shall reap with
joyful shouting. He who goes to and fro weeping,
carrying his bag of seed, shall indeed come again with
a shout of joy, bringing his sheaves with him. (Psalm 126:5–6)*

The Lord's deliverance of Israel from captivity was an
occasion of celebration. After seventy years in Babylon,
it was like a dream to be returning to Jerusalem. The
fact that God would actually intervene and restore them after
generations filled them with joy and laughter as they praised
the Lord. Their restoration was also a testimony of God's
power and goodness among the other nations. When they
observed Israel being restored to the Promised Land, the
nations around them recognized it was not these weak people
who had been subjected to servitude who had brought it
about; it could only be explained by the Lord's mighty hand.

So it is when we are delivered and restored to the Lord
from captivity in sin. It should bring joy and laughter to our
lives, for we know we do not deserve it, and it is not due to
our own work and efforts. But also it should be a testimony
to others of God's grace and power to save. When people see
the change in our lives once we have been restored to walk
with the Lord, His power and goodness should be evident.

> **It is those who shed tears of sorrow
> over sin who are the most joyful in
> experiencing redemption.**

However, the psalmist then makes a strange request in
verse 4: *"Restore our captivity, O LORD."* Having been delivered, why would they pray to be restored to captivity? It can
be understood only in the context of the following verses.

They were filled with such joy only because they had known suffering and sorrow. One who doesn't go through the valley of suffering and rejection cannot really appreciate the blessings of a prosperous and abundant life. Only one who has been through a serious illness can fully appreciate being restored to health. It is easy to take God's blessings for granted. Chinese Christians are being severely persecuted for their faith. Pastors are being arrested and tortured, but the church in China is flourishing and growing. They tell believers from abroad, "Please don't pray that the persecution cease lest we become weak in our faith and lethargic like the churches in the West." It is those who shed tears of sorrow over sin who are the most joyful in experiencing redemption. Those who labor faithfully without results can better appreciate the harvest when it comes.

As we seek to sow the seed of the gospel and witness to a lost world, those who will see results are those who go out with a heart that is literally broken over the lostness and darkness in which the peoples of the world are held in bondage. When we see people without Jesus, whether in a Muslim country, an unreached people group, or among people walking the streets in America, tears should come to our eyes because we recognize their captivity to sin. But as we carry the gospel and sow the seed faithfully, those who are broken and weep over the lost will have the greatest joy in seeing them saved.

PRAYER: *Lord, break my heart for those in captivity to sin. May their deliverance and salvation be a testimony of Your power. Give me a passion for witnessing and sowing the seed of the gospel that I might experience the joy of the harvest.*

The Lord's Help in Any Endeavor

Key Verse: Unless the LORD builds the house,
they labor in vain who build it; unless the LORD guards
the city, the watchman keeps awake in vain. (Psalm 127:1)

This verse has probably been used as the slogan and theme for every church building program in history! As a congregation initiates plans for new facilities, they are reminded that their efforts will be futile unless the Lord is in it. The application is much broader, and, in fact, applies to all of life. We may not be building a house, but any endeavor without the Lord is not likely to be successful. As reflected in other Psalms, we observe that the wicked seem to prosper; those who do not acknowledge God in any way appear to be successful, but that is a judgment from a limited and temporal perspective. For those who know God, His lordship needs to be acknowledged in everything we do. We do not attempt any task without assurance that it is in obedience to His will and with confidence He will guide us and bless us. We can take every precaution to assure our safety and protection, but our only guarantee is the presence and protection of the Lord. He is the one who guards our health and keeps us safe.

I am reminded that my task is not building a house, but the projects I undertake and the work I do will be in vain unless they are of God. My personal efforts will be futile unless I have God's help and blessing. It is in vain for one to work long hours and overextend himself to fulfill responsibilities if it is only in one's own strength that he labors. I can remember as a teenager quoting verse 2 to my parents when they would try to get me up on days I wanted to sleep in: *"It is vain for you to rise up early."* We are reminded that long hours of work and painful, exhausting labor without the Lord are fruitless, but when the Lord is involved, He blesses us even as we sleep, obviously giving us renewed strength in our rest.

*Any endeavor without the Lord
is not likely to be successful. His
lordship needs to be acknowledged
in everything we do.*

The following verses speak of the blessing of children as a gift of the Lord. Such references obviously led to the Jewish concept that barrenness was punishment from the Lord. Perhaps the entire Psalm is not so much about building a literal house as it is about building a home. Without the Lord it is unlikely a family will prosper and be blessed. One can engage in all kinds of personal efforts to protect his family, but the Lord will guard the sanctity of the home. Children are, indeed, a blessing from the Lord, but if they are to be as a reward and others will speak well of them, they must be nurtured in righteousness and the ways of the Lord. Israel had been instructed in Deuteronomy 6:7, *"And you shall teach [the Lord's commandments] diligently to your sons and shall talk of them when you sit in your house."* Ephesians 6:4 tells us, *"Do not provoke your children to anger; but bring them up in the discipline and instruction of the Lord."* Many parents would acknowledge their frustration in dealing with the rebellion and independent spirit of an adolescent and their need for the Lord to help in the challenge of raising children who will be a blessing and will walk with the Lord.

PRAYER: *Lord, thank You for the gift of my children, for they are truly a reward and blessing. Thank You for offsetting my own failures to nurture them in Your Word and for calling them to serve You. Guide them as they build their families for Your glory. I pray that my work and every endeavor will be evidence that You are the One doing it.*

Conditions for God's Blessing

*Key Verse: How blessed is everyone who fears the LORD,
who walks in His ways. (Psalm 128:1)*

Everyone would like to receive blessings from the Lord.
Even those who do not believe in God or have a personal relationship with Him often invoke the blessings
of a "higher being" and seem to acknowledge, especially in
times of need, a nonhuman, divine power in the universe. Of
course we know God as a personal God who has revealed
Himself through Jesus Christ and has even chosen to live
within those who believe on Him. He delights in blessing
His people, but there are two contingencies for receiving His
blessing: fearing the Lord and walking in His ways. Fear is
not synonymous with being afraid of punishment or daily
being driven by guilt; it is an awe and reverence that stimulate a love and desire to please and honor our Lord who is
exalted over all the earth. He has given thorough instructions
regarding His way of life; it is not a legalistic obedience of
commandments as much as it is a heart that is inclined to follow His precepts. Three specific blessings are implied for
those who fear the Lord and walk in His ways.

God will bless their labor, their work, or life's vocation so
that they will benefit from the fruit of their own work. There
is a sense of fulfillment and security in being able to earn a
good living and provide for one's family. No one relishes
being out of work and unable to support his own needs.
Living beyond one's means and becoming dependent on bor-
rowing and credit has put many in bondage and deprived
them of the joy of being self-sufficient. One who has a secure
job and adequate income to provide for one's family will be
happy and recognize it is because of the Lord's blessings.

> *Walking in God's ways is not legalistic obedience of His laws as much as it is a heart that is inclined to follow His precepts.*

God has also promised to bless and prosper the land when His people honor Him and follow His will. This is a collective blessing that goes beyond a response to one person's faithfulness, but Jerusalem was assured of prosperity and peace only as a result of God's blessings. When we stand firm in our convictions in fear of the Lord and walk in His ways, it should have an influence on others and give them encouragement to the point of infecting society by our witness and bringing God's blessings.

While we may seek God's blessings in many endeavors, the most valued is His blessings on our family. One can be successful in business, may obtain wealth, status, and recognition; but if there is no unity and love within the home, any sense of blessing is elusive. Children are the legacy of one's life. One may retire from a successful career and leave a significant inheritance, but children and grandchildren who honor him and follow his testimony and example of walking with the Lord are the greatest blessing one could hope for. Such a man who fears the Lord will have a wife who is loved and blessed and will be fruitful in nurturing the atmosphere of the home to honor the Lord. And, as any grandparent would testify, the pleasure of grandchildren is one of the greatest blessings God provides in the later years of life.

PRAYER: *Lord, thank You for my family and the blessings of a loving wife and children who are a heritage that honors You. May I always fear You and walk in Your ways, not out of a selfish desire for blessings but that You might be honored in the life I live.*

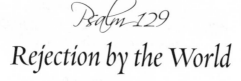

Rejection by the World

Key Verse: "Many times they have persecuted me from my youth up; yet they have not prevailed against me." (Psalm 129:2)

We need to realize that the Christian life will always be incompatible and out of step with the world. First John 5:19 says, *"We know that we are of God, and the whole world lies in the power of the evil one."* This world is the province of Satan's activity and dominion, but we are assured of victory. We have confidence that God's all-sufficient grace will be available. Jesus told His disciples in John 16:33, *"In the world you have tribulation, but take courage; I have overcome the world."* As long as we are in this present world, we will experience tribulation, but all the opposition and adversity we encounter cannot prevail because we are in Christ.

Israel had always had those who attacked them and sought to oppress them. As the chosen people of God, they were called to righteousness and a solitary devotion to the true and living God. They did not fit in with the surrounding cultures and lifestyle. They were not respected for their unique convictions but were persecuted throughout their history. A child who chooses not to participate in some mischievous activity conspired by his playmates will be taunted and ridiculed. A young person who values purity and seeks to honor God will not fit in with the crowd. And though the repercussions may not be physical, the ostracism and condescension will be felt just as severely.

We will experience tribulation, but all the opposition and adversity we encounter cannot prevail because we are in Christ.

Too many Christians seek to straddle the fence and find some middle ground of compromise in order to be accepted by neighbors and colleagues at work. No one wants to appear pious and judgmental, and the pressure to fit in as one of the "good ole guys" is not always subtle. To resist that temptation in order to be true to the Lord is to be subjected to ridicule and disdain by others. The secular media is becoming more blatant in their scathing verbal persecution of people of faith.

Defensiveness is counterproductive, and our only resource is to trust in the Lord and His righteousness. We must be faithful to stand for truth, uncompromising in our convictions, regardless of the consequences—trusting the Lord for vindication. We must be confident that one day the cords of their power and influence will be severed. The false hope they place in humanistic values of self-sufficiency and self-gratification will wither as grass on a housetop. The philosophy of life to which they are committed will produce no fruit. And when they eventually stand before the judgment of the Lord, there will be no one to bless them.

We have to put up with a lot of injustice in the world. People take advantage of our goodness, defraud us, and ridicule us for our faith, but they will not prevail. We are blessed in the fact that suffering is an opportunity for God to act in our lives and provide strength and grace to withstand persecution.

PRAYER: *Lord, I do feel out of step with the world. Give me strength to remain faithful and not to compromise for the sake of avoiding the ridicule and persecution by others. Give me confidence of Your grace and the fact that You will eventually judge those who do not trust in You.*

The Lord's Desire to Save Abundantly

Key Verse: Hope in the LORD; for with the LORD there is loving-kindness, and with Him is abundant redemption. (Psalm 130:7)

Those of us who were raised in a Christian environment and came to know Christ at an early age probably don't realize the depths of sin out of which God has saved us. But others have had to experience the pain and degradation that sin brings into their life before they cry out in despair for help and forgiveness. Some ignore the consequences of sin, choosing their own, independent way of life and living contentedly a lifestyle absent of any accountability. It is only when the convicting power of God's Holy Spirit brings them to an awareness of their separation from God that there is a willingness to turn to Him and plea for His mercy.

Sooner or later everyone needs to realize that no one has any merit or goodness to stand before God without being judged and condemned. The prevailing concept of most people is that we should have no fear of God's judgment as long as our good deeds outweigh our bad. But God's judgment will not be on the basis of our relative goodness. His holiness and righteousness are the standard, and no iniquity can be accepted into His presence. All of our good deeds and worthy motives do not wipe out even a small percentage of sinful actions and a heart that is impure. So, were it not for God's grace and willingness to forgive, no one could stand before Him and hope to be justified.

> *God's nature is one of mercy and grace because His greatest desire is to save us and restore us to fellowship with Him.*

The realization that our hope for salvation is totally dependent on God's mercy and loving-kindness—and His provision in Jesus Christ—is essential in motivating us to call upon Him and receive the redemption from sin He provides. Our only hope is in Him, and that hope is based on believing the truth and the reliability of what He has told us in His Word. Have you ever spent a restless and sleepless night waiting for the dawn, knowing that day would bring a different perspective and relief from anxiety? That is like the struggle of the soul when one senses his bondage to sin and comes to the conviction that Christ is the answer. Striving to come to that point of faith when God will bring peace and assurance is like a watchman in the night looking forward to the dawn when the dangers and potential threats vanish with the sunlight.

Like Israel, our only hope for salvation, and the only possibility of standing justified on the day of judgment, is in the Lord. Just as He continually forgave Israel when they transgressed His laws and lived in iniquity, He forgives us, for He is a loving God. His nature is one of mercy and grace because His greatest desire is to save us and restore us to fellowship with Him. No matter how far we sink in the depths of sin, He not only offers salvation, but He offers it abundantly! Even for those of us who are saved and find ourselves away from God in sin, we can know that God doesn't forgive grudgingly; we will not be saved "by the skin of our teeth" but with an abundant redemption.

PRAYER: *Lord, my sins must be so ugly to You. I am unworthy to come before You and stand in Your presence. Thank You for Your loving-kindness that is poured out in abundance because I believe Your Word, and You are the hope and assurance of my salvation.*

Psalm 131

The Danger of Pride

Key Verse: O LORD, my heart is not proud, nor my eyes haughty; nor do I involve myself in great matters, or in things too difficult for me. (Psalm 131:1)

Pride is probably the most subtle and devious sin to which we are subjected. It is not as much manifested in actions as it is hidden away in our attitude. It is so prominent because it is the natural expression of the flesh or that self-centered life that is opposed to the Spirit. Every desire for acceptance and recognition is driven by pride. Concern for what people think about us is an indication of pride. It is detestable to God because it stands in opposition to His being the center of our life and the focus of our devotion. Glorifying Him should be our desire. God will not share His glory with another, and we are told in James 4:6, *"God is opposed to the proud, but gives grace to the humble."* Being proud not only subjects us to retribution from God; it cuts off the flow of His grace that we so desperately need. However, one who is proud has an air of self-sufficiency and usually would not even acknowledge the need for God's grace.

> **Pride is probably the most subtle and devious sin to which we are subjected and is detestable to God.**

Also, one who is proud is usually condescending toward others. Those who are conceited and get a "big head" because of an honor or an accomplishment are most vulnerable to subsequent failure and embarrassment; arrogance is blind and distorts one's perception of reality. This is a particular danger among those who have been blessed with a deep spiritual experience. Satan even uses that to create a haughty spirit of looking down on others who aren't as spiritual. There is even a danger of taking pride in humility, or more accurately a pseudo-humility, feeling that there is something spiritual about a low self-esteem. We should not be conceited about our own abilities, but we also should recognize that God has blessed us and gifted us to be profitable and bring glory to Him.

In fact, we should accept our status, opportunities for service and leadership, even those that may bring the attention and acclaim of others, but everything we do should be for God's glory. We should accept our place in the body of Christ and in society, being good stewards of our work and ministry, but not with ambition that is driven by self-gain. Too many people have been victimized by the "Peter principle" in which they rise to find themselves in a position or responsibility, due to ambition, for which they are not equipped; life becomes filled with stress, and failure is inevitable.

Contentment is a desirable trait. Paul said in Philippians 4:11, *"I have learned to be content in whatever circumstances I am."* An unweaned child is restless in his mother's arms, constantly stirring and nuzzling his mother's breast, wanting to be nursed. But a weaned child sits contentedly on her lap, confident that his needs will be met. Our soul should be like that, quiet and composed, because of our confidence and hope in the Lord. We should not be restless and ambitious, always looking for a better job, advancement, and greener grass on the other side of the fence. Be faithful in where God has placed you, serve Him faithfully, and with genuine humility rest in Him.

PRAYER: *Lord, I am so vulnerable to pride and ambition. Don't let me do anything that will infringe on Your glory, but help me serve You contentedly as a trusting, dependent child.*

A Purpose and Passion in Life

*Key Verse: "I will not give sleep to my eyes, or slumber
to my eyelids; until I find a place for the LORD, a dwelling
place for the Mighty One of Jacob." (Psalm 132:4–5)*

It is sad that many people flounder through life, bouncing
from job to job and from one interest to another. They
flow with the momentum wherever circumstances may
take them, directionless and simply earning a living without
any sense of significance and fulfillment because they have
never identified a life purpose. Without a vision and a clearly
identified purpose, there is a lack of focus and discipline in
life. There is no overriding future destiny that helps determine decisions and career choices.

God had given David a sense of calling and divine destiny, and David had a covenant relationship with Him. He
was committed to fulfilling God's purpose in obedience. This
was not only for the sake of his personal success but also for
the blessing of his sons and the generations that followed. He
wanted them to learn from God's testimony. The focus of his
life was not just serving faithfully as king of Israel but being
worthy of the promise that the Messiah would be a descendant of his throne and reign forever.

> **Without a vision and a clearly defined
> purpose, there is a lack of focus and
> discipline in life.**

God had chosen Israel as His covenant people with a special purpose to serve Him and to be His representative and
witness. He had chosen Zion, or Jerusalem, as His holy city
and the dwelling place of the ark of the covenant that symbolized His presence in the midst of His people. In response

to having been called and chosen by God and blessed with the privilege of the Messiah coming through his lineage, David developed a passion for building the temple as an appropriate and honorable dwelling place for the Lord. He wanted a place where the priests of God could serve in righteousness and the godly ones of Israel would worship with joy. It would be a place that would remind them that their salvation and strength came from the Lord. This became the priority and focus of His life to the point that he was unwilling to indulge in comfort for himself or even rest until there was a dwelling place for the Lord. We know that David was not allowed to build the temple, but this passion and purpose carried over to his son and was eventually fulfilled.

Just as David had a passion for finding a dwelling place for God in Israel, we should have a passion for finding a dwelling place for God in the midst of all the peoples of the world. Our desire should be to see the gospel planted that the nations would know their salvation is from the Lord and they could worship Him with joy. That is God's desire and purpose, and it should be the focus of those of us, like David, who have the privilege of knowing Him and having a personal relationship with Him. But it is evident that we will never devote ourselves to that task until we are driven by a passion, such as David's, that supersedes our own comforts. God will not dwell among the nations until we are willing to forego personal ambitions and dedicate ourselves passionately to that purpose.

PRAYER: *Lord, help me realize that You have a plan and purpose for my life and devote myself fully to Your calling. As David had a passion for the temple as a dwelling place for God in the midst of His people, I pray You will give me a passion to find a place for You among all the peoples of the world and allow nothing to divert me from that purpose.*

Psalm 133

Relating to One Another in Unity

*Key Verse: Behold, how good and how pleasant it is
for brothers to dwell together in unity! (Psalm 133:1)*

Dissension, controversy, and broken relationships among God's people may be the greatest detriment to our witness to a lost world that desperately needs to see evidence of God's redeeming grace in our lives. If knowing Christ does bring about a changed life, then it should be apparent in our relationships with one another. Living together in unity is a blessing of the Lord that makes life good and relationships pleasant. It is a distinct contrast with anger, bitterness, and grudges that foment ill will because it is something that is produced by the Holy Spirit and reflects the nature and character of God. But people can sit together in church and maintain a pretense of cordial relationships with one another without truly being spiritually bonded in hearts that are united in love.

A great deal of discussion is focused on criticism of differences among Christians and various denominations as if unity should be the supreme objective. Jesus Himself did speak of His desire for unity in John 17 and that His followers would be "one." However, the unity of which He spoke was based on truly knowing the Father, being sanctified in His truth, and being perfected in a love that glorifies Him. Those who present unity as the greatest good usually advocate it at any cost, even a willingness to compromise truth. The shallow ecumenical unity of seeking to unify various streams of faith is accomplished only by each one having to give up certain unique convictions; God is not glorified when the teachings of His Word are relinquished for the sake of getting along with others. True unity comes from a common sanctification of God's Spirit in response to faithfully holding to His teachings and His Word.

IN THE SECRET PLACE

> *If knowing Christ does bring about a changed life, then it should be apparent in our relationship with one another.*

Not only is unity like the anointing oil of God's Spirit, but it is the Holy Spirit that leads us in practical ways in order to maintain the kind of unity that will glorify Him. When an offense has brought about dissension or severed a relationship, we are instructed in Matthew 18 to go to the offending brother and seek reconciliation. If that is not successful, we are to enlist others as witnesses and mediators in the appeal and finally submit the issue to the body of Christ. In the Sermon on the Mount, Jesus tells us that even if we have done nothing wrong but someone has been offended or has a difference with us, we cannot sincerely engage in worship until we have taken initiative to be reconciled and unified with our brother. Disunity is so prevalent because it is a natural characteristic of our fleshly nature to defend ourselves, to stand up for our rights and our opinions, and to protect our reputation and self-esteem, which may be threatened by others. This is why the Spirit would lead us to a relationship of mutual submission to one another, and *"through the grace given . . . every man . . . not to think more highly of himself than he ought to think . . . give preference to one another"* (Rom. 12:3, 10).

PRAYER: *Lord, disunity is so characteristic of our world, depriving You of glory and us of Your blessing. Give me a heart of love that strives for unity among my family, colleagues, and those with whom I may disagree. Let me be an instrument of reconciliation by yielding my rights and being mutually submissive in fellowship with others.*

Blessing God by Faithful Service

Key Verse: Lift up your hands to the sanctuary,
and bless the LORD. (Psalm 134:2)

This is the third Psalm of the last four that has only three verses. But the message of these few brief verses is significant. We are to bless the Lord. It is awesome to think that God, who is all powerful and sovereign over the universe, the One who is all sufficient and has no needs or lacks anything, can be blessed by us. He longs for our worship and for us to serve Him. We are told to *"lift up [our] hands to the sanctuary"* (v. 2). It is not the building or place that is holy, that is to be revered and worshipped but the fact that the sanctuary is the place of God's habitation. We often call the worship centers at our churches "sanctuaries" because they are supposedly the places where God meets His people. It should not be just this special place of worship, but we should be so aware of God's presence that the whole world is seen as His sanctuary. Our bodies should be, and are, the sanctuary of God's presence. First Corinthians 3:16 says, *"Do you not know that you are a temple of God, and that the Spirit of God dwells in you?"* So we are to lift up hands in worship to the Lord.

Lifting up our hands in prayer and worship is becoming a more common posture for praise and worship. It is unfortunate that many look on this gesture with disdain as a show of spirituality rather than as an expression of a genuine focus on God. We are instructed to lift up our hands because this is a symbol of submission to one who is exalted. It is a reaching out in desire for the fullness of God's Spirit to be received and welcomed into our lives, but it also represents an attitude of surrender to Him. It is amusing to realize this is an analogy of Wild West outlaws who have been caught and raise their hands in surrender. It means they are no longer going to fight and resist arrest; they have thrown down their weapons and have nothing in their hands. God is blessed, indeed, when we lift our hands in worship as a genuine demonstration that we hold nothing of merit in ourselves but come in total surrender and submission to His lordship.

> *God is blessed when we worship, holding nothing of merit in ourselves but come in total surrender and submission to His lordship.*

This Psalm is directed to those *"who serve by night in the house of the Lord"* (v. 1). There were always Levites, or priests, on duty in the tabernacle and later in the temple. Since there were so many of them, they served on a rotation basis. Those serving at night were not in a prominent position such as those who led the ceremonies and conducted the sacrifices when the people gathered during the day, but they served an important function. They are like so many of God's servants today who serve behind the scenes. They are not on the platform before others, preaching sermons, leading others and getting high profile recognition. They are like many in the church and in any organization who perform menial tasks and routine functions that are necessary. Whether secretaries, custodial staff caring for facilities, those who provide business services for missionaries, technical support, and a plethora of other services, they are servants of the Lord, and their service blesses the Lord. Those who are faithful in their service, though unseen and never receiving the acclaim of others, will be blessed by the Lord.

PRAYER: *Lord, may I be as those servants who worship and stand before You through the night, faithful at all times. As I lift my hands in submission to You, may it not just be a physical posture but represent the surrender of my life. May my worship truly bless Your name.*

Psalm 135

Created for Praise

Key Verse: For I know that the LORD is great, and
that our Lord is above all gods. Whatever the LORD
pleases, He does. (Psalm 135:5–6)

Praising the name of the Lord is the primary purpose for which God has called us as His people, and we should remember that it is why we gather with the people of God in church to worship. Certainly we are strengthened and encouraged by a message from the Word of God, but we come together *in the courts of the house of our God* (v. 2) to sing praises. We would like to think that we go to church as a privilege and because of the sincere desire of our heart rather than as an obligation. However, as servants of the Lord, we have a responsibility to worship and praise the Lord corporately in His house. He is exalted and worthy of our praise, and His name represents all that is good and lovely.

First Peter 2:9 says, *"[We] are a chosen race, a royal priesthood, a holy nation, a people for God's own possession."* And it is for the purpose of *"proclaim[ing] the excellencies of Him who has called [us] out of darkness into His marvelous light."* We must not succumb to the attitude that we go to church for what we can get out of it and become negligent in attendance if we find the worship boring and the sermon meaningless. The purpose of worship is to focus on the Lord and express the praise to Him that is due.

> **Praising the name of the Lord is the
> primary purpose for which God has
> called us as His people.**

We are reminded of the greatness of the Lord that is the source of wind and rain. In His sovereignty He controls the natural world and everything in heaven and earth. He is the one who sent the plagues on Egypt and delivered His people; He empowered Israel in battle and was responsible for their defeating the pagan tribes that stood in the way of their possessing the Promised Land. The heritage that Israel received from the Lord was for all generations, and the heritage of salvation in belonging to Him that we receive is everlasting. That is not because of our worthiness but because of His goodness, and it pleases Him to save us. God will judge His people, but it will be with compassion because we have trusted in Him and become His servants who praise and bless His name.

As in Psalm 115, we are once again reminded that idols are nothing. They have no life; neither are they able to bless and give life to anyone. They are simply the objects that man has created by his own hands to be the devotion of his life. In contemporary life, what represents the focus and passion of our life? There are those who have been successful in business or politics who literally worship their status and success; these things are the driving force of all they do and the priority of their life. Others have finally acquired their dream home or an expensive, luxury automobile and, in essence, worship their possessions. One's family, a fanaticism with sports, or anything that dominates our time and attention and becomes the driving passion of our life can become an idol. Those who create them and trust them become like them, lacking in substance and life. God is above all and is absolutely sovereign, doing whatever He pleases. And what pleases Him is doing what will bring glory and praise to Him; so all of us, at all times, personally and collectively, are to revere and bless the Lord.

PRAYER: *Lord, I am Your servant, and I recognize Your greatness and worthiness is to be praised. Don't let me esteem anything in this world above You. You do whatever pleases You, and I will be faithful to bless and praise You in my worship personally and in fellowship with other believers.*

Psalm 136

God's Everlasting Mercy

*Key Verse: Give thanks to the God of heaven, for His
lovingkindness is everlasting. (Psalm 136:26)*

Currently there is a great deal of controversy in churches over the style of music and worship. Those who have sung the traditional, well-known hymns in four-part harmony have been critical of the newer preference for praise choruses, many of which are sung repetitively. In a rather condescending way, these worship choruses, which are often faithful expressions of scriptural truth, are referred to as 7–11 songs, that is, seven words sung over and over eleven times. Well, that is nothing new. Psalm 136 is an ancient antiphonal song of praise in which the same five words are repeated twenty-six times, in fact, in every verse. *"For His lovingkindness is everlasting"* is a more contemporary translation of this familiar phrase in the King James Version, *"For His mercy endureth forever."*

Realization of His goodness and that He is above all gods should elicit a heart of praise and giving thanks to the Lord. To be aware of His abundant mercy should cause us to sing of His loving-kindness continually. Experiencing His grace is not just once and for all; His love and kindness are not provided only until He loses patience with us, but they go on and on. It is His nature, and it is eternal. This hymn reviews the history of God demonstrating His loving-kindness to show that it is truly everlasting. Each creative act and the wonders He performed were testimonies of His loving-kindness. His deliverance of His people from Egypt, bringing them across the Red Sea, leading them through the wilderness, and overthrowing pagan kings to provide Israel a heritage all affirmed His mercy and love and that it was ongoing and endless.

> *We need to be reminded that*
> *God is worthy of praise for all He*
> *does for us—all the time!*

We need to be reminded that God is worthy of praise for all that He has done for us throughout our lives. He created us and gave us life. He redeemed us from our sin and made us His own special possession. He has brought us through the rebellious years of adolescence and youth and matured us as adults. He has blessed us with families and a significant and fulfilling life. He never grows impatient but is always beside us to deliver us out of our troubles and rescue us from adversaries who would come against us. The concept of His mercy "enduring" reflects perseverance; He endures our continued failures and perseveres in His mercy, whether we are worthy or not. He is the one who has blessed us with a secure job and steady income that we can have food, and His provisions are not just sufficient but in abundance. As 2 Peter 1:3 says, *"His divine power has granted to us everything pertaining to life and godliness."* So, with that reality in mind, we should also be continuously acknowledging and singing His praise as *"the Lord of lords . . . who alone does great wonders"* (vv. 3–4). As a familiar cliché expresses it, "God is good all the time! All the time God is good!" His loving-kindness is truly everlasting and is always available.

PRAYER: *Lord, You are worthy of all worship and honor and praise. You are great and powerful to remember me and be merciful to me in times of need. You have demonstrated Your compassion in my life so many times; You are truly good all the time. May I never cease to praise You and worship You because Your loving-kindness is truly unending.*

Psalm 137

When We Lose the Song

*Key Verse: How can we sing the LORD's song
in a foreign land? (Psalm 137:4)*

Over the last few days I watched weather reports as a
hurricane approached and swept across Florida. In
the aftermath of the storm, residents who had evacu-
ated returned to find their homes and everything they owned
destroyed. The television newscasts showed their tears and
their grief even as they expressed resolve to rebuild, but all
they had left were memories. Such was the situation of the
children of Israel who had been carried away into captivity in
Babylon. In collaboration with the neighboring tribe of
Edom, Babylon had razed Jerusalem; their beautiful holy city
had been destroyed. Finding themselves as foreigners in
Babylon, subjugated as slaves to their new masters, they had
lost the song in their hearts. Their harps hung unused on the
willow trees; in their grief they could not sing as they remembered the former glory of Jerusalem and all they had left
behind.

The song in our hearts gives evidence of faith, a sense of
the Lord's presence and confidence in His providence. We have
all had those days when a praise chorus is constantly on our
brain, and we find ourselves whistling or quietly singing the
lyrics. The song is a testimony of a joy that cannot be sup-
pressed. On the other hand, we have gone through times of
heavy hearts due to grief or pressures and concerns when we
couldn't sing if we tried. There is no joy, and we don't feel like
singing in our misery, especially when we remember better
times when we were free from current burdens and pressures.

Many missionaries have arrived overseas and lost their
joy. When they lose the perspective of their calling as a privilege of sharing the gospel with a lost world and begin to think
of themselves, the joy evaporates. It is hard to sing in a foreign land where the heat is stifling, the crowds are irritating,

one struggles to communicate in a strange language, and normal amenities that were always taken for granted are lacking. As one remembers how wonderful and comfortable life was in America, the pity party commences, and the last thing we feel like doing is singing praises to the Lord.

> *The song returns to our hearts when*
> *we relinquish our burdens to the Lord*
> *and remember His faithfulness.*

But Jerusalem was more than just their home and a beautiful city. It represented the habitation of God and His presence in the midst of His people. Without Jerusalem and the place of worship, it was likely that they would forget God. Though they could not sing their songs of joy, they prayed that they would not forget God although in a foreign land. It would be better for them to become lame and their tongue unable to speak than to forget God and the place He was worshipped. In their misery and suffering, Israel prayed for recompense upon their captors; yet their greatest need was not to be liberated but for the song of the Lord to return. An experience in 2 Chronicles 29:27 tells us, *"When the burnt offering [sacrifice] began, the song to the LORD also began."* We will find the song returns to our hearts when we relinquish our burdens to the Lord, sacrifice all that is meaningful to us, and remember the Lord and His faithfulness.

PRAYER: *Lord, I often go through times when it is difficult to sing spontaneous songs of joy and praise. I feel I am in captivity to so many pressures and burdens. Restore an awareness of Your presence and confidence in Your faithfulness so I can sing Your praise.*

Approaching God in Humility

Key Verse: For though the LORD is exalted, yet He regards the lowly; but the haughty He knows from afar. (Psalm 138:6)

M any of the Psalms reflect situations in which it is difficult to praise the Lord. When one is overcome by enemies, experiencing suffering, and times of distress, or has rebelled in sin, praise is absent. It is hard to acknowledge the Lord and focus on Him. Praise is a confession of God's lordship and worthiness to be exalted. It reminds us of His providence, which puts the circumstances of life in perspective, and literally becomes the access into His presence. This Psalm begins, as many, with an affirmation and commitment to praise the Lord, but note that it is *"before the gods"* (v. 1); this is so that no other gods, including man-made ones, will infringe on our worship and devotion. It is also not perfunctory worship but *"with all my heart"* (v. 1) and in a spirit and attitude of submission, *"I will bow down"* (v. 2).

We praise God for who He is—because of His character, His holiness, and His exaltation. But we thank Him for what He does in His providence, loving-kindness, goodness, and power. The psalmist's praise evolves into thanksgiving because:

- He had experienced God's loving-kindness and recognized His truth.
- God's Word was revealed and magnified by the faithfulness of His promises.
- He had called upon the Lord, and God had answered.
- The Lord had given boldness and strength to his soul.

We praise God for who He is—because of His character and holiness; we thank Him for what He does in His providence, goodness, and power.

He was also filled with praise, as am I, because of the vision and prophetic promise of verses 4 and 5. One day, *"all the kings of the earth will give thanks to Thee, O LORD . . . and they will sing of the ways of the LORD."* This is contingent on their hearing the words of God or, as we often express it in our mission strategies, having access to the gospel. The gospel is the power of God to save and to draw people to Christ. But as we are reminded in Romans 10, they can't call upon Him or believe on Him if they have never heard of Him. It is imperative that we proclaim the Word of God to every tribe and tongue and that the Scripture be provided in every language, that God might be exalted among the kings and rulers and all the peoples of the world.

We must never become presumptuous regarding the Lord's blessings or allow the privilege of access and intimacy with Him to compromise our respect for His holiness and exalted nature. We must always worship Him with humility and a sense of unworthiness. With this attitude we will not readily sin and presume God will forgive us, but always be broken over sin and remorseful regarding the ugliness in our heart and attitude. That is what allows God to meet us and respond with grace. He is always opposed to the proud. One who is arrogant and self-sufficient cannot know and experience His help, but He will *"stretch forth [His] hand"* (v. 7) on behalf of the lowly.

PRAYER: *Lord, You are worthy of all praise and thanksgiving. Deliver me from pride that I may come into Your presence humbly and worthy to receive Your grace and help. Don't let me become presumptuous and take Your mercy for granted, but lead me to walk in submission to You and worship You with all my heart.*

Living within God's Providence

Key Verse: Search me, O God, and know my heart; try me and know my anxious thoughts; and see if there be any hurtful way in me, and lead me in the everlasting way. (Psalm 139:23–24)

It is so awesome to realize that God in His providence is all-knowing and cares about us and every detail in our life. Liberal theologians have developed a contemporary theology of "theism" which declares that God doesn't know the future because it has not yet happened. That is a blatant denial of the Word of God and testimony of Scripture. The word *providence* comes from the Latin, *pro-video,* which means to see beforehand. God, in His omniscience knows everything that is going to happen to us and is able to use it for His purpose. Many seem to have the opinion that the world is so big and God is so busy that He cannot be concerned about the details of our life; but Jesus said that He even knows the number of hairs on our head and sees every sparrow that falls.

Not only does God know our every action; He even knows our thoughts. He is aware of the direction our path of life will take and understands our ways, even our inclinations and why we do what we do. He knows what we are going to say even before a word is uttered. One of the greatest deterrents to involvement in sinful activity when I was young was the fear of my parents finding out about it. I did not do things that I would not want them to know about. It is startling to realize that God knows everything we do and say, but rather than that being something we fear, we should understand it is for the purpose of His guiding and blessing our life for His purpose. He has put a hedge around us and laid His hand upon us. God is determining the circumstances, and even when He lets down that hedge of protection, as He did with Job, so that we are afflicted with adversity, it is for our greater blessing and His glory. God is in control!

> *Not only does God know our every action; He even knows our thoughts and the direction our path of life will take.*

That is a concept that is difficult for us to grasp, but there is absolutely nowhere we can go to get away from the presence and oversight of God. Just as time is an element of the created world, so is light and dark. God is not deterred by darkness; neither can we hide our sin in the dark and secret recesses of our heart. When we go through dark trials and times of uncertainty, God is still there upholding us and leading us.

This Psalm totally dispels the position of abortion-rights advocates that life begins at birth rather than conception. God formed us in our mother's womb, took our genetic makeup and determined the course of our life long before we were born. Though our days are preordained, we shouldn't think of ourselves as a puppet with every action predestined, but He knows how we will respond to His love and guidance because His thoughts toward us are so precious. The psalmist begins with an affirmation that God *"has searched me and known me"* (v. 1), and he closes with submission to Him and a subsequent plea to *"search me . . . and know my heart"* (v. 23). How assuring to know that if He discerns any *"anxious thoughts"* (v. 23) or *"hurtful way"* (v. 24), He will lead us in the way of truth.

PRAYER: *Lord, You created me for a purpose and know my every action and thought. It is precious to know You think of me and have planned every event and decision of my life. May I stand in awe of Your providence; cleanse my heart and always lead me in Your way.*

Psalm 140

Responding to Abuse

Key Verse: I know that the LORD will maintain the cause of the afflicted, and justice for the poor. (Psalm 140:12)

S ome people are simply contentious! I have had my share of relating to people who were against everything and everybody. It did not matter what the issue was; whether because of low self-esteem or sense of rejection that dates back to their childhood, they seemed to have an inherent anger that was manifested in attacking others. Being in a leadership role, I have also had to deal constantly with people who had a problem with authority. Though attacks were often personal, it really didn't matter who was in leadership or what their position was; it was just not the nature of some to show respect. I have always accepted the fact that many will disagree with me and have even encouraged freedom for that to be expressed, but some degree of respect is expected.

First Peter 2:13 tells us to be respectful and submissive to those in authority, even pagan rulers. How much more should that be true of our relationship with godly people whom God has placed in a position of servant leadership? Our inability to show respect and express disagreements with grace is a reflection of our self-centered, carnal nature; and those who are in bondage to this kind of attitude and demeanor can be cruel and vicious. Church fellowships are not exempt from dissension and the disruption they cause, nor are pastors free from their attacks. People allow baseless perceptions to grow into evil assumptions and circulate poisonous rumors devised to hurt and entrap the innocent.

Let God deal with the wicked who may abuse and malign us, and He will guard our hearts and minds with abiding peace.

God, who is the strength of our salvation, is the one who covers our head in times of battle when we come under attack and are victims of malicious talk. The head is most vulnerable not only physically but in the sense that we are often entrapped and defeated by the thoughts that dominate our thinking and attitudes. Our only solution is to turn to the Lord as our defense in supplication and allow Him to deal with our enemies. To be defensive or counterattack is a "no-win" solution and brings us down to the same level of those who devise evil and are self-serving. Philippians 4:6–7 tells us to *"be anxious for nothing, but in everything by prayer and supplication with thanksgiving let your requests be made known to God. And the peace of God, which surpasses all comprehension, shall guard your hearts and your minds in Christ Jesus."* It doesn't say that God will necessarily answer our requests, but He will guard our hearts and our minds (*He covers "my head in the day of battle,"* v. 7) to provide an abiding peace.

Let God deal with the wicked who may abuse and malign us. Be confident that He comes alongside of us to stand with us as He will *"maintain the cause of the afflicted and justice for the poor"* (v. 12). But we have a responsibility to be conscientious to walk in righteousness and maintain an "upright" attitude toward others as we are always in God's presence. We should give thanks to Him regardless of what we may experience.

PRAYER: *Lord, sometimes I seem to be surrounded by people with evil intent, seeking to entrap me with criticism, and stirring up strife. Uphold me, defend me, and provide justice in the turmoil I feel, that I might rely on Your strength and dwell in Your presence.*

Psalm 141

Guarding Our Words

Key Verse: Set a guard, O Lord, over my mouth; keep watch over the door of my lips. Do not incline my heart to any evil thing. (Psalm 141:3–4)

E ven those who are conscientious about their walk with the Lord, live a righteous life, and have gained a significant level of victory over sinful actions and behavior, find it is difficult to maintain control over the spoken word. It is so easy to utter a thoughtless remark, a sarcastic comment, or a cutting rebuke without realizing that it is inappropriate and contrary to the love and grace we should be expressing. Jesus explained that the real problem with our words is that they reveal what is in our heart. In Matthew 15:11 and 18 He clarified it is *"not what enters into the mouth [that] defiles the man, but what proceeds out of the mouth [comes from the heart], this defiles the man."* James 3:8 observes, *"But no one can tame the tongue; it is a restless evil and full of deadly poison."* That is why we must rely on God to put a guard over our mouth. But it is not just a matter of refraining from unwholesome words; we need God to guard our heart so we are not inclined to anything that is evil or unholy to which expression may be given.

> **The real problem with our words is that they reveal what is in our hearts.**

This is so important because we can be circumspect and conscientious in our devotion to the Lord and obedient in everything we do, but if we fail in the words we utter, it nullifies everything else and defies the sanctification we should exhibit. Always speaking with integrity and truth, avoiding casual slang that is associated with swearing even though we may not actually use a crude or lewd word, or foregoing

---

insensitive criticism and gossip are all ways that God would lead us. James 3:2 says, *"For we all stumble in many ways. If anyone does not stumble in what he says, he is a perfect man, able to bridle the whole body."* This is obviously where we are most vulnerable and represents our greatest need for the Lord's help. It is not something we can do on our own and in our own strength.

After we are told in Ephesians 4:26–27 to get over our anger lest we give an advantage to Satan, verse 29 says, *"Let no unwholesome word proceed from your mouth, but only such a word as is good for edification . . . that it may give grace to those who hear."* In this context the verse that follows indicates that we grieve the Holy Spirit when we do otherwise. So it is not just a matter of speaking evil of someone; we should ask God not to allow a word to escape our lips that is not wholesome but only that which blesses and edifies others.

Throughout the Psalms, the repetitive plea that God would hear our prayer and heed our supplications reminds us that we should not be presumptuous that God is always at our beck and call. He is always present and delights in blessing us and granting our petitions. But this is contingent on our prayers being in accord with His will and what is glorifying to Him, not just because we want our perceived needs fulfilled. That is why our prayers should be as incense offered to Him and with a heart of submission as symbolized by uplifted hands. While the snares of the wicked and those who would have ill will toward us are painful, it is the snares of our own carnal hearts from which we need deliverance. God is our only hope. We must look to Him to be our refuge and defense.

PRAYER: *Lord, the truth of this Psalm is convicting. I confess my failure in words that reflect the flaws in my heart. Guard my lips and give me a heart that is pure. May all I request in prayer be submissive to Your will.*

Deliverance from Despondency

Key Verse: When my spirit was overwhelmed within me,
Thou didst know my path. (Psalm 142:3)

L ife is filled with challenges and problems. More often
than not we find ourselves struggling with a financial
crisis, an unexpected illness or prolonged health need,
or family issues that leave us distraught and helpless. We may
walk through the valley and persevere until we find hope,
experience God's grace, and eventually get on top of these
problems. However, it is devastating when our spirit is overwhelmed with depression and anxieties, and we cannot even
identify the reason. When we have been in such a situation,
we can readily identify with the desperation of the psalmist
as he cries out to the Lord, pleads in supplication, pours out
his complaint, and declares his trouble.

Invariably, one of the reasons we sink so low is that we
feel no one understands or is sensitive to what we are feeling
and going through. People may ask us, "What's wrong?"
A friend or spouse may offer to help, but our inability to
understand and articulate what we are feeling makes it difficult to communicate and for others to respond. The "perse-
cutors" may not be persons or physical adversaries but
situations that produce worry, such as an accusing conscience
or disappointments that have eroded our faith and sense of
God's presence. They put our souls in a prison of helplessness
and despondency, and we recognize it is a situation that is
too strong for us to overcome on our own.

> **When our souls are in a prison of**
> **helplessness and despondency,**
> **God knows everything that is**
> **happening and where it is leading.**

We have two things that give us hope and on which we can rely. One is the fact that God knows our path. His providence that was so beautifully expressed in Psalm 139 reminds us that He knows everything that is happening to us and where it is all leading. He understands our dilemma and the trap that we walked into and is also aware of the solution. He is our refuge, not only from sin but day by day *"in the land of the living"* (v. 5). He heeds our cry and is the source of the fullness of blessing He desires for us.

The other factor that is our hope and deliverance is the fact that we are surrounded by a support group and those who love us. We may feel that no one cares, but a part of God's bountiful mercy is not just what He does but what He does through others. When we are reminded of the fellowship of believers of which we are a part and what a blessing this is, a sense of meaning and assurance will return along with a spirit of thanksgiving.

One other inescapable impression from this Psalm is the fact that multitudes of people in our community and all over the world are crying out as the psalmist in verse 4, *"No one cares for my soul."* While we usually are focused on our own needs and struggle with depression, we need to be sensitive to so many who feel lonely and rejected and that society has passed them by. While unreached people groups and a world in darkness may not be conscious of their lostness, their futile search and vain religious expressions are testimonies that no one cares enough to reach them with the gospel.

PRAYER: *Lord, it is assuring to know You know my path and care for my soul. Thank You for friends and family who provide love, support, and encouragement in times of need. Make me sensitive to the fact that so many people live in despondency and loneliness with no one to care and let me be Your instrument to let them know of Your love and deliverance.*

Psalm 143

Experiencing Personal Revival

*Key Verse: Let me hear Thy lovingkindness in the morning;
for I trust in Thee; teach me the way in which I should walk;
for to Thee I lift up my soul. (Psalm 143:8)*

I find this Psalm to be one of the most relevant to my personal experiences. I'm sure I am not alone as one who sometimes goes through times of spiritual dryness. There are times I don't feel an intimacy with God, and there is a lack of joy and sense of victory day by day. Doubts plague my mind, and I find that I am vulnerable to carnal attitudes. *"My spirit fails"* (v. 7), and *"my soul longs for [God], as a parched land"* (v. 6). Why do we often feel that the flow of living water has been extinguished and the vitality of our faith has vanished? We plead with the psalmist that God would hear our supplications because it seems our prayers are just empty, perfunctory words that don't get past the ceiling. We have all been there from time to time. So what is the solution?

First, we should recognize our sinful nature. Perhaps Satan, the accuser, has put us on a guilt trip; our enemy delights in crushing our spirit, robbing us of the peace and joy God has given us in Christ and leading us into dark times of doubt. The last thing we want is for God to judge us, for we have no merit whatsoever. We come to Him in honesty, confessing and acknowledging what we feel, confident He will respond based on His faithfulness and His righteousness. Second, we should *"remember the days of old."* Think about when God has worked in our lives before; recall how He has blessed and reached out to us, proving His power and faithfulness in the past.

> *In times of spiritual dryness, we must come to God in honesty, confessing and acknowledging what we feel, confident He will respond.*

In addition to these, beginning in verse 8, we come to a sequence of requests that outline the solution to our dilemma of feeling dry spiritually and separated from God. We should focus our thoughts on the Lord each morning and begin the day with these appeals but with a commitment to fulfill the condition that is a contingency for each one.

Appeal: *"Let me hear Thy lovingkindness."*
Condition: *"For I trust in Thee."* (v. 8)

Appeal: *"Teach me the way in which I should walk."*
Condition: *"For to Thee I lift up my soul."* (v. 8)

Appeal: *"Deliver me, O Lord, from my enemies."*
Condition: *"I take refuge in Thee."* (v. 9)

Appeal: *"Teach me to do Thy will . . . let Thy good Spirit lead me."*
Condition: *"For Thou art my God."* (v. 10)

Appeal: *"O Lord, revive me . . . bring my soul out of trouble."*
Condition: *"For I am Thy servant"* and *"for the sake of Thy name."* (v. 11, 12)

PRAYER: *Lord, I lift up my soul to You and long to see Your face. Pour out Your Spirit and loving-kindness as water on the parched and dry ground of my life and restore me to the blessing of an intimate relationship with You. Deliver me, revive my soul, and teach me the way I should walk, led by Your Spirit.*

Psalm 144

Being the People of God

Key Verse: How blessed are the people . . . whose God
is the LORD! *(Psalm 144:15)*

M an is nothing compared to the greatness and sovereignty of God who is eternal and all-powerful. We are like a mere breath or a passing shadow, and that is pretty insignificant! Just the fact that God would be mindful of us and take an interest in us is an awesome reality. After all, He is the one to which the heavens bow down; He spawns the lightning flashes across the sky and causes the mountains to quake. Yet He calls us out of a world that is alien to Him to be His people. He rescues us from evil and delivers us from the storms of life and from a world that lives in the deceitfulness and falsehood of sin. Like David, this should elicit a submissive spirit on our part toward Him and be reflected in songs of praise in our hearts.

Truly we are blessed to be the people of God and to be the recipients of His grace and blessings. We should be humbled and filled with thanksgiving; there is no place for pride in thinking we are anything within ourselves or are worthy of God's attention. There is an abundance of blessings to the people who are faithful to acknowledge His lordship and whose hearts are inclined to worship and praise Him. Their lives will be fruitful in sons and daughters who honor the Lord; subsequent generations will thrive and serve Him. God will prosper His people with a plentiful harvest of crops, and their cattle will reproduce and multiply in abundance. He provides not only sufficiency but wealth and prosperity for His people. And the streets of their cities will be safe from crime.

> *There is an abundance of blessings*
> *to the people of God who acknowledge*
> *His lordship and are faithful to*
> *worship and praise Him.*

While these references are usually applied collectively as an appeal to our nation or community to be the people of God and to live according to His righteousness, we must not overlook the aspect of His being a personal God. While He is concerned that His people honor Him and live in obedience to His commandments—acknowledging His lordship—He delights in revealing Himself and relating to us individually. Notice the personal pronouns as God is *"my rock . . . my lovingkindness . . . my fortress . . . my stronghold . . . my deliverer . . . my shield!"* (vv. 1–2). He is concerned for each of us who belongs to Him. We can trust Him to provide whatever we need in protecting us from temptation and harm. He is the refuge in which each of us can find shelter and respite when the battle and storms of life get rough. He personally desires to train and equip us to fight the spiritual battles that we will invariably face. His Holy Spirit indwells each of us to nurture us, mature us, and sanctify us as the people of God. We do not subdue the enemy because of our power and ability but only because God acts on our behalf.

It is not just about us as those who have been set apart to be blessed as the people of God; neither was it about David or the nation of Israel. God desires that all peoples become those whose God is the Lord. Our witness and the prosperity and success we enjoy should be a testimony of God's favor and blessing that would cause other peoples to come under submission to His lordship.

PRAYER: *Lord, help us to be the people of God who are worthy of Your blessings. Help me to reflect Your lordship, recognizing that You are all that I need. I ask this not out of a desire for personal blessing and prosperity but as a testimony of Your grace. I pray that our nation would fear You and live in submission to You.*

Worthy of Praise

Key Verse: The LORD *is gracious and merciful; slow to anger
and great in lovingkindness. The* LORD *is good to all, and
His mercies are over all His works. (Psalm 145:8–9)*

A s we get to the final six Psalms of this lengthy collection of hymns and meditations, mostly attributed to David, they move into a focus of praise and an attempt to articulate the glory and exaltation of which God is worthy in our lives and worship. Psalm 145 is a reminder of Psalm 116, which was a meditation on "I love the Lord, because . . ." Here is a similar expression, "I bless and praise the Lord, because . . ." It is an extensive listing, similar to Psalm 103, of why the Lord is worthy of praise.

When we meditate on God's glorious splendor and majesty, we quickly realize that His greatness is "unsearchable" or cannot be defined or fully comprehended. Every day we are to praise the Lord and acknowledge His greatness, and those days will flow into eternity in which God will be praised forever and ever. God's mighty acts and power will be the focus of our testimony and witness in the world and are to be passed on from generation to generation. I remember often singing the words of a popular hymn, "Count your many blessings; name them one by one." We should be overwhelmed as we recount the times His abundant goodness was evident; thoughts of His righteousness precipitate joyful shouts of glory and praise!

---

*Every day we are to praise the Lord
and acknowledge His greatness; those
days will flow into eternity in which
God will be praised forever.*

Among the reasons we cannot be restrained in speaking of God's glory, talking about His power, and testifying of His mighty acts are these:

- The Lord is gracious and merciful.
- The Lord is slow to anger and great in loving-kindness.
- The Lord is good to all.
- The Lord's mercies are evident in all His works.
- The Lord sustains all who fall and raises up those who are bowed down.
- The Lord provides food (physical needs) to all who look to Him in faith and trust.
- The Lord satisfies the desires (necessities of life) of every living thing.
- The Lord is righteous in all His ways and kind in all His deeds.
- The Lord is near to all who call upon Him.
- The Lord will fulfill the desire and save all who fear Him.
- The Lord protects and keeps all who love Him.
- The Lord will judge and destroy the wicked.

God created the world and *"all flesh"* to recognize His lordship and to praise and bless His name. We can be personally responsible only for our own attitudes, words, and actions, so with our mouth we should speak of His praise and make known His glory.

PRAYER: *Lord, You are worthy of all praise, and Your greatness is beyond comprehension. Let my heart be filled with Your love and my words and actions testify of Your power and glory to all the world and successive generations.*

Psalm 146

Seize the Day

Key Verse: I will praise the LORD while I live; I will sing praises to my God while I have my being. (Psalm 146:2)

We are not long for this world! Life passes quickly, and we should realize that we have a stewardship and responsibility to use the time God has given us appropriately. I have always had a self-image that was much younger than my actual age, but after passing a half-century of life and rapidly moving toward what is the traditional age of retirement, my perspective has begun to change. I realize that time is limited for accomplishing God's purpose for my life. Like others, I want to finish well and enjoy a productive ministry in my latter years.

But I have come to understand one of the subtle diversions of the enemy is to get us to procrastinate and think we have plenty of time to serve God and fulfill His will. Satan is delighted for us to make plans and have good intentions about the future as long as we never get around to them. We are always in a mode of making preparation and establishing the foundation of family and career for what we are "going to do." We ignore the reality that we have been given only the present for serving the Lord. We must do what we are "going to do" each day, or we will find that the future has passed and our most noble plans and intentions are unfulfilled.

---

*We must do what we are "going to do"
each day, or we will find the future
has passed and our plans and
intentions are unfulfilled.*

Whatever God's will and direction for life, vocationally and otherwise, it is to be lived for the praise of His glory. Certainly we will have an endless opportunity to praise the Lord and worship Him throughout eternity in heaven, but it is this life and earthly existence that God has given us to serve Him. One day this body will return to the grave, and all opportunity will be past. I was impressed by the testimony of one of our younger missionaries who died in a traffic accident; a few weeks earlier she had written in her newsletter about all she had been doing in witness and ministry. It had not been without hardship and suffering, but she said, "It has all been for His glory. . . . I would not change a thing if I could!" We never know when our life might end. We all anticipate living until our eighties or beyond and to die a natural death, but if life should be cut short, our desire should be to live in a way that we have no regrets; we would not change a thing because we have walked in obedience and our life has been one of praise to the Lord.

This would, indeed, be the passion and driving purpose of our life if we would just be aware of God's greatness and mercy and realize it is being manifested in practical ways in the world each day.

- He made heaven and earth and is faithful to the end.
- He executes justice for the oppressed and gives food to the hungry.
- He opens the eyes of the blind and lifts up those who are bowed down.
- He loves the righteous, protects the stranger, and cares for those in need.
- He thwarts the way of the wicked and reigns forever.

PRAYER: *Lord, my hope is in You. I will not trust in man and the things of earth, for You are sovereign and reign forever. Help me to be a good steward of the life You have given me. In every activity and endeavor may I live to the praise of Your glory, constantly aware of the practical ways Your greatness and mercy are revealed.*

Psalm 147

A People of Praise

Key Verse: *The* LORD *favors those who fear Him, those*
who wait for His lovingkindness. (Psalm 147:11)

We think of praise of God as singing or worship, whether verbally or in our hearts. Praise is complimenting, affirming, exalting, and acknowledging the greatness of someone or what they have done. When we praise the Lord, it is accompanied by a sense of joy, confidence, and assurance; this is in contrast to feelings of discouragement and doubt. Therefore, we find that praise is pleasant. It is becoming, or appropriate, for us to praise the Lord for *"great is our Lord, and abundant in strength"* (v. 5).

It is good for us to praise the Lord because this is a testimony and response that we fear and revere Him and hold Him in proper esteem as One who is holy and exalted. That relationship generates a faith and confidence to wait (the same word in Hebrew as "hope") for God's loving-kindness which is manifested (1) in what He does for His people, (2) what He provides for His people, and (3) in fulfilling His purpose through His people.

God draws His people together and builds them up. He takes a scattered people with diversified, self-centered interests and unifies them as His people, even drawing in the outcasts and misfits. He brings wholeness to their bodies and spirits, healing the brokenhearted and binding up their wounds. He knows each of them personally and cares for them. God told Abraham that His descendants, God's people, would be as numerous as the stars in the heavens. Just as *"He counts the number of the stars [and] gives names to all of them"* (v. 4) so He knows His people. He supports those who are afflicted and mistreated and will deal with the wicked because His understanding is total and complete without any flaw.

> *The world and everything in it was*
> *created for the blessing and use of*
> *many to serve and glorify the Lord.*

God has provided the world as an environment and blessed place of habitation for His people. A lot of environmentalists go to the extreme in exalting nature itself, but man is God's highest creation; the world and everything in it should be protected, but it was created for the blessing and use of man to serve and glorify the Lord. Throughout the Psalms we consistently see how the glories of nature make us aware of God and His greatness. He creates the clouds that bring rain that makes the grass grow. Providing for the birds and beasts is all a part of the life cycle He created, but the mountains and strength of animals are not His delight; He is delighted with those who fear Him and put their hope in Him.

Finally, God is worthy of praise because He has chosen to fulfill His purpose through us, His people, just as He did Israel. He gives us strength, blesses our children and successive generations, gives peace to the land, and satisfies our needs that His Word and His commands might be spread throughout the earth. He desires that His statutes and ordinances be scattered like ashes that blow in the wind and snow that covers the ground and melts, flowing like water through the land. Just as He did to Jacob and the children of Israel, God has uniquely blessed us in giving us His Word and truth; He is worthy of our praise.

PRAYER: *Lord, I praise You not simply because it is good, pleasant, and appropriate but because You have chosen me as Your own to fear You and trust in Your loving-kindness. I pray that all people will recognize Your power and grace and live for Your praise and glory.*

Psalm 148

We Live to Praise

*Key Verse: Let them praise the name of the LORD,
for His name alone is exalted; His glory is above
earth and heaven. (Psalm 148:13)*

Praise of the Lord is to permeate every aspect of the universe. It would be impossible to define the scope of God's dominion and lordship, but in an effort to be as comprehensive as possible, the psalmist emphasizes that everyone and everything is to praise the Lord. Eight times in the first four verses he expresses in the strongest imperative that we are to praise the Lord. God desires that we love Him, that we serve Him, that we fear Him, that we are obedient to His commandments, and that we live for Him, but the overarching priority is to praise Him. All else that we do is for the purpose of His praise; it is to glorify, exalt, and bless His name. This is God's desire for (1) all the hosts of heaven, (2) all of creation on the earth, and (3) all mankind.

We don't have any problem thinking of heaven as a place of praise. Our traditional understanding of God's heavenly kingdom is a place where we all will be gathered around the throne of God, praising and giving glory to Him for all eternity. That may sound somewhat boring to some, but there will be no distraction from our focus on Him. Even in this life everything that is not focused on God is some kind of earthly distraction that has to do with our existence and carnal needs and relationships, none of which will exist in heaven. God is looking forward—as we should be as well—to that day when we will be with Him and join the hosts of heaven in praising Him purely and completely, but He created the angels and heavenly hosts to praise Him even now. Our limited ability to comprehend the highest heavens can be only inadequately equated with the stars, which are the highest and most distant things in our realm of knowledge. All that is a part of the heavenly kingdom was established forever to give praise to God.

---

*God desires that we love Him,
serve Him, fear Him, and live for
Him, but our overarching priority
is to praise Him.*

Even that which is created and temporal in the earth is to praise the Lord. All the created order is a testimony to God's wisdom and greatness, from the fish in the depths of the sea to the birds of the air and everything that lives upon the earth. Even the inanimate features of nature, including the mountains, hills, and trees, testify to God's glory and reflect praise to Him. Interestingly, the forces of nature that defy man's control and can be destructive; fire, hail, snow, and stormy wind, give evidence of a higher power in the universe that should be acknowledged and worshipped. Could it be that God allows natural disasters to occur to make us aware of our weakness, to prove that man is not supreme, and to turn our hearts to Him?

Primarily, however, people were created and given life to praise the Lord. Young men, old men, women, and children are to recognize that God is exalted and to praise Him. Even those who have attained the highest status and authority among men—kings, princes, and judges—are to come in submission before the Father and give praise to Him.

PRAYER: *Lord, I exist to praise Your name, for You are exalted over heaven and earth and have created all things for Your glory. I look forward to that day when I will be part of a vast heavenly host praising Your name forever. But may every aspect of my life be for Your praise as long as You give me life upon the earth.*

A People for God's Glory

Key Verse: For the LORD *takes pleasure in His people; He will beautify the afflicted ones with salvation. (Psalm 149:4)*

As has been expressed so frequently, God called Abraham and set apart the children of Israel as His chosen people, not for their blessings and benefit but to serve Him and live to the praise of His glory. Among all the peoples of earth, they were to enjoy a special relationship with Him; they would recognize God as their Maker and would acknowledge Him as their King and absolute authority. This would be a relationship that would bless them, elicit songs of joy and response in worship. Psalm 102:18 refers to a *"generation to come; that a people yet to be created may praise the* LORD." I believe this is a reference to those who are Christians. Not only the historic tribes of Israel but those who have been redeemed by the blood of Christ become the people of God. The Lord takes pleasure in His people who worship and praise Him; He takes those who are afflicted by sin and restores them to become those who are beautiful and purified in His sight through the salvation that He has provided.

> *It is an honor to be among those who know the Lord and are counted as His people, chosen to worship and praise His name.*

It has been my experience to have many cross-cultural worship experiences and to be blessed by the diverse expressions of singing and praising the Lord. My heart has been stirred by the exuberant songs of believers in India accompanied by drums, cymbals, and tambourines. One senses a genuineness of praise as Africans put their whole bodies into rhythmic dances and movements. The beauty and harmony of Hispanic choruses in Latin America reflect hearts that are in touch with God and have experienced God's grace. It was an emotional moment to attend the largest church in Korea when twenty-five thousand people in attendance all prayed simultaneously; the murmur of voices being lifted to the Lord was like the sound of a mighty wind sweeping over the congregation. Whether through these experiences, our normal American styles of worship, or listening to the elaborate instrumentation of a philharmonic orchestra playing familiar anthems, the Lord takes pleasure in the music and expressions of worship. Those who belong to Him—His congregation—have a new song in their hearts that cannot be restrained!

In contrast to the "godly ones of Israel" are those who do not acknowledge God's lordship. One day God will bring vengeance and judgment upon those who have rejected Him and have not given Him the praise and glory to which He is due. Especially those who have been leaders and people of influence, who have been responsible for leading people astray and depriving them of knowing the Lord, will experience a severity of punishment. I'm not sure what part we will play in this, whether the godly ones who have glorified the Lord will actually be instruments of vengeance, or whether the contrast of our devotion and praise with those who are lost will be the testimony that will seal their fate. Nevertheless, it is an honor to be among those who know the Lord and are counted as His people. Let us never forget that it is for the purpose of exulting in God's glory, worshipping Him in song and praising His name.

PRAYER: *Lord, I am so blessed to be among the redeemed and to have the privilege of worshipping and praising You. Give me a song in my heart to celebrate Your glory. In contrast to those who do not know You, let the joy of my heart be a testimony that I belong to You.*

Praising God All the Time

*Key Verse: Let everything that has breath praise the L*ORD*.*
*Praise the L*ORD*! (Psalm 150:6)*

There is a tinge of emotion as I come to this final Psalm. Although I will read these reflections over and over, just as I have and will continue to read and meditate on the Psalms themselves, I feel that a long and intimate visit has come to a close. Of all that can be said of God, the greatness of His power, the holiness of His character, and the faithfulness of His loving-kindness, and about our pilgrimage of knowing Him, it can only be summed up by the admonition to praise Him. All the world, and everything He has created, is to praise Him. The inanimate grandeur of nature is for His praise. The miraculous creation of living things is to praise Him. We are to live our lives as a testimony of His love and our devotion to Him. We are to praise Him for His greatness and sovereignty and for His mighty deeds in the world and in our own lives.

We praise the Lord at church, *"in His sanctuary"* (v. 1), as we gather with His people to worship, but we are also to praise the Lord out in the world, *"in His mighty expanse"* (v. 1). We are to praise Him all the time. It is not just all created beings that breathe that are to praise the Lord, but with every breath of life we are to praise Him. It is not just the musical instruments of piano and organ, drums and trumpets, guitars and violins that are to be expressions of praise, but whatever instruments are in our hands are to be implements of worship that are used for His glory—the dishes and pots and pans in the kitchen, the tractors and plows on the farm, the computers and cell phones in our office. Wherever we are and whatever we do, there is not a moment or activity that should not be devoted to the Lord and be for His glory.

> *Wherever we are and whatever we do,*
> *there is not a moment or activity*
> *that should not be devoted to the*
> *Lord and for His glory.*

We should comprehend day by day as we live and breathe what the apostle John grasped in the Book of Revelation. *"Worthy art Thou, our Lord and our God, to receive glory and honor and power; for Thou didst create all things, and because of Thy will they existed, and were created . . . Worthy is the Lamb that was slain to receive power and riches and wisdom and might and honor and glory and blessing . . . for Thou was slain, and didst purchase for God with Thy blood men from every tribe and tongue and people and nation"* (Rev. 4:11; 5:12, 9). God created us, redeemed us, and is worthy of our praise. He created the whole world and died for the sins of all peoples. He is worthy of our total devotion and all the honor and blessing and glory we can give in living for Him.

PRAYER: *Lord, You are not only my Savior and Master; You are my life and my all. As an unworthy servant I acknowledge Your power and glory. I am a recipient of Your grace and daily expressions of Your loving-kindness. You are merciful and forgiving when I sin; You are my strength when I am weak. You are my joy when I am sad and my hope when I am discouraged. You are my refuge, my fortress, and my shield when I am tempted and when my carnal nature threatens to take control. You are my light to guide me as I walk in obedience to Your will. You are exalted and worthy of my praise and worship. I lay my life at Your feet as an offering, lift my hands in submission as Your servant, and give You my heart to be filled by Your presence that I might live for Your glory alone.*